Debby Sjogren

Visit UnveilinGLORY's exciting website to learn about our wonderful new curricula for all ages, K-12th: www.UnveilinGLORY.com/homeschool

The Dog Walk

ISBN: 978-0-9862066-7-2

Designed by Bob Sjogren.

Debby Sjogren
Mission Minded Publishers
4663 Crown Hill Rd.
Mechanicsville, VA 23111
debby@mmpublishers.com

To obtain additional copies, contact UnveilinGLORY at 804.781.0386 or visit their website at www.UnveilinGLORY.com.

Dear student, parent, teacher or youth leader,

Only God is perfect.

Though we, at Mission Minded Publishers, have tried and tried (and tried!) our best to make this workbook free of error, there are certainly some mistakes somewhere in these 300+ pages. Please forgive us and help us find those mistakes.

If you find typos or errors, please email me and let us know what page you found them on and what the typo or error was. I would greatly appreciate it so we can make the next edition that much better.

Since there are websites referenced in this curriculum which can be very difficult to exactly type in, we have put them in a .pdf document on the UnveilinGLORY website. If you go there and download it, you can simply "click" and go directly to the website without having to type in any characters! (www.UnveilinGLORY.com/content/view/77)

I also want to give many thanks to Annette Burkett and Jody Gadra for their excellent editing, and a huge shout-out to my husband, Bob, for all the hours he spent on the computer making this curriculum look great.

Seeking to glorify God in our products,

Debby Sjogren

Debby Sjogren
President, Mission Minded Publishers
debby@mmpublishers.com

P.S. Please check out the website of UnveilinGLORY, Inc. for new materials if you enjoyed this curriculum. We have an array of creative, life-changing curricula at this web address: www.unveilinglory.com/homeschool.

My Homeschooled Family

God has blessed my husband, Bob Sjogren, and me with four amazing children! We homeschooled all four of them for a total of 19 years. (Actually, I homeschooled them, but my husband did coach the basketball team! ☺)

Thanks to God's grace and their hard work, all four of them have now graduated with bachelor's degrees in either Media Arts, Spanish, English, Religious Studies, or Communication Studies from either James Madison University or Christopher Newport University as of May 2016.

Our oldest son, Luke, is married to his beautiful wife, Hannah, and they have had two children. Lovable Layla Hope is their firstborn daughter born in 2014, and their firstborn son, Hudson Ishmael, now plays on the streets of Heaven after only living one day here on earth: November 28, 2015. We all miss you so much, Hudson, but will see you again one day! Our younger three adult children are Elise, Abby, and Hunter.

We have had three dogs as a family, a beagle named Jaime Sue, a lab-mix named Jasmine, and finally a Golden Retriever who still lives with us named Jenne Jewel. We had two cats because our kids begged and prayed for them. But personally, I really like dogs. ☺

I grew up in Alabama (Roll Tide!), but my husband and I have lived in Mechanicsville, Virginia, for almost 18 years now. We have just celebrated 30 years of marriage.

God is good, all the time.

From the Author: A Letter to the Student

Welcome to UnveilinGLORY's middle school curriculum titled, *The Dog Walk.* This material is designed for 6th – 8th graders. The curriculum contains 90 lessons, and I have presented it in such a way that if you do 3 lessons per week, you will finish this Bible Curriculum in 30 weeks. Each lesson should take you between 30 – 45 minutes.

The Dog Walk was written for you, the student, to be able to work through this curriculum independent of your teacher or parent. As a middle schooler, I knew it was time to begin to make my faith in God my own. So I would like to challenge you to do the same. Of course, your parent or teacher is welcome to go on this "walk" with you or alongside of you, but I hope you are ready and responsible enough to take the challenge to truly become devoted to Jesus, follow Jesus, and learn to speak of Jesus over the course of the next 30 weeks. And my biggest prayer for you is that you will keep on *The Dog Walk* with Jesus as your Master for the rest of your life. I started on this "walk" when I was 13 years old and I am so glad I did!

Along with this workbook, you will need the following to complete this middle school curriculum:

- *Emma's Story* by Bob Sjogren and Stephani Jenkins
- *The Positive Dog* by Jon Gordon
- *I Heard Good News Today 3: Faith Adventures with God* by Charissa Roberson
- EvangeCube by E3 Resources

All of these items listed above are included in UnveiliGLORY's middle school curriculum kit.
So, you should have them in your kit unless you purchased this workbook separately from someone else. If you don't have one of these items, please call 804.781.0386 and order the missing item from the list above.

A few other suggested items that this author recommends you have your parent or teacher purchase to fully complete this workbook include:

- one package of 3" x 5" index cards (about 40) or one spiral-bound of index cards
- one plastic box that holds recipe cards or index cards (optional)
- one composition book with lined pages or a blank-book journal to use for your devotional times in God's Word (optional)

How to use this curriculum:
The curriculum's lessons should be completed three times per week, thus you will finish the 90 lessons in 30 weeks (3 X 30 weeks = 90 lessons). Each lesson includes reading assignments, questions to answer, sometimes activities to complete, and often times a Scripture to be memorizing (only one per week!). At the end of each week, you will be asked to quote your memory verse to someone else. Please do quote your verse and have them initial the box or line when asked. Accountability is a good thing when you are trying to "hide God's Word in your heart!"

On the third day of most weeks, you will be asked to train another person in what you have learned that week. I have called it your "Dog Training Day." I am very excited about this part of *The Dog Walk*! Why? Because I have seen in my own life that when I have to teach something to someone else, I learn it so much more myself and I can then truly begin to live it out in my own life. So at the beginning of those weeks, you may need to plan ahead to train a friend or family member that week.

Sometimes you will be instructed to go to a computer and research using a website or an APP. If you need help, please ask your parent or teacher to guide you through this part of your assignment. On our website, www.UnveilinGLORY.com/content/view/77, look under the heading "Middle School Curriculum" and find the PDF document. Download it for free and you'll have links you can click on to easily access those websites.

Several times throughout this curriculum, you will be asked to give feedback to this author or perhaps another author. Especially, the last week will be a review week. If you can send your review answers to me, it will be most helpful for us as we will try to implement any suggestions you have made to make *The Dog Walk* even better in the future.

Throughout this curriculum workbook, after some of the questions, you will see a footnote-sized numeral like this: [641]. That small numeral signifies a correct answer that you may check against your own answer. These answers can be found beginning on page 318 in our "Answer Key" section in the back of this workbook.

If you have any questions, please feel free to call me at our UnveilinGLORY office at 804.781.0386. If I am not there, our office manager will be glad to give me your message or question, and I will return your call as soon as possible. Or you can always email me at debby@mmpublishers.com, and I will respond as soon as I can.

Ready for a life-changing journey? Then, let's begin *The Dog Walk!*

For God's glory and our joy on this journey with Him,

Debby Sjogren

Mrs. Debby Sjogren
Author, *The Dog Walk*
President, Mission Minded Publishers
Curriculum Writer & Editor, UnveilinGLORY
804.781.0386
debby@mmpublishers.com

From the Author: A Letter to the Parent or Teacher

We, at UnveilinGLORY, are delighted you have chosen to use our new middle school curriculum titled, *The Dog Walk,* this coming year with your child/student! This material is designed for 6th – 8th graders. The curriculum contains 90 lessons, and I have presented it in such a way that if your student completes 3 lessons per week, he/she will finish this Bible Curriculum in 30 weeks. Each lesson should take your student between 30 – 45 minutes.

The Dog Walk was written for the students to be able to work through this curriculum independent of you, their teacher or parent. As a middle schooler, I knew it was time to begin to make my faith in God my own. So I would like to challenge you to give your student the opportunity to do the same. Of course, you are very welcome to go on this "walk" with them, but I hope your student will be ready and responsible enough to take the challenge to truly become devoted to Jesus, follow Jesus, and learn to speak of Jesus over the course of the next 30 weeks. While writing this curriculum, my prayer for your student has been that they will keep on *The Dog Walk* with Jesus as their Master for the rest of their life. I started on this "walk" with Jesus when I was 13 years old and I am so glad I did!

Along with this workbook, your student will need the following to complete this middle school curriculum:

- *Emma's Story* by Bob Sjogren and Stephani Jenkins
- *The Positive Dog* by Jon Gordon
- *I Heard Good News Today 3: Faith Adventures with God* by Charissa Roberson
- EvangeCube by E3 Resources

All of these items listed above are included in UnveiliGLORY's middle school curriculum kit.

So, you should have them in your kit unless you purchased this workbook separately from someone else. If you don't have one of these items, please call 804.781.0386 and order the missing item from the list above.

A few other suggested items that this author recommends your student should have to fully complete this workbook include:

- one package of 3" x 5" index cards (about 40) or one spiral-bound of index cards
- one plastic box that holds recipe cards or index cards (optional)
- one composition book with lined pages or a blank-book journal to use for their devotional times in God's Word (optional)

How to use this curriculum:

The curriculum's lessons should be completed three times per week, thus your student will finish the 90 lessons in 30 weeks (3 X 30 weeks = 90 lessons). Each lesson includes reading assignments, questions to answer, sometimes activities to complete, and often times a Scripture to be memorizing (only one per week!). At the end of each week, they will be asked to quote their memory verse to someone else. Please do ask them to quote their verse and have someone initial the box or line when asked. Accountability is a good thing when one is trying to "hide God's Word in one's heart!"

On the third day of many weeks, your student will be asked to train another person in what they have learned that week. I have called it "Dog Training Day." I am very excited about this part of *The Dog Walk*! Why? Because I have seen in my own life that when I have to teach something to someone else, I learn it so much better myself, and I can then truly begin to live it out in my own life. So at the beginning of those weeks, you may need to help your student plan ahead to make an appointment to share what they are assigned to teach another person that week.

Several times throughout this curriculum, they will be asked to give feedback to this author or perhaps another author. Especially, the last week will be a review week. If you can make sure your student sends their review answers to me, it will be most helpful for us as we will try to implement any suggestions they have made to make *The Dog Walk* even better in the future.

Sometimes your student will be guided to use a website or a suggested APP for further clarification, to enhance their learning experience, or even as a part of their lesson. Hopefully, you will be able to guide them, and sit beside them if necessary, during these components of the curriculum. On our website, www.UnveilinGLORY.com/content/view/77, look under the heading "Middle School Curriculum" and find the PDF document. Download it for free and you'll have links you can click on to easily access those websites.

Throughout this curriculum workbook, after some of the questions, you will see a footnote-sized numeral like this: [641]. That small numeral signifies a correct answer that you may check against your student's answers. These answers can be found beginning on page 318 in our "Answer Key" section in the back of this workbook.

If you have any questions, please feel free to call me at our UnveilinGLORY office at 804.781.0386. If I am not there, our office manager will be glad to give me your message or question, and I will return your call as soon as possible. Or you can always email me at debby@mmpublishers.com, and I will respond as soon as I can.

Ready for a life-changing journey for your student? Then, let's begin *The Dog Walk!*

For God's glory and our joy on this journey with Him,

Debby Sjogren

Mrs. Debby Sjogren
Author, *The Dog Walk*
President, Mission Minded Publishers
Curriculum Writer & Editor, UnveilinGLORY
804.781.0386
debby@mmpublishers.com

From the Author: A Letter to a Youth Leader

We, at UnveilinGLORY, are delighted you have chosen to use our new middle school curriculum titled, *The Dog Walk*, this coming year with your students! This material is designed for 6th – 8th graders. The curriculum contains 90 lessons, and I have presented it in such a way that if your students complete 3 lessons per week, they will finish this Bible Curriculum in 30 weeks. Each lesson should take your student between 30 – 45 minutes.

The Dog Walk was written for the students to be able to work through this curriculum independently. As a middle schooler, I knew it was time to begin to make my faith in God my own. So I would like to challenge you to give your students the opportunity to do the same. Of course, you are very welcome to go on this "walk" with them, but I hope your students will be ready and responsible enough to take the challenge to truly become devoted to Jesus, follow Jesus, and learn to speak of Jesus over the course of the next 30 weeks. While writing this curriculum, my prayer for your students has been that they will keep on *The Dog Walk* with Jesus as their Master for the rest of their lives. I started on this "walk" with Jesus when I was 13 years old and I am so glad I did!

Weekly Discussion Group Time: I would recommend you have them do the 3 lessons per week at home, and then during your weekly discipleship time you can have them discuss and share with one another what God taught them that week and how they have grown in their relationship with Jesus. As the curriculum develops, you will see many great opportunities to plan servant evangelism events with them or aid them in planning outreach times to practice using their Evangecubes.

Along with this workbook, each student will need the following to complete this middle school curriculum:

- *Emma's Story* by Bob Sjogren and Stephani Jenkins
- *The Positive Dog* by Jon Gordon
- *I Heard Good News Today 3: Faith Adventures with God* by Charissa Roberson
- EvangeCube by E3 Resources

All of these items listed above are included in UnveiliGLORY's middle school curriculum kit.
So, each student should have them in their kit unless you purchased this workbook separately from someone else. If they don't have one of these items, please call 804.781.0386 and order the missing item from the list above.

A few other suggested items that this author recommends your students should have to fully complete this workbook include:

- one package of 3" x 5" index cards (about 40) or one spiral-bound of index cards
- one plastic box that holds recipe cards or index cards (optional)
- one composition book with lined pages or a blank-book journal to use for your devotional times in God's Word (optional)

How to use this curriculum: Each lesson includes reading assignments, questions to answer, sometimes activities to complete, and often a Scripture to memorize (only one per week!). At the end of each week, they will be asked to quote their memory verse to someone else. Please do ask them to quote their verse when you meet for your discussion group times. I would recommend starting off your group by having each member quote the verse for that week's lesson. Accountability is always a good thing when anyone is trying to "hide God's Word in one's heart!"

On the third day of many weeks, your students will be asked to train another person in what they have learned that week. I have called it "Dog Training Day." I am very excited about this part of *The Dog Walk*! Why? Because I have seen in my own life that when I have to teach something to someone else, I learn it so much better myself, and I can then truly begin to live it out in my own life. So at the beginning of those weeks, you may need to help your students plan ahead to make an appointment to share what they are assigned to teach another person that week. During your weekly discipleship times, it will be great to have them report on how the "Dog Training Session" went that week.

Several times throughout this curriculum, they will be asked to give feedback to this author or perhaps another author. Especially, their last week will be a review week. If you can make sure your students sends their review answers to me, it will be most helpful for us as we will try to implement any suggestions they have made to make *The Dog Walk* even better in the future.

Sometimes your student will be guided to use a website or a suggested APP for further clarification, to enhance their learning experience, or even as a part of their lesson. Hopefully, you will be able to guide them, and sit beside them if necessary, during these components of the curriculum. On our website, www.UnveilinGLORY.com/content/view/77, look under the heading "Middle School Curriculum" and find the PDF document. Download it for free and you'll have links you can click on to easily access those websites.

Throughout this curriculum workbook, after some of the questions, you will see a footnote-sized numeral like this: [641]. That small numeral signifies a correct answer that you may check against your student's answers. These answers can be found beginning on page 318 in our "Answer Key" section in the back of this workbook.

If you have any questions, please feel free to call me at our UnveilinGLORY office at 804.781.0386. If I am not there, our office manager will be glad to give me your message or question, and I will return your call as soon as possible. Or you can always email me at debby@mmpublishers.com, and I will respond as soon as I can.

Ready for a life-changing journey for your students? Then, let's begin *The Dog Walk!*

For God's glory and our joy on this journey with Him,

Debby Sjogren

Mrs. Debby Sjogren
Author, *The Dog Walk*
President, Mission Minded Publishers
Curriculum Writer & Editor, UnveilinGLORY
804.781.0386
debby@mmpublishers.com

Table of Contents

Week 1: Day 1

Lesson 1

Hello, students! My name is Mrs. Debby Sjogren and I have been married to Mr. Bob Sjogren for over 30 years. Over a period of 19 years, I have had the privilege of homeschooling our four children: Luke, Elise, Abby and Hunter. I grew up in the Deep South, mostly Tennessee and Alabama, and received a Bachelor's Degree in Education from The University of Alabama. ROLL TIDE ROLL!!!

Here I am with my husband!

Well, enough about me...let's jump into our first lesson in *The Dog Walk*.

I wrote this workbook specifically for you! I want to encourage you, as the student, to dive into these lessons yourself. It is fine to do this as a family or with a group of friends, but you will grow taller and stronger in your faith and personal relationship with God if you make this curriculum truly "your own" challenge to accept. So, I challenge you today: learn to walk like a dog this year so that you can continue throughout the rest of your life! You will never regret it—I promise.

One reason I am so excited about this study is because it was in these middle school years of my own life that I really began to question, struggle and even ignore my faith in God for a short time. Then, finally, at age 13, God truly met me one night at a Jr. High church camp near Birmingham, Alabama, and my life has never been the same.

That night, in early July, a college-aged camp counselor, Joe Bancroft, told his story of trying many, many different paths to finding true peace in his heart. As a teen in high school, he had tried smoking cigarettes, drinking alcohol, being good in sports, and even some drugs to find deep joy and peace in life. Then he looked at our group of 30 kids that night and said with great emotion, “Until I tried Jesus, I never found the inner peace and joy I was looking for!”

I listened very intently because in 5th grade my parents moved our family from Florida to Alabama, so I had to make all new friends and start a new school. (Homeschooling wasn’t even thought of back then in the early 1970s!) I had always gone to church, walked the aisle to give my heart to Jesus in 4th grade and had great Christian friends in Florida. But then—we moved. We did find a new church, but it was huge and I didn’t like the kids there. My new school was well respected, but my new friends at school and in my neighborhood were not following Jesus. I desperately wanted new friends. I wanted to “fit in,” right? So in the 6th grade, I began following the wrong crowd to become popular. We all had bad attitudes toward our teachers, and we made many bad decisions that seemed like fun at the time. Back then, even 12-year-olds could buy cigarettes at the local drugstore, so my friends and I would buy them and say it was for “our parents.” Then we would sneak out of our houses at midnight and meet to smoke our “cigs.” We thought we were really “cool,” but the fun lasted for only a short time.

You see, I was basically a smart kid, but that year I started coming home from school with bad grades and bad conduct reports, even a “D+” one time. My parents were not happy. My mother even discovered and read my diary where I had written all about “sneaking out at midnight” and WHOA! She was not happy with me! I truly felt terrible on the inside—I loved my parents and didn’t want them to be so disappointed in me. *But God wasn’t taken by surprise!*

I can now see that God was using these terrible events to soften my heart and prepare the “soil” of my heart to be “fertile ground” so I could receive the forgiveness that came through believing and receiving the free gift of salvation. It was through accepting the death and resurrection of Jesus Christ as a payment for **all** of my sins that my friendship with Him would begin at that Jr. High Camp!

Here are my fun and crazy four “kids” in their birth order: Luke, Elise Abby and Hunter!

So, how does all of this relate to ***you***? Well, in the next 89 lessons in this workbook you will learn a lot of what I learned during those middle school years that caused me to keep walking with God and following my Savior and Lord, Jesus Christ, ever since I was 13 years old.

1. Do you ever feel like you are just "hanging onto your parents' faith"?

    Circle one: Yes or No

2. Have you ever had to move and change your housing or your church or your group of friends? Circle one: Yes or No If "Yes," how did you feel about that big change?

____

____

3. Do you struggle with being disrespectful to any authority in your life right now like I did at age 12?

    Circle one: Yes or No

If you answered "yes" to any of the above questions, I want to encourage you to not give up. We are about to start a great adventure of learning to "walk like a dog" for the rest of your life. Are you ready?

Circle one: Yes or No

2 Corinthians 5:17 (ESV)

Therefore, if anyone is in Christ, he is a new creation.
The old has passed away; behold, the new has come.

Write out 2 Corinthians 5:17 in your favorite version to memorize this week:

___

___

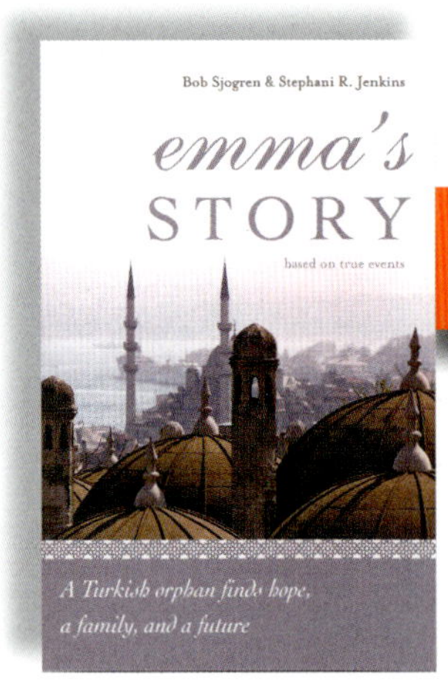

Today's Reading To Grow Your Faith

Emma's Story:
Read Chapters 1—4
(**Answer Key** begins on page 318.)

1. What was the job of the angel, Grace, in Chapter 1 to help Tara?[1]

___

2. Whom was God speaking to in their hearts in Arizona?[2]

___

3. Who appeared more powerful in Chapter 3, God or Satan?[3]

___

4. Who were Tara plus Becky and Graham all trying to help in Turkey?[4]

___

Week 1: Day 2

Lesson 2

Why Learn to Walk Like a Dog Anyway?

So, you may be asking (especially if you have not done our elementary curriculum called *Cat and Dog Attitudes*), "Why in the world does this author want me to 'walk like a dog'? That is ridiculous!!!"

No, I don't want you to get down on ***all fours*** and literally walk like a dog. But in your attitude towards God, towards people, and towards your daily life activities, ***I do want you to walk like a dog, and not a cat.*** It all starts with a joke that Gra'ma Sjogren told our family at the dinner table one night:

A dog says: *You pet me.*
You feed me.
You shelter me.
You love me.
YOU MUST BE GOD!

A cat says: *You pet me.*
You feed me.
You shelter me.
You love me.
I MUST BE GOD!

Hopefully, you laughed—or at least snickered? Even if you are a cat lover, you probably do know that most cats are super soft and charming, but very independent and all about what they want and when they want it. On the other hand, most dogs are very loyal to their masters and will come running, fiercely wagging their tails, whenever they see the one they love walk into the house!

Hopefully, you are now asking, "How does this joke apply to me?" That's a good question.

Let me explain: the dog and the cat are both Christians. They both go to church or youth group. They both could be homeschooled. They both read their Bibles and pray. However, their ***heart attitudes*** are very, very different.

The heart attitude of the Dog Christian says, "Thank you, Jesus, for all that you have done and do for me every day! You loved Your Father so much that you died for His Glory and also for my eternal joy if I follow You. I want to honor You and follow You today and the rest of my life. I want to live to make You famous, not myself."

But the heart attitude of the Cat Christian says, "Thank you, Jesus, for all that you have done and do and will do for me the rest of my life! You love me so much that You died for me, You are building a mansion for me, and You are coming back for me one day to take me to the streets of gold where no one suffers or ever cries again! Wow! Will you just keep on blessing me every day? Will You make ***me*** famous?"

Do you see the difference? Let's talk about this difference with a few questions:

Answer These Questions:

1. What was the same in the heart attitudes of the Dog Christian and the Cat Christian?[5]

____

____

2. What was different between the heart attitudes of the Dog and the Cat?[6]

____

____

3. Honestly, right now in your own heart, what percentage are you a:

Dog Christian? __________ %

Or a Cat Christian? __________ %

} Remember the numbers should add up to 100%. ☺[7]

4. Now are you beginning to understand just why this curriculum is titled, *The Dog Walk?*

Circle one: Yes No Maybe

2 Corinthians 5:17 (ESV)

Therefore, if anyone is in Christ, he is a new creation.
The old has passed away; behold, the new has come.

Keep saying this verse over and over, until you can say it from memory to your parent or a friend or sibling by the end of the week. One way that helps me to memorize a Bible verse is to write it on a 3" by 5" index card and tape it onto my bathroom mirror. Then, every time I brush my teeth or wash my hands, I keep repeating the verse: first with my eyes open, then with them both closed!

Activity For Today

A butterfly is a perfect example of a new creation. It starts off as a caterpillar and then weaves a cocoon, and changes into a beautiful butterfly. In its second stage of life, it is a "new creation."

This is exactly what happens to us when we accept Christ into our lives. We become a "new creation" just like 2 Corinthians 5:17 is telling us.

Draw a picture of a beautiful butterfly on the next page.

My Butterfly

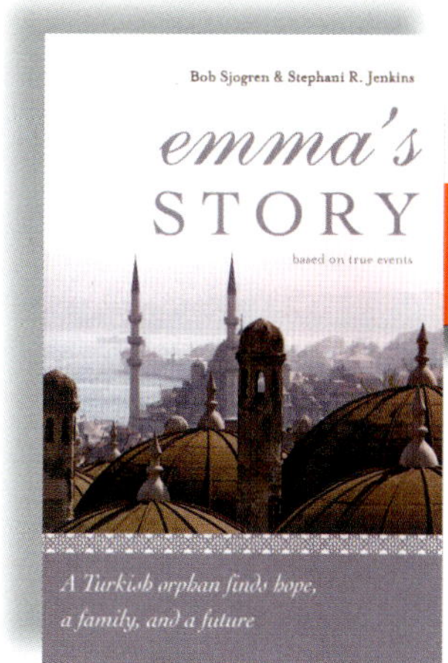

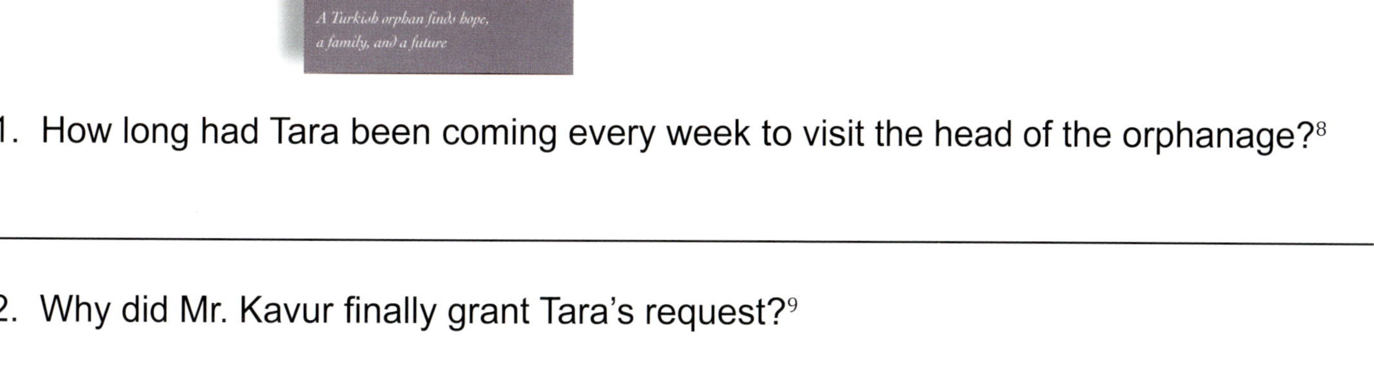

Emma's Story

Read Chapters 5-8

1. How long had Tara been coming every week to visit the head of the orphanage?[8]

____

2. Why did Mr. Kavur finally grant Tara's request?[9]

____

3. Whom did God use to connect Graham and Becky in Arizona to Tara and the orphanage in Turkey?[10]

____

4. What caused the problem in customs as the Bates entered Turkey?[11]

____

5. What did the angel called Hope whisper to Bahar when she was afraid?[12]

____

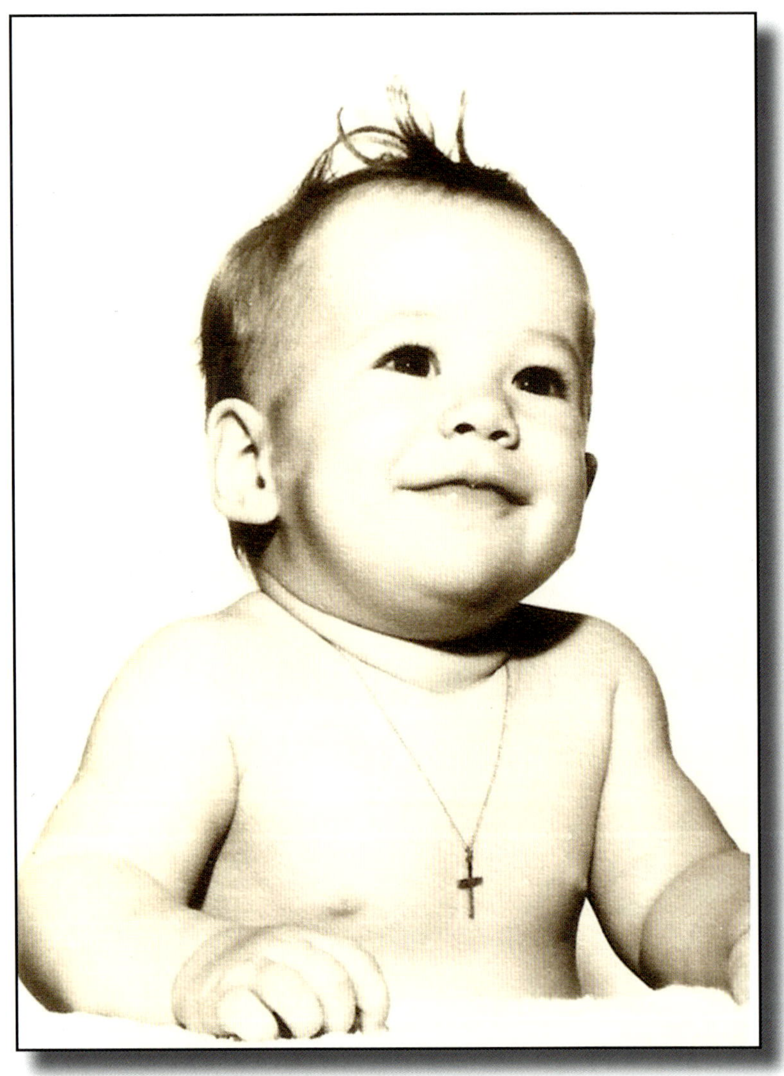

Here I am when I was a baby.
Do I look anything like
your baby picture?

I remember praying the prayer when I was six years old!

I hunger for God, I thirst for Him, and I see the fruit of His Spirit in me.

How They Know They Are Believers

What are the Dog and the Cat relying on to ensure they are believers? [13]

____

____

Making Sure You Are A New Creation

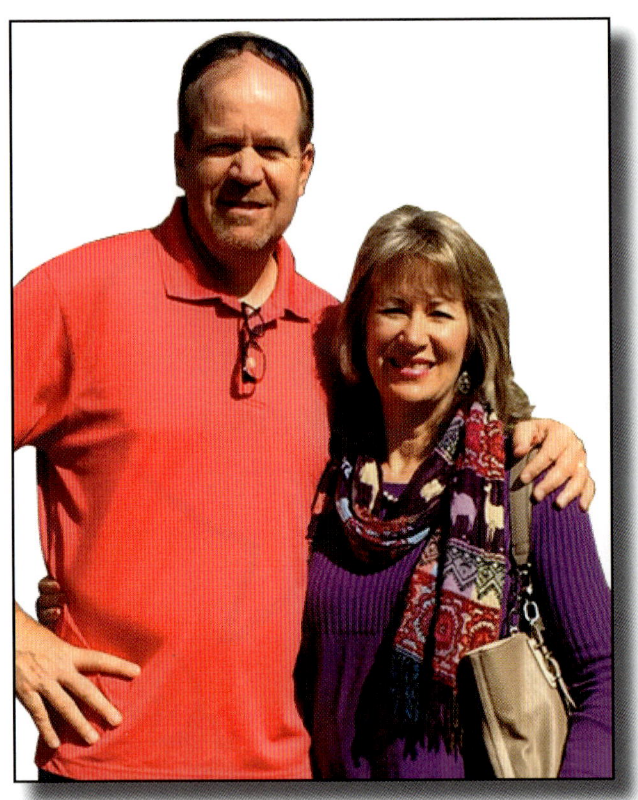

After 30 years of marriage, we still go out on dates!

Let's go back to my Jr. High church camp story, okay? I never really finished it, did I?

So, that night when I heard the college camp counselor, Joe Bancroft, share his story, I immediately thought to myself, "I want that inner peace deep in my heart that Joe was talking about." But I didn't want to pray with him at the end of his talk because I needed to think about this a little more.

When I climbed into my bunk bed that night (yep, I had the top bunk of a three-level bunk bed), I was looking straight at the wooden ceiling. I literally said out loud, "If you are real, Jesus, will you come into my heart, forgive all my sins (I knew I had done plenty of them lately), and show me You are there?" Then I just went to sleep.

You know what happened, right? Jesus Christ ***truly did*** hear my heart's cry in that little bunk bed on July 3rd. (I can always remember the date because the next day we watched fireworks over the lake at church camp to celebrate the 4th of July!!!) You are probably now asking, "How? What changed? How did you know He came into your life?"

The answer to your question is found in our Memory Verse for this week: "...if anyone is in Christ, he is a new creation. The old has passed away; behold, the new has come." (2 Cor. 5:17) You see, when I got out of my third-story bunk bed the next morning, I truly felt differently on the inside. ***I had peace in my heart! I was forgiven! I was now a "New Creation" in the words of the Bible.*** And "the old was gone; the new had come" came true pretty quickly when I felt strongly that I was supposed to tell my cabin's female camp counselor, Jill Worsham, about a little "secret" I had in my duffel bag. I'm sure she was ***very*** surprised when I said to her later that day, "I don't need these anymore" and then I proceeded to hand her a pack of cigarettes that was missing a few. She was surprised but happily took them and we had a great talk right then and there about the brand new "me" with Jesus now in my life. Thankfully, she asked me to meet with her weekly for the rest of the summer so I could grow in my new relationship with Jesus Christ.

Two things happened when I got home from church camp. First, I discovered my mother and her friends had been praying for a year that I would choose to follow Jesus as my Lord and Savior. Secondly, when I began to share with my "friends" in my neighborhood that I still wanted to hang out with them, but I had made a decision to follow Jesus with my life, they thought I was weird and called me a "Jesus Freak." Of course, it hurt my feelings as first, but years later I can see that it was that summer of loneliness that taught me that Jesus Christ could be my BFF (Best Friend Forever). I have ***never*** regretted making that choice! So, in the next weeks of our curriculum, together we will be discussing how to truly make Jesus your BFF, plus the power of praying for others!!!

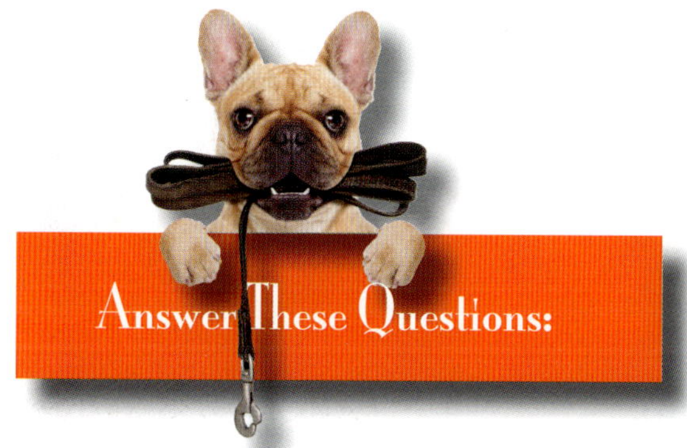

1. Have you ever personally asked Jesus to come into your life and started a journey towards a true friendship with Him—towards living like a Dog?

Circle one: Yes or No

2. If not, you can do that right now, if you are ready: ***Simply have an honest talk with Jesus like I did in my bunk bed.***

You can ask Him if He is real to come in and take over your heart like I did, or you can tell Him you believe in Him as God. Then you can thank Him for dying on the cross to make the payment for all of your sins —past, present, and future, and ask Him to come into your life as your Lord and Savior. Then you can declare to Him that you really want to start living your life for His Glory and not your own, that you want to follow Him just like He asked his disciples to do when He walked on this earth. You can ask Him to be your BFF like I experienced the summer of my 13th year! This is how you start *The Dog Walk*!

3. If you are not ready to make that commitment to follow Jesus Christ, that's okay. But know that anytime you are ready, He is waiting to welcome you into this friendship that John 15:13–15 describes.

Read John 15:13-15. Check the box after you have done that. ☐

4. What is the greatest example of love according to verse 13?[14]

____

5. In vs. 14, what does Jesus call us if we follow His commands?[15]

____

6. If we are friends of Jesus, what will He "make known to us" (vs. 15)?[16]

____

So are you ready to begin *The Dog Walk*? Next week we will find out the key, foundational Scripture for walking like a Dog the rest of your life!

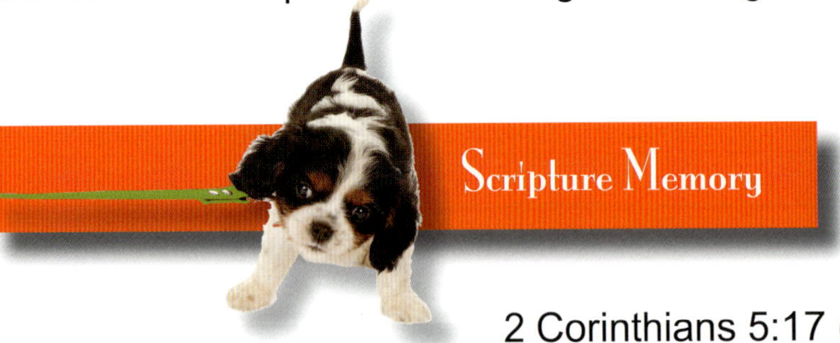

2 Corinthians 5:17 (ESV)

"Therefore, if anyone is in Christ, he is a new creation. The old has passed away; behold, the new has come."

Today: Quote your memory verse to your parent or teacher.

Put a check in the box after you have successfully quoted the Scripture. ☐

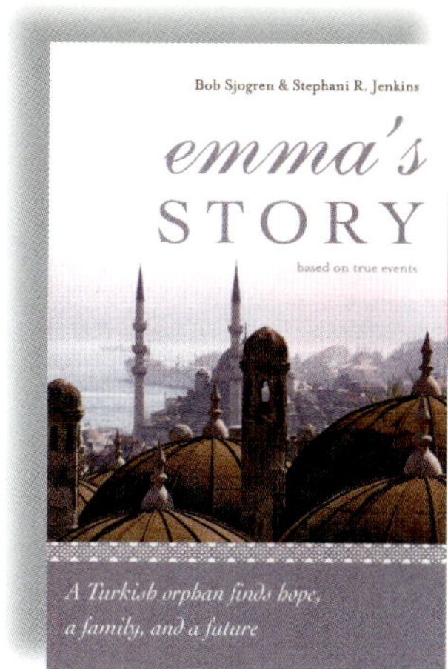

Today's Reading To Grow Your Faith

Emma's Story:
Read Chapters 9–12

1. On page 35, who is "reclaiming his hold" in the orphanage through allowing Tara, Graham, Becky, and George to start a ministry there?[17]

____

2. On page 38, what caused the demons to back away from the group of people?[18]

____

3. What phrase did Tara whisper gently over and over to the handicapped children?[19]

____

4. On page 46, what was the angels' battle cry to push out Satan's demons?[20]

____

This is my sister and me at Christmas.

How do you like my neon green legs?

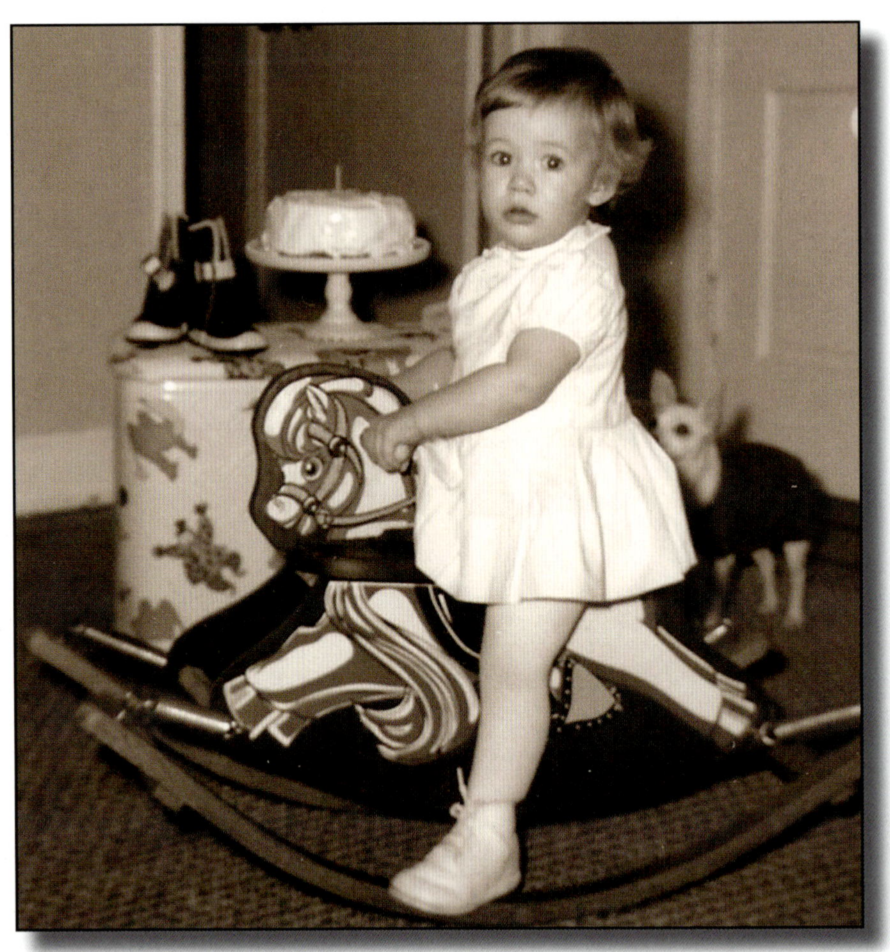

Can you guess how old I was here?
(Hint, look at the candles on the
cake in the background.)

Week 2: Day 1

Lesson 4

The Most Important Command of Our Master

Dogs have masters, but Cats have servants. Ever thought about that?

Dogs really want to please their master, right? Last week we learned that Jesus wants to call us "friends" not servants in John, chapter 15. He clearly stated how to be His friend in John 15:14, "You are my friends if you do what I command you." So, today we will be looking into the ***most important command*** of our Master for Dog Christians.

Now, let's be honest, there are ***a lot*** of commands in the New Testament...WHOA, how do we remember them, or even attempt to "do" all those commands?

Thankfully, Jesus really is our BFF! He decided to make it simple for us to remember His ***most important command*** as His followers or friends. Jesus told us a story about a very religious and smart person. Luke and Matthew both call him a lawyer—someone who was very important in his community. After listening to Jesus debate some of the religious leaders in the Temple one day, the lawyer asked Jesus a loaded question, "Which is the most important of all the commandments?" (Mark 12:28–34)

And what did our Master, Jesus Christ, answer him? Mark 12:30–31 (ESV)

> 30 *And you shall love the Lord your God with all your heart and with all your soul and with all your mind and with all your strength.*
>
> 31 *The second is this: You shall love your neighbor as yourself.*

Let's *dissect* that verse a little, okay? (I know this isn't Biology class, but I just liked the way that word sounded, don't you?)

Why in the world did Jesus tell us to love the Lord our God with four different parts of ourselves? As you begin to look deeper into the meaning of each of those, you will understand the importance of these four distinctions and how it does help us, as His friends, to truly love God with our whole selves.

Love the Lord your God with ***All Your Heart***:

The word ***heart*** is *kardia* in Greek (the language in which the New Testament was written), and the definition is best described as "the center of spiritual life including our thoughts, passions, desires, appetites, affections, or purposes." Wow! That is really talking about what make you ***you*** deep inside, right?

(Look up in a dictionary any of those words you don't understand to get the full meaning of the word ***heart***.)

Love the Lord your God with ***All Your Soul***:

The Greek word for ***soul*** is *psyche*, and its definitions include: the breath of life or our feelings. Only ***you*** can know how you truly feel about something or someone, right?

Love the Lord your God with ***All Your Mind***:

The Greek word for ***mind*** is *dianoia*. The definitions include: your understanding or way of thinking. Hmmm...let's *think* about that one a little...haha!

Love the Lord your God with ***All Your Strength***:

The Greek word for ***strength*** is *ischys.* The definition includes these words: ability, force, and might.

Ever thought about lifting weights to help you love God more? Me neither.

(Mark 12:30-31)

Since this is your memory verse for this week, please fill in the blanks below:

"And you shall _____________ the Lord your ____________

with all your _________________ and with all your ________________

and with all your ________________ and with all your ___________________.

The second is this: You shall ____________ your _________________________

as ______________________." (Mark _____: 30-_________)[21]

Suggestion:

Search for the song by Lincoln Brewster called "Love The Lord" on YouTube (www.youtube.com).

I have often memorized Bible verses by putting them to music. The chorus of this song ***really*** *helps me remember this verse so much easier.*

So, let's answer a few questions now to apply these definitions to this most important verse for *The Dog Walk*, following our Master's greatest command:

1. Since your ***heart*** is the "center of who you really are deep inside," write a list of 1-3 people or things you love the most right now:

1. ______________________________

2. ______________________________

3. ______________________________

2. Since your ***soul*** means "your feelings," right now in your life what would be something or an event for you to get really excited about?

____

3. Since your ***mind*** in the Greek means your "understanding" or "way of thinking," what person or book or movie would you say has most influenced the way you think about God?

____

4: According to the Greek word for ***strength***, our "ability or power" to love God must be able to grow stronger. Can you name one new habit you could possibly begin that would perhaps ***strengthen*** your love for God?

____

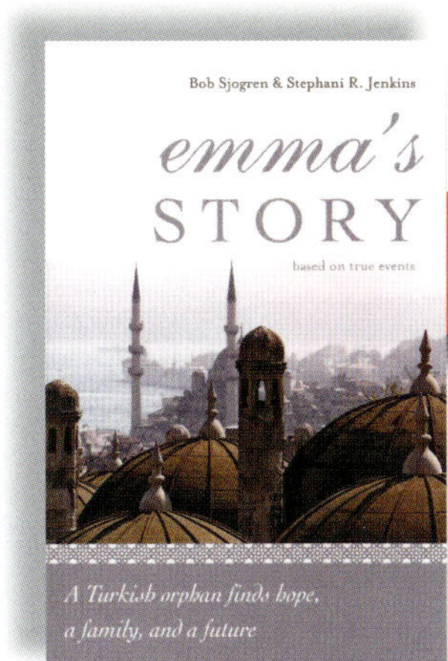

Today's Reading To Grow Your Faith

Emma's Story:
Read Chapters 13–16

1. What did Graham and Becky name their new ministry to the orphans of Turkey?[22]

____

2. Who wanted to steal God's glory from the story of Bahar's life?[23]

____

3. With whom was Bahar taken to live after her mother died?[24]

____

4. What major geological catastrophe happened in this chapter?[25]

____

"Just mailed the
cat to Indonesia!
~Awesome Day!"

Do any of you have a space
between your front teeth
like I do?

Week 2: Day 2

Lesson 5

Our Master's Most Important Command (Part 2)

So yesterday was a ***long*** lesson, wasn't it? We had to really work our brains to dive into the first half of our *Memory Verse* for this week. Isn't it cool to learn Greek words in middle school? I bet you had no idea you were so smart. Great job!!!

Now, let's focus on the second half of that same Scripture. When you think about the second half of our Memory Verse, have you ever asked yourself the question: *just who is my neighbor?* Well, in Luke's reference to this same story, he follows the lawyer's question with another story to answer that very question! Guess which *parable* Jesus told him? The Parable of the Good Samaritan! Why that story? There is a reason. And I'm sure you can't wait to find out, right, my fellow Dogs?

Read Luke 10:25-37. Check the box after you have read it! ❑

So, imagine going to a grocery store to buy some food. As you're about to turn into the entrance, you see a man lying on the side of the parking lot in the back. You can tell he's been beaten and bruised. Then you see two religious people, like your Youth Pastor and your Church Elder or Deacon, pass right by the hurting, almost dying man — and totally ignore him! Can you believe it? Then, a *Samaritan* (someone from a different culture and probably not at all religious) saw the hurting man, stopped immediately and kindly helped him in many ways including giving money and showing great compassion. That's the context of the story. Let's get back to the Scriptures.

Then Jesus asked the all-important question to the lawyer: "Which person who passed by the hurting man, *do you think*, proved to be his *neighbor*?"

What would ***your*** answer have been? ________________________________.

The wise lawyer answered Jesus, "The one who showed him mercy." Then Jesus replied, "You go, and do the same." Wow! That really hits us between the eyes, doesn't it? And it probably did the same to that lawyer!

As some people say, it is fun and easy to follow Jesus by going to church or youth group with all my friends, but to reach out to someone who looks or dresses or speaks differently from me? Now that's a different story. But the Samaritan, *someone of a different culture from the hurting person,* is the true "hero" of this story.

The "one who showed mercy" is the person in the story that Jesus says we are to follow his example in order to "love your neighbor as yourself." That kind of love is what Jesus is asking of *us* to begin *The Dog Walk*. Are you ready?

1. According to Jesus' definition, who is your *neighbor* right now?

____

2. To whom do you feel Jesus wants you to show mercy or kindness in your life right now? (Perhaps it is a family member or someone in your homeschool co-op or neighborhood that you find very hard to love. Ask God who He wants to be your neighbor, the one who needs you to show them mercy this week.) Write that person's name here:

____

Now pray for an opportunity to be kind to them this week. Check the box after you have prayed for this opportunity. ☐

(Mark 12:30-31)

[30] *And you shall love the Lord your God*
with all your heart and with all your soul
and with all your mind and with all your strength.

[31] *The second is this: You shall love your neighbor as yourself.*

Suggestion:

Memorizing Scripture doesn't always have to be hard. In our last lesson, we talked about memorizing verses to music. Today, we're going to find another way.

You can memorize Scripture through making pictures! Yep, you—you can draw pictures. This is called a rebus. A rebus is a representation of a word or phrase by pictures, symbols, etc. that suggest that word or phrase. Here's my husband's rebus of Colossians 3:23—the rebus is the pencil drawing, not the typed words:

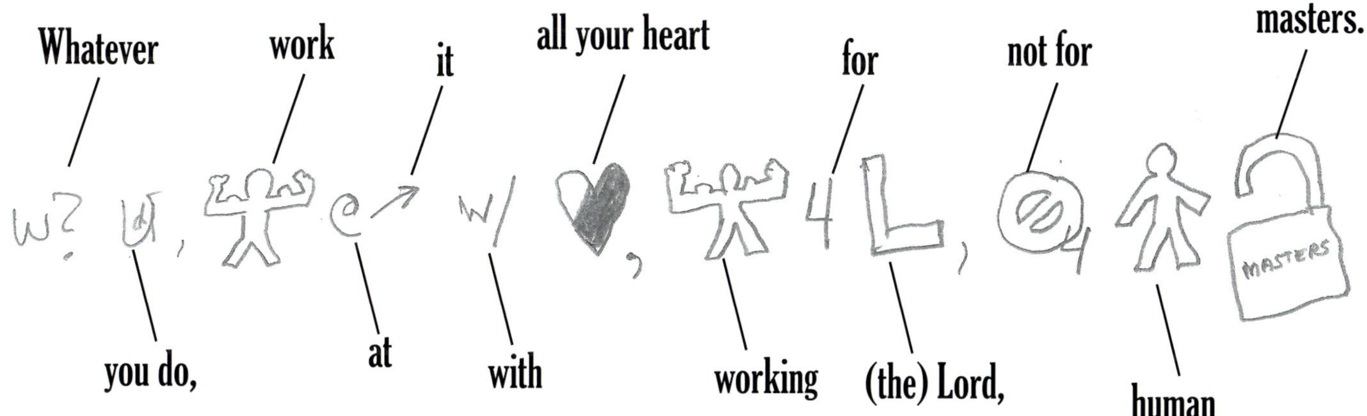

Notice that it doesn't have to be professional looking at all. You can use stick figures if you want! It doesn't matter because only you will be seeing it. Therefore make it any way you want. (And there's no need to write the explanation.) The key is to be sure that you can understand it and as a result, memorize it!

Now on the next page, make a rebus of Mark 12:30-31.

My rebus of Mark 12:30-31:

So, I wish I could see your way cool REBUS of the Memory Verse (if you want, ask your parent to scan it to me at debby@mmpublishers.com).

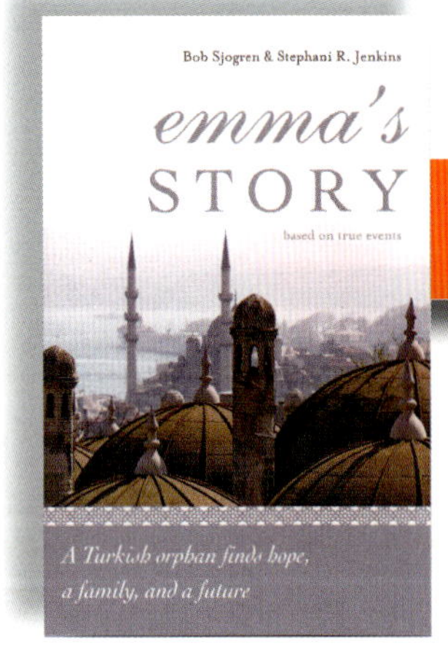

Today's Reading To Grow Your Faith

Emma's Story:
Read Chapters 17–20

1. What is the name of Becky's daughter?[26] ______________________________
2. What animal did God use to rescue Bahar from the rubble of the earthquake?[27]

   ____

3. What is the name of the teams that Becky takes over to the orphanage?[28]

   ____

4. What did Amy and Mark wish they could do for Bahar after they got home?[29]

   ____

Cartoon Day
Week 2: Day 3
Lesson 6

I'm leaving because of you!
Excuse me, but can we talk please? We need to work through this to honor God.

When Cats And Dogs Have People Problems In Church

How is the Cat not loving their neighbor? [30]

____

____

Who's Got the Power?

Well, I hope you have been a good *neighbor* this week as you have been memorizing *The Most Important Command* from our Master, Jesus, as we begin *The Dog Walk*.

Write what happened when you "showed mercy or kindness" to the person God put into your heart or mind earlier this week:

___

I hope you sensed God smiling at you when you *lived out loud* His love to another person this week! He really smiles when we love that person that can perhaps really annoy us or that person that is so different from us. It's easy to just "pass by" even though they may be sad or lonely or just need a friend.

When I was in middle school and high school, I was a cheerleader for a few years. I loved it! It was so much fun getting the audience to yell for our athletes, especially in the gym for our basketball team. We often did a "Call and Response" cheer where the students and parents had to yell a reply to our question. And one of our cheers we would yell to our fellow students was:

Cheerleaders: ***Who's got the power?***
Reply: ***We've got the power!***
Cheerleaders: ***Who's gonna win?***
Reply: ***We're gonna win!***

Well, today's lesson is titled, "Who's Got the Power?"

Why did I use that title? Because your Memory Verse for the week is nearly impossible to live out or obey if you aren't plugged in to the true ***Power Source***.

Let's quote your memory verse together right now: Mark 12:30–31

And you shall love the Lord your God with all your heart and with all your soul and with all your mind and with all your strength.
The second is this: You shall love your neighbor as yourself.

Place a check in the box after you have quoted it to someone else. ☐

Now please open your Bible or Bible App and read this verse out loud:

I John 4:19

(Now don't you wish ***that*** was your Memory Verse for this week? It's only 7 words! Too bad, but you aren't in ***first grade*** anymore ☺.)

Seriously, this verse, "We love because He first loved us," is ***very key***.

You are right if you feel it is next to impossible to walk like a Dog Christian if we have to totally obey Mark 12:30-31 in our own power or strength.

But we don't, do we?

When you ask Jesus to forgive you of all your sins—and He does, then you open the door of your heart and invite Him in—He comes in to stay.

Guess what happens? His ***Spirit***, which contains ***His power*** to love God and others, fills your heart and life to the fullest. But sometimes that power "leaks" out of us.

So, think of it like a laptop computer, like this one I am typing on right now. It has been plugged in and the battery is fully charged. But now, as I'm working on our porch without it being plugged in, the battery is slowly draining. Eventually it will die and it won't be able to work or fulfill the purpose it was created for.

Do you understand my analogy? We need to stay plugged in to God—meeting with Him on a regular basis—if we want the ***power*** to love Him and love our neighbor. ***This is a must if you want to live life like a Dog Christian and not like a Cat Christian.***

How do you like my new Dog Walk cheer? Find one person to call and respond:

You: ***Who's got the power?***
Reply: ***God's got the Power!***
You: ***Who you gonna love?***
Reply: ***God and our neighbors!***
You: ***Who gets the Glory?***
Reply: ***God gets the Glory!***

And so you are now ready to truly begin ***The Dog Walk***!

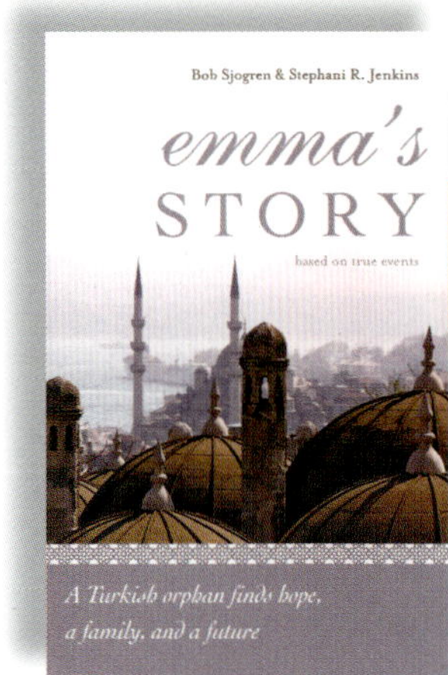

Today's Reading To Grow Your Faith

Emma's Story:
Read Chapters 21–24

1. Did Bahar's uncle give permission for Amy to adopt her?[31]

____

2. What practical gift was Least of These able to provide for Gulistan?[32]

____

3. About how many trips to Turkey had Becky flown in the past two years?[33]

____

4. What is the new name that Adam told Bahar the Bates and Sneeds have given her?[34]

____

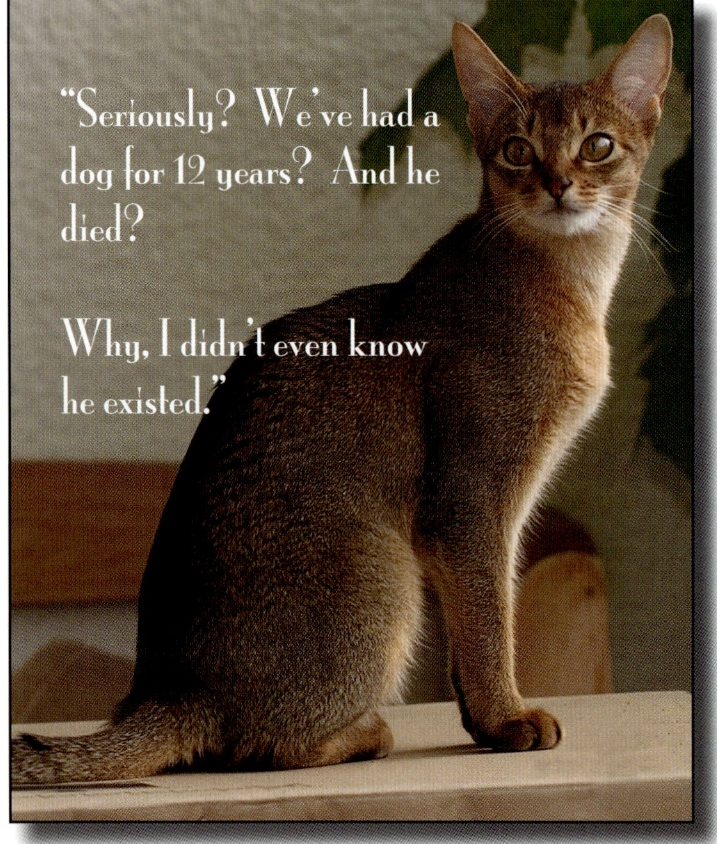

"Seriously? We've had a dog for 12 years? And he died?

Why, I didn't even know he existed."

Photo by: Marin Bahmann, via Wikimedia Commons

Week 3: Day 1

Lesson 7

Plugging Into God Every Day

Hey fellow Dogs! I am really excited about this new week of growing through *The Dog Walk!* Last week we jumped into studying our foundational verses for our walk as Dog Christians. Can you still say them? "And you shall ***love*** the Lord your God with ***all*** your _________ and with ***all*** your ___________ and with ***all*** your _______ and with ***all*** your _______________. And the second is this: ***love*** your _________________ as yourself." (Mark 12:30-31). (*Hope you knew how to fill in all those blanks, my friends!)* [35]

One simple way to remember how to live out loud that ***Most Important Command*** from our Master (Jesus) is found on a T-shirt that my son, Hunter, received his freshman year at college. Various groups, churches, organizations and ministries love to give away free T-shirts to college students to promote their organizations! But this slogan was the best one I have seen to live out on our Dog Walk! It says: ***Love God. Love People. Repeat***. Now that about sums it up, doesn't it?

Well, today we are discussing how to "plug into God" every day! We will be studying an Old Testament passage that will hopefully guide and challenge you in your conversations with God. I will introduce you to an interesting website on prayer created by my husband, Bob Sjogren, a few years ago. We will be using it often in this curriculum for the next few weeks.

Read Ezekiel 36:26–27 (ESV) below that the website is based upon:

26 *And I will give you a new heart, and a new spirit I will put within you.*
And I will remove the heart of stone from your flesh and give you a heart of flesh.

27 *And I will put **my Spirit** within you,*
*and **cause you** to walk in my statutes and be careful to obey my rules.*

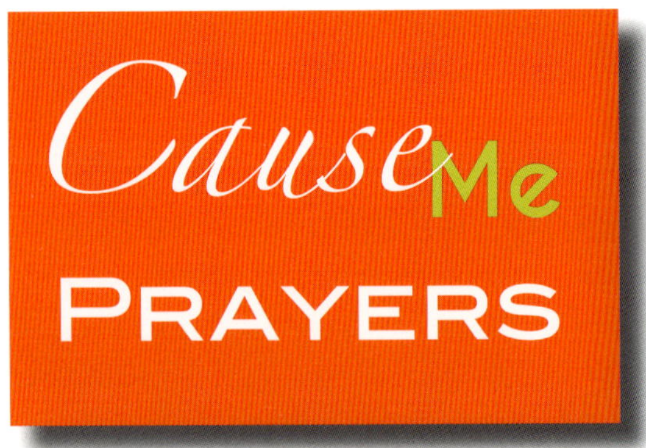

First, let me ask you a question...do you ever ask God for help? Yes or No? Let's be honest, of course you do! Well, in my husband's teaching called "Cause Me Prayers," he opens our eyes and heart up to a new way of talking to God as Dog Christians. These "Cause Me Prayers" teach us to depend on God 100% each day—thus, we learn how to daily "plug into God!"

Practically speaking, list 3–5 areas or people in your life that you might have a struggle with right now. Examples: math, little sister, honoring mom, friends, etc.

1. ______________________________
2. ______________________________
3. ______________________________
4. ______________________________
5. ______________________________

So, normally when you talk to God about one of these people or areas of your life, what do you say? Probably something like these prayers:

*Dear Jesus, please **HELP** me do better in math, or*
*Dear God, **HELP** me honor my parents today, or*
*Dear Jesus, **HELP** me love my annoying little sister, or*
*Dear God, **HELP** my basketball team win our big game tonight!*

Relate to any of these prayers? I have a ***big*** question for you: When you ask God to help ***you*** be better in math or in obeying parents or loving siblings, aren't you really saying, "God, I can love my sister 60% (or maybe 40% or 75%) today, so please give me the extra 40% of the love I need for her." Without realizing it, you are trying to do it in your own power and strength.

Instead think of "plugging into God" and asking Him to love her through you 100%. This way you are just His vessel of love for her—and He gets 100% of the glory! Do you see the difference?

So, when we apply our verse for this week, Ezekiel 36:27 (on the left page), the power source is very different. And the person who gets the GLORY for the answer is very different! With "help me" prayers, we can be *too proud of ourselves* and only give God a little of the glory for answering and helping *us* do it! But with "cause me" prayers, God gets *all* the glory because He accomplished 100% of our requests *through* us. Which type of prayer request wording do you think Dogs will want to pray? Yep, "Cause Me Prayers!"

Let's practice talking to God about the 3–5 people or areas on your list on the page on the left.

Example: Dear Lord, please **<u>CAUSE</u>** <u>me to give You glory</u> by obeying my mom today.

Now talk to God about your list above using the words from Ezekiel 36:27. Remember to replace the words "help me" with "cause me to give You glory" by...

1. ____
2. ____
3. ____
4. ____
5. ____

Great job! It may seem weird at first, and the words really don't matter as much as your own ***heart attitude***. Now let's go to our "Prayer to Go" website and read a few other God-centered prayers: www.prayertogo.com

When you get to the home page, you will see colorful looking iPod minis—that's what you saw on the previous page. **Click** on the neon green one that says *"Preteen Prayers"* on it. Then read or listen to, by **clicking the arrow to the right of the stars,** at least five of the prayers. Then rate each one by choosing a number in the blue drop-down box and then clicking "Vote."

Check the box when you are done. ❑

Go to www.prayertogo.com and look under ***Prayer Resources*** on the right side of the home page. Click on Video / 8 Teachings.

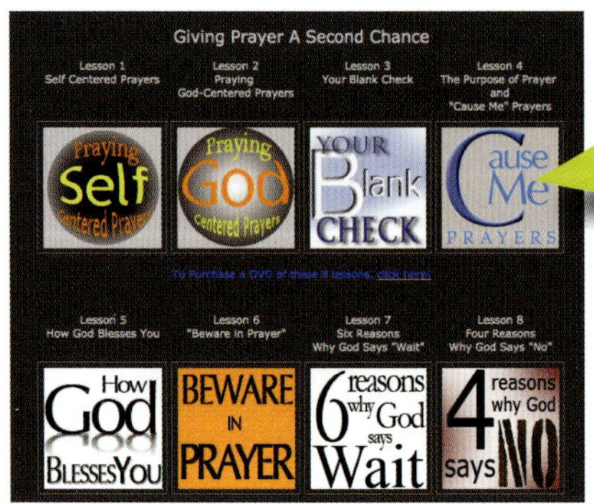

Then click on the topic "Cause Me Prayers." You can watch a video of my husband, Bob Sjogren, teaching on our Memory Verse for this week. See if your mom or dad will watch it with you. It's very powerful!

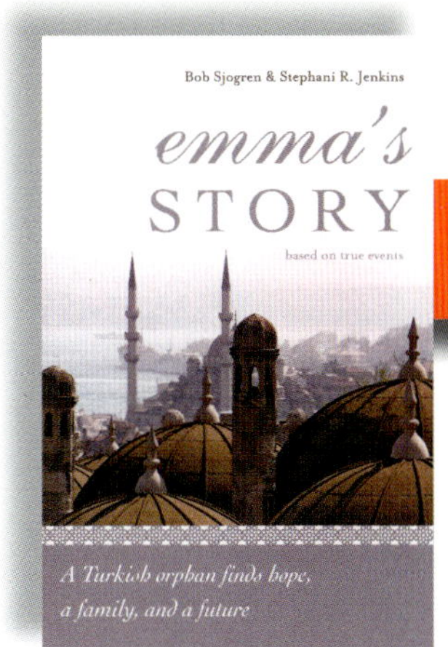

Today's Reading To Grow Your Faith

Emma's Story:
Read Chapters 25–28

1. Which angel had God sent to guard Becky against the demon called Suffering?[36]

____

2. What are the names of the twin girls who are hoping to be Bahar's sisters?[37]

____

3. Who went with Amy to help her try to adopt Bahar?[38]

____

4. Why was it such a big deal that Amy and Mark wanted to adopt "Emma"?[39]

____

"But the bird always comes this time of day. I don't get it—where is he?"

By Karelj (Own work) [Public domain], via Wikimedia Commons

Here I am in 5th Grade.

Do you think I changed much one year later in 6th grade?

Week 3: Day 2

Lesson 8

Praying Cause Me vs. Help Me

Today, we will begin with learning your Scripture Memory Verse for this week:

Read again Ezekiel 36:26–27 (ESV):

26 *And I will give you a new heart, and a new spirit I will put within you.*
And I will remove the heart of stone from your flesh and give you a heart of flesh.

27 *And I will put my Spirit within you,*
*and **cause** you to walk in my statutes and be careful to obey my rules.*

Understanding a verse helps me remember and live it out much better. So, let's answer a few questions today:

1. ***Who*** puts the new heart and new spirit within us? [40]

____

2. Does "heart of stone" refer to a person who cheerfully obeys God—Yes or No? [41]

____

3. When God changes our hearts from "stone" to "flesh," what words can best describe a person with a soft heart towards God? [42]

____

4. Who or what does God put "within us" to cause us to obey Him? [43]

---

5. So then, who is actually responsible for our obedience to God? [44]

---

6. Finally, do you think if you ask Him, God will cause you to walk like a Dog? Why or why not?

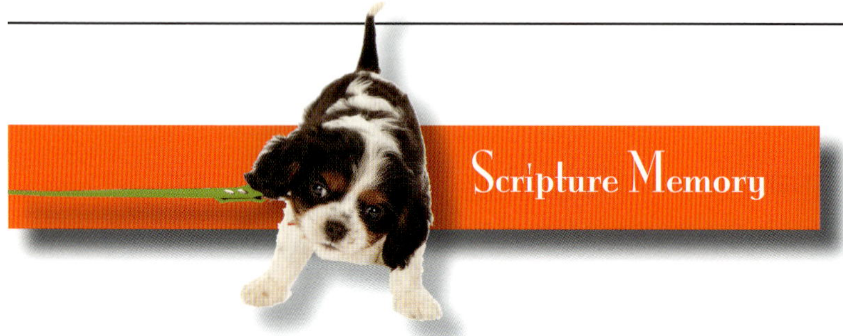

Take 5 minutes to begin memorizing Ezekiel 36:27 (ESV) below. Either review it in your mind, write it out underneath the verse, or make a rebus.

27 And I will put my Spirit within you, and cause you to walk in My statutes and be careful to obey my rules.

I saw this bumper sticker on someone's car.
I'll bet there's a cat one too!

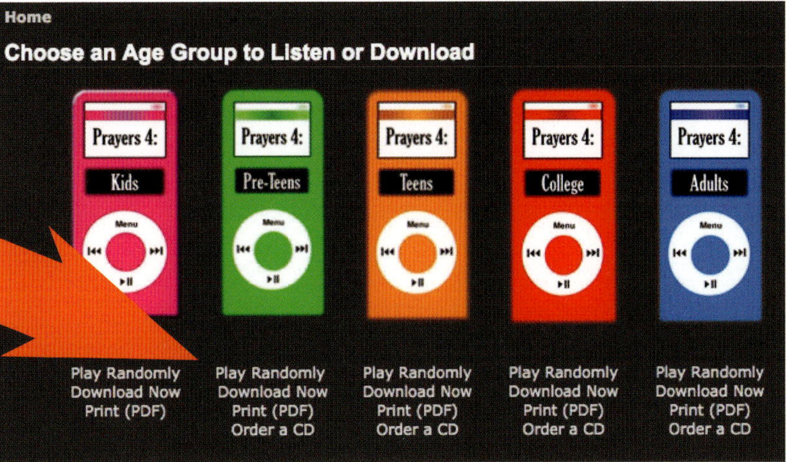

Now, go back to the website: www.prayertogo.com Read or listen to 10 more prayers today and rate them.

Write the one prayer you liked the most today here:

____

Finish today's lesson by practicing your own "cause me" prayers that you wrote out on page 33. Remember, to pray "cause me" for God's glory, not your own.

Think of five areas of your life or your family or in the world that you feel God wants you to talk to Him about today. Then write "Cause Me" prayers for them.

1. ____

2. ____

3. ____

4. ____

5. ____

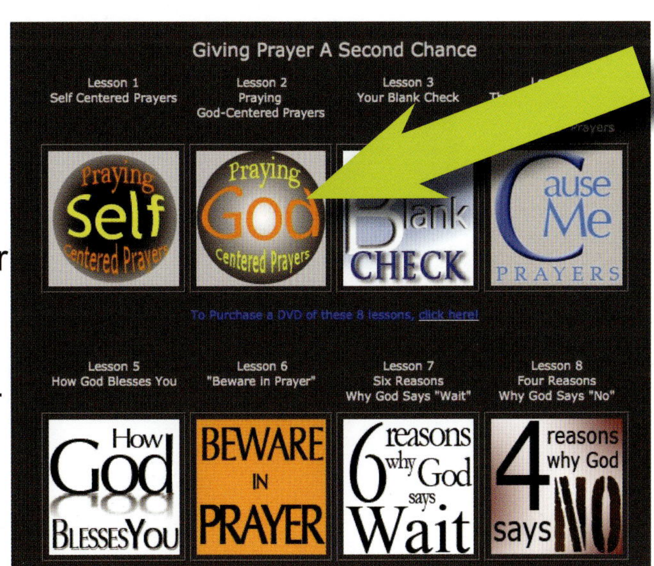

Go to www.prayertogo.com and look under PRAYER RESOURCES on the right side of the home page. Click on Video / 8 Teachings.

Then click on the topic "Praying God-Centered Prayers". You can watch a video of my husband, Bob Sjogren, helping you to understand what kind of prayers Dogs pray!

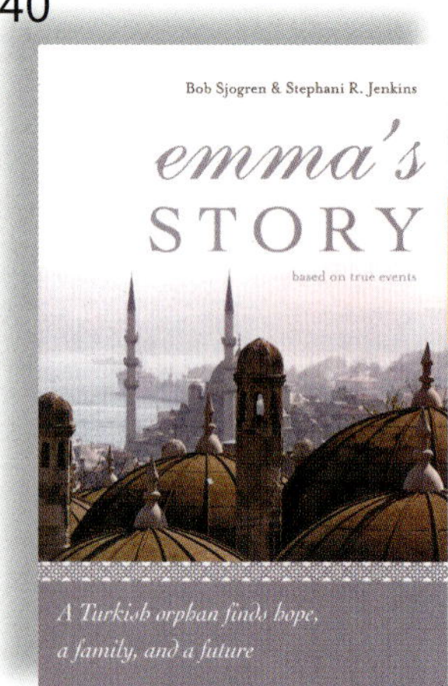

Bob Sjogren & Stephani R. Jenkins
emma's
STORY
A Turkish orphan finds hope, a family, and a future

Today's Reading To Grow Your Faith

Emma's Story:
Read Chapters 29-32

1. What was the name of the woman that Least of These paid to feed the children?[45]

2. What was the name of Amy's translator?[46]

3. Which demon has been working hard against this adoption process?[47]

4. On pg. 123, what did Mrs. Basar think the Americans wanted to do to Emma?[48]

Shhh. We're hunting wabbits!

LORD, MAKE HIM HAPPY, HELP HIM TO BE GOOD, HELP HIM GET GOOD GRADES, BLESS HIM LORD.

LORD, MAKE HIM HOLY, CAUSE HIM TO DELIGHT IN YOU, LET HIM TOUCH THE NATIONS, GIVE HIS FUTURE SPOUSE THE SAME HEART.

How Cats And Dogs Pray For Their Kids

The Cat's prayer is not incorrect, but what is it missing? [49]

____

____

The Pressure is OFF

With the Holy Spirit living inside of us ***causing us to live the Christian life***, the pressure is ***off,*** right? Sometimes as Christians, we think we have to do all the work to be obedient and good and perfect for God to love us and be pleased with us. But in reality, we simply need to keep "recharging our spiritual battery" (plugging into Him) daily to get His power to live the Christian life.

I hope you have learned this week that, according to the Scriptures, God Himself is the One Who puts His Spirit within you. This is what the Dog Walk is all about! We all need to open our hearts to Jesus as our Master and begin *The Dog Walk* living for His Glory and not your own.

Since I know you're serious about being a Dog, let's get practical. Name one area where, without realizing it, you are not depending on God 100% and as a result, are robbing God of the glory due to His name?

____

Cat Christians often think that they have to live the Christian life in their own power and strength and then add a little "thanks to God" for the small role He does. But Dogs want to shine the spotlight on God. Trusting in Him 100% makes us flashlights that point people to Him and how great He truly is!

Now, write a "Cause Me" prayer for the area in which you are not depending 100% upon God.

____

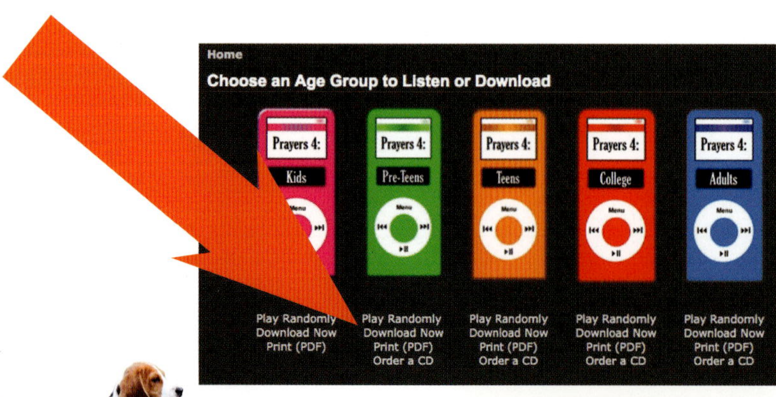

Now, go back to the website: www.prayertogo.com

Read or listen to 10 more prayers today and rate them.

Well, I hope you are enjoying this new way of praying or talking to God this week.

Can you quote Ezekiel 36:27 now? Take this workbook to one person in your family. Say your memory verse below, and have them check the box after you have said it correctly. ☐

27 *And I will put my Spirit within you, and cause you to walk in My statutes and be careful to obey my rules.*

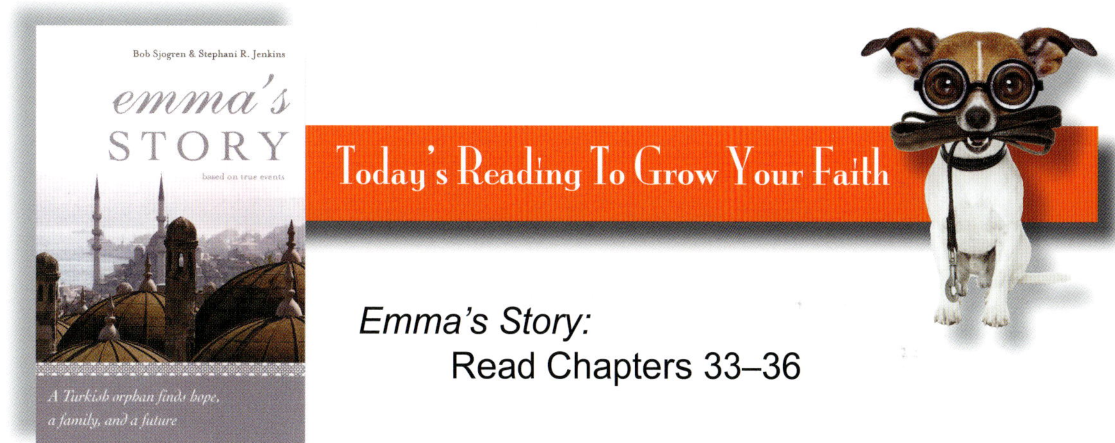

Bob Sjogren & Stephani R. Jenkins
emma's
STORY
A Turkish orphan finds hope, a family, and a future
Today's Reading To Grow Your Faith

Emma's Story:
Read Chapters 33–36

1. Which two demons were working very hard against Amy and her daughter, Beth?[50]

____

2. What is the name of the kind, Muslim driver for Amy and the ministry?[51]

____

3. Who helped Beth finally work through her problems about adopting Emma?[52]

____

4. Which grandchild of Becky and Graham was being attacked in this chapter[53]

____

Here I am at 13 years old.
This photo was taken the
summer when I came to know
Jesus personally!

(Sorry the quality
is so poor.
It is a very old picture.)

Week 4: Day 1

Lesson 10

Finding JOY on our Dog Walk

When I was about your age, I remember having days where I was happy and then some days where I felt kinda down—maybe bored or maybe even lonely. During one of those times, my mother noticed my mood had changed and asked me what was wrong. I really had no good answer, so I just said, “I don’t know, Momma, but some days I feel really great and some days I feel sad.”

Well, that day my wonderful mother (even though I didn’t always think she was wonderful during my middle school years, truth, right?)—okay, let’s start over. On that day, my wonderful mother taught me a simple but profound truth. I call it the “Secret to Joy.” And it is so simple, but you can miss it so easily—especially if you are living your life as a Cat Christian. Let me explain the secret: Live out **J-O-Y** !

What do I mean? Your focus each day must be in that order: **J-O-Y**

Because if you turn it around, you just get “Yoj”. And what is that? Nothing. Boring. Weird word. Blehhhhh! “Yoj”—even that word looks and sounds depressing. But a lot of people who call themselves Christians live a life of “Yoj”. Usually they are ***all*** Cats...or sometimes Dog Christians who have forgotten the “Secret to Joy!”

Well, you must now be asking, “How do I live out **J-O-Y**?” The secret is that each of those letters represent who we plan our lives around each and every day.

J = Jesus
O = Others
Y = You

So, once I learned this “secret” from my mother, I tried to begin each day thinking like a Dog Christian would think:

First, how can I honor Jesus today? Or bring glory to God today?
Second, how can I bless others today? Who needs me to encourage them?
Third, what are my own needs or desires for today?

I promise you, if you plan your day in that order, you will find **JOY** instead of what often happens when you plan your day in this order: *You, Others, Jesus* or "Yoj." It has been true in my life for over 40 years! And I taught it to my four children, too. I challenge you to live it out this week. Put it to the test. Pass it on!

I taught my kids the "JOY" principle when they were this young.

1. **Jesus**: What is one attitude you can choose to have or action you can choose to do that will truly honor and glorify **Jesus** this day? (Read Matthew 5:1-16 if you need ideas.)

____

2. **Others**: Who do you feel needs a kind word or a good deed from you today? Next, what will you do to express it to them?

____

3. **You**: What is one need you have or goal you want to accomplish today?

____

John 10:10 (ESV)

The thief comes only to steal and kill and destroy.
I came that they may have life and have it abundantly.

1. Who do you think "the thief" is for us today as followers of Jesus?[54]

____

2. Who is the "I" in our memory verse?[55]

____

3. What does the word "abundant" really mean?[56]

____

Begin to memorize this verse as you draw two contrasting pictures in the boxes below.

Draw a Thief Stealing	Draw a Person with an Abundance of Something

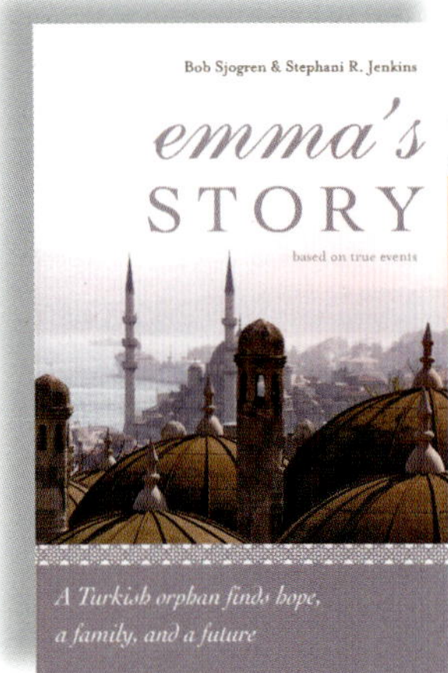

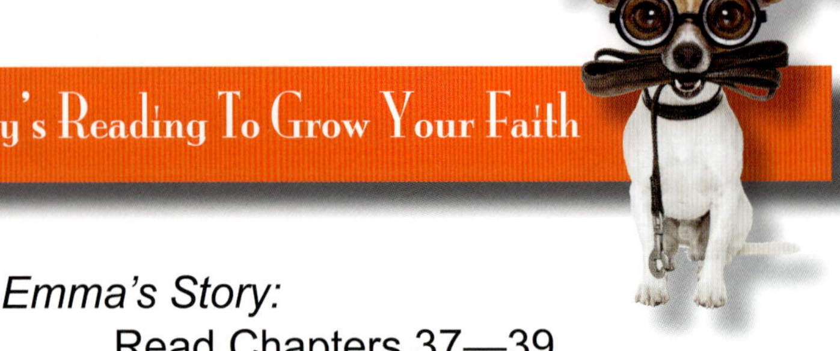

Emma's Story:
Read Chapters 37—39

1. What happened that softened the hearts of young Graham's classmates?[57]

___

2. Who was there to encourage Amy when she felt like giving up?[58]

___

3. Whom did God send to fight Chaos and Confusion when the traffic was so bad?[59]

___

Week 4: Day 2

Lesson 11

Finding JOY on our Dog Walk (Part 2)

Well, we only spent one day on planning your day to live out *The Dog Walk's* "Secret to JOY." Do you think that was enough? I don't. I think a second time would be helpful to really help it become a part of our lives. So let's do it again ***today.*** Fill out the J-O-Y section below one more time for a new day.

1. **Jesus**: What is one attitude you can choose to have or action you can choose to do that will truly honor and glorify **Jesus** this day? (Read Matthew 5:1-16 if you need ideas.)

____

2. **Others**: Who do you feel needs a kind word or a good deed from you today? Next, what will you do to express it to them?

____

3. **You**: What is one need you have or goal you want to accomplish today?

____

Now, go put your "Secret to JOY" into action for today! Check the box when you have completed all three JOY givers! ☐

1. Did you experience more JOY in your life when you practiced living out our "Secret to Joy" in your last lesson? Circle: Yes or No

2. Explain what happened in your heart or life or attitude that day when you truly put **Jesus** first, **Others** second, and **Yourself** third in your thoughts and plans for that day.

____

____

3. Have you had a "Yoj" type of day this week? Circle: Yes or No

4. If "yes," explain what happened and how you felt when you lived your day with your focus in this order: **Yourself** first, **Others** second (or not at all), and **Jesus** third (or not at all).

____

5. Did you have true joy in your life or heart when you chose that path for that day? Circle: Yes or No

John 10:10 (ESV)

The thief comes only to steal and kill and destroy.
I came that they may have life and have it abundantly.

Fill in the blanks to help you memorize your weekly verse:

The ____________ comes only to ______________ and ___________ and

_____________________. I came that ___________ may have _____________ and

have it ____________________________.[60]

Take one minute and thank Jesus right now for His promise of abundant life—both now here on earth and for all of eternity in heaven with Him. Place a check in the box after you have done it. ☐

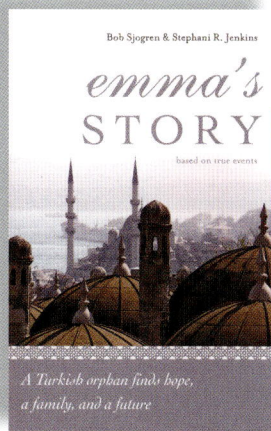

Today's Reading To Grow Your Faith

Emma's Story:
Read Chapters 40-Epilogue

1. Back in the USA, what did God remind Beth to do when her mother and uncle in Turkey were trying to get to the orphanage before it closed for the weekend?[61]

____

2. After finally being adopted, what was Bahar's new full name?[62]

____

3. Epilogue: Finish this quote, "Remember that no matter what obstacles you face in

life, _________ __________ ____________ ___ ________!"[63]

I was in high school for all of these pictures.
Which do you think came first,
the short or long hairstyle?

Can you pick out which one is me?

Copernicus was wrong. The world (and God) revolves around us.

Aa Bb Cc Dd Ee F

COPERNICUS

Cat's Schooling 101

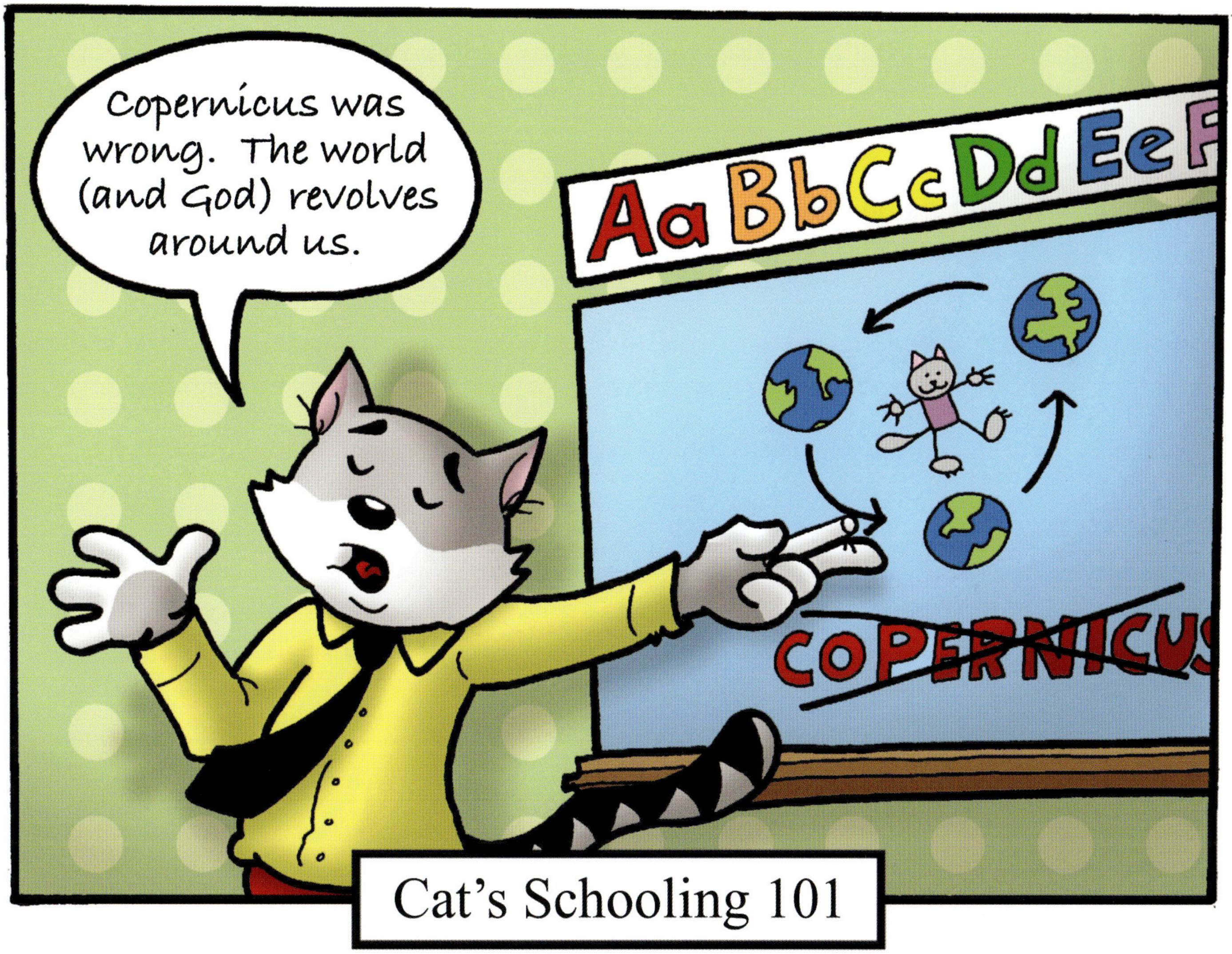

Describe a time when you thought everything was all about you. [64]

____

____

Finding JOY on our Dog Walk (Part 3)

Experts say that you need to do something 30 days in a row before it becomes a habit. I'm not making you do it 30 days in a row, but I am hoping and praying that thinking through J-O-Y does become a habit for you. So, you guessed it, we're going to go through it one more time! This is the last day of this week's focus of our Dog Walk—planning your day to live out our "Secret to JOY!" But I hope you think through it every day of your life!

1. **Jesus**: What is one attitude you can choose to have or action you can choose to do that will truly honor and glorify **Jesus** this day? (Read Matthew 5:1-16 if you need ideas.)

___

2. **Others**: Who do you feel needs a kind word or a good deed from you today? Next, what will you do to express it to them?

___

3. **You**: What is one need you have or goal you want to accomplish today?

___

Now let's roll like the NIKE ads, and **JUST DO IT!**

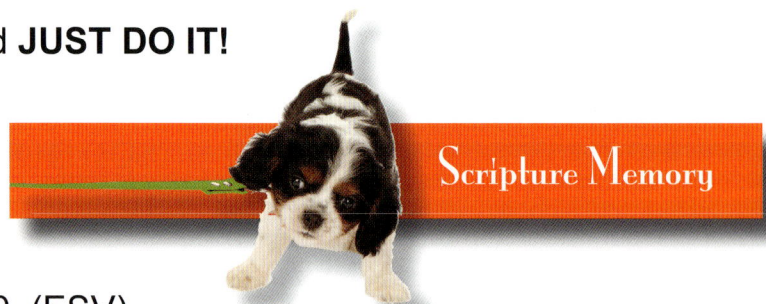

Scripture Memory

John 10:10 (ESV)

The thief comes only to steal and kill and destroy.
I came that they may have life and have it abundantly.

Quote this verse to one family member and then check the box. ☐

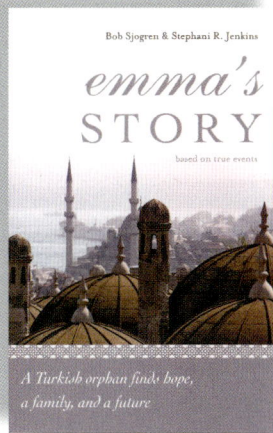

Today's Reading To Grow Your Faith

Emma's Story:
Final Project

You read about Stephani Jenkins on page 162 in your last lesson. She was close to your age when God gave her the desire to write a book before she graduated from her homeschool high school. But that was over 10 years ago, Stephani is now married to Chris, and God has blessed them with three little boys. She started her first "official" year of homeschooling in the fall of 2015.

Your Final Book Project: Write a letter to Stephani Jenkins and her family sharing how *Emma's Story* has affected your prayer life or changed your life!

Here is her email address: stephani.jenkins@gmail.com

If you want to send her a handwritten letter, please mail it to our office, and we will send it on to her home address:

Mrs. Stephani Jenkins
c/o Mission Minded Publishers
4663 Crown Hill Road
Mechanicsville, VA 23111

Stephani and Chris Jenkins

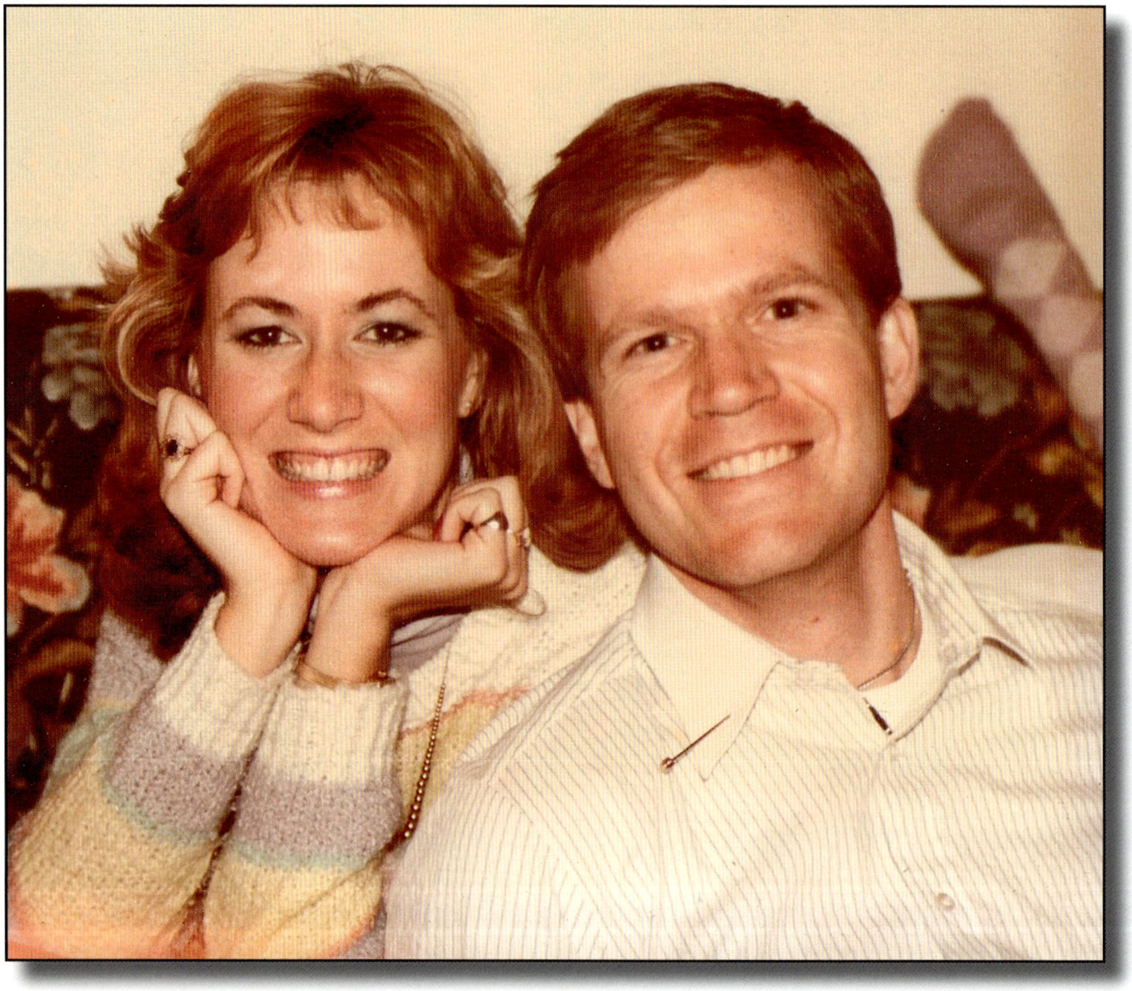

This picture was taken when I first met my husband.
I was 25 years old. He was 26.

Week 5: Day 1

Lesson 13

How's Your PMA?

Actions follows Attitude—ever heard that saying? Well, it is often true and even God's Word points to its truth in the 4th chapter of Philippians. We will look at that a little later...

But speaking of *Attitude*, I have another story to tell you from my middle school years.

When I was finishing elementary school and heading into 6th grade, I had the privilege of going to a summer camp each year for three years. Because I lived in Alabama, my parents picked a Christian-based place called *Camp Winnetaska*. I have a lot of fun memories from my week there each summer and one of the memories involves *Attitude*.

Positive
Mental
ATTITUDE

Camp Winnetaska had a large gym at the top of a hill where all the campers would gather every morning after breakfast. And every morning the Camp Director would call us together with his whistle. I can still remember the loud, shrill sound of the whistle he blew as we started our day's activities.

After he blew the whistle, he would shout zealously: "How's your PMA? And all 200 campers would loudly answer, "Boy, are we enthusiastic!"

What does PMA stand for? *Positive Mental Attitude.*

He was trying to get us to learn that ***actions follow attitude***. This means that if you start off your day with a positive attitude, you're probably going to have a positive day! Pretty neat huh!

But the opposite is true as well. If you start off your day with a negative attitude (some people call it, "waking up on the wrong side of the bed!"), then you're probably going to have a bad day.

Learning about all of this is our next section in *The Dog Walk!*

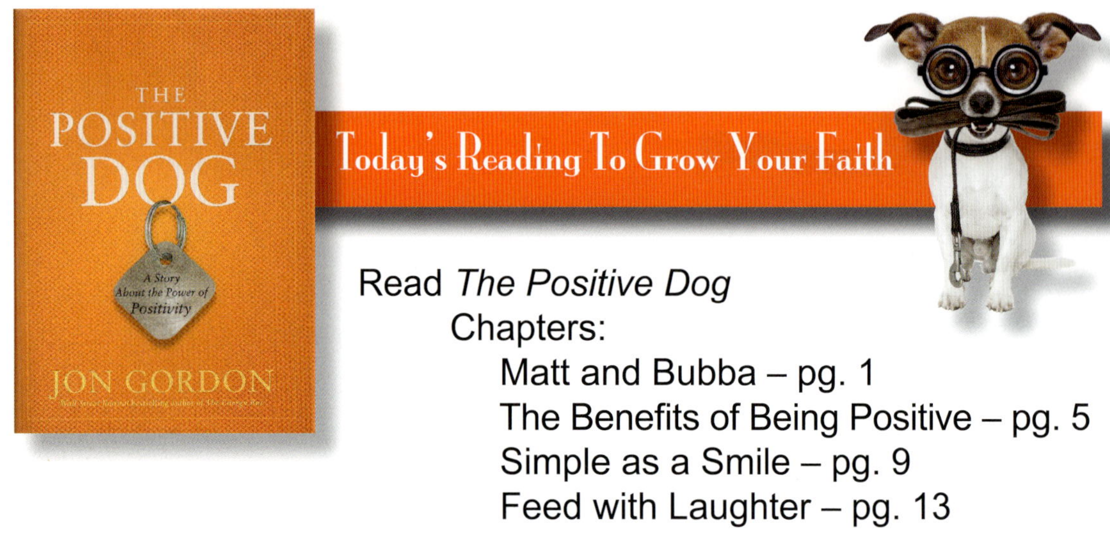

Read *The Positive Dog*
Chapters:
- Matt and Bubba – pg. 1
- The Benefits of Being Positive – pg. 5
- Simple as a Smile – pg. 9
- Feed with Laughter – pg. 13

Answer these questions from today's reading:

1. According to Bubba on page 3, what two types of dogs do we all have inside us?[65]

____

2. According to research, name six benefits of *Positivity (or a positive attitude)*.[66]

   1. ___________________________________
   2. ___________________________________
   3. ___________________________________
   4. ___________________________________
   5. ___________________________________
   6. ___________________________________

3. On page 10, what can be the "source of our Positivity?"[67]

____

4. What "is a powerful way to feed the positive dog in us each day?"[68]

____

5. What are the 3 "dog bone" quotes Bubba wants Matt to remember?[69]

1. ____

2. ____

3. ____

Psalm 118:1 (NIV)

Give thanks to the Lord, for he is good; his love endures forever!

Finish today's lesson teaching one of your siblings or friends Camp Winnetaska's morning chant: **How's Your PMA? "Boy, are we Enthusiastic!"** You start it off to them first and then have them start it off to you.

My husband loves to garden.
This is one of the watermelons he grew.
Umm, it was tasty!

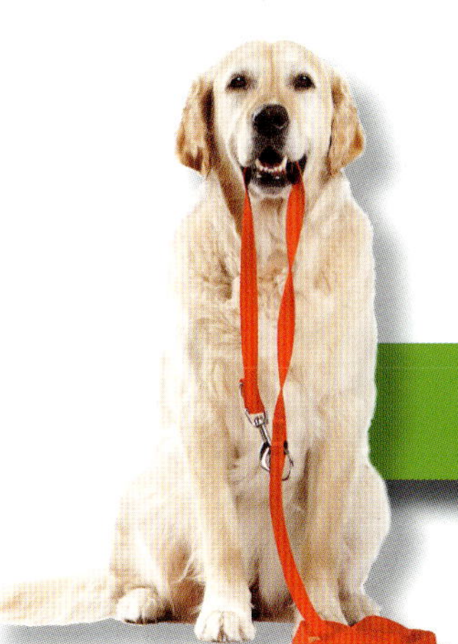

Week 5: Day 2

Lesson 14

Learning Life Lessons with Mrs. Debby

Attitude of Gratitude

The Positive Dog is not the only book that talks about the benefits of being positive. There are many other books and many other people who have created phrases that will point you in the same direction.

Read the six below and put a check mark in the box you like the most!

- ☐ *Yesterday is not ours to recover, but tomorrow is ours to win or lose.*
  Lyndon B. Johnson

- ☐ *Keep your face to the sunshine and you cannot see a shadow.*
  Helen Keller

- ☐ *Find a place inside where there's joy, and the joy will burn out the pain.*
  Joseph Campbell

- ☐ *Your attitude is like a box of crayons that color your world. Constantly color your picture gray, and your picture will always be bleak. Try adding some bright colors to the picture by including humor, and your picture begins to lighten up.*
  Allen Klein

- ☐ *You cannot have a positive life and a negative mind.*
  Joyce Meyer

- ☐ *Worrying does not empty tomorrow of its troubles, it empties today of its strength.*
  Corrie ten Boom

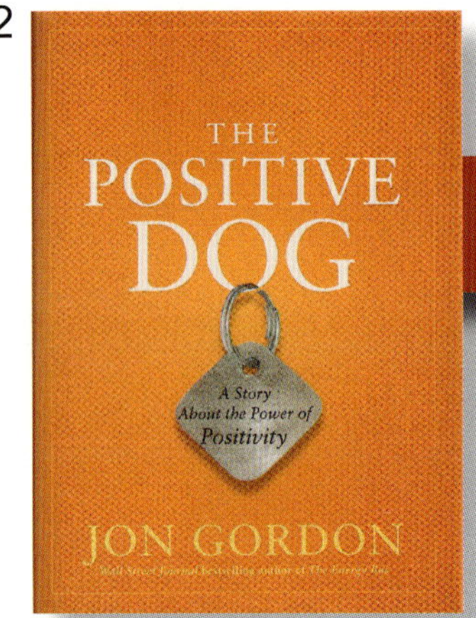

Read *The Positive Dog*
Chapters:
Take a Thank-You Walk – pg. 17
Build Your Gratitude Muscle – pg. 19
A Day of Gratitude – pg. 23

Answer these questions from today's reading:

1. On page 17, what type of thoughts, besides humorous ones, feed the positive dog?[70]

___

2. On page 18, what does Bubba say we want to start our day thinking about?[71]

___

3. What kind of walk did Bubba recommend for Matt to take each morning?[72]

___

4. On page 25, what is the "ultimate food for those who want to be more positive"?[73]

___

5. What 3 "dog bone" life lessons had Bubba taught Matt in these chapters?[74]

   1. ___
   2. ___
   3. ___

Psalm 118:1 (NIV)

Give thanks to the Lord, for he is good; his love endures forever!

Wow God. This is so cool. How did You ever think this up? Every drop is praising You.

Oh rats. Now it's too wet to do anything outside. My plans are ruined.

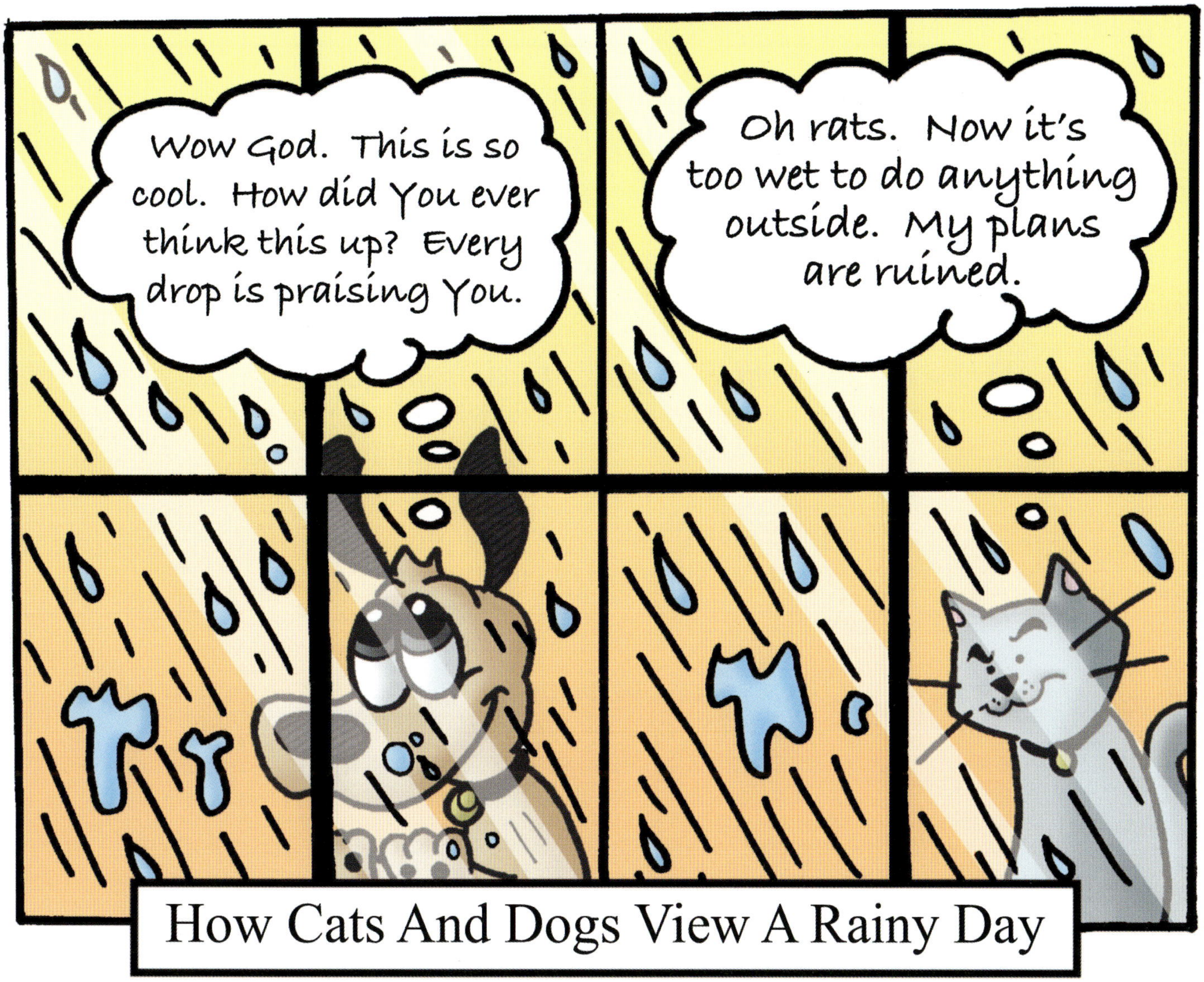

How Cats And Dogs View A Rainy Day

Which one would "Bubba" be proud of and why? [75]

____

____

Get To vs. Have To

Did you like the quotes from the last lesson! Some of them are really good! In fact, they can change the way a person thinks. Lots of people have said positive things that others have quoted. But the original idea of "Positive Thinking" comes from—you guessed it, the Bible!

God knows that if we think positively, that our lives are going to be better. Hence, He is constantly encouraging us to hide His Word in our hearts (memorize Scripture) so our lives will be positive.

Look at the following Scripture and place a check by the one which encourages you the most!

- ☐ *For I know the plans I have for you," declares the Lord, "plans to prosper you and not to harm you, plans to give you hope and a future.*
  Jeremiah 29:11

- ☐ *And we know that in all things God works for the good of those who love him, who have been called according to his purpose.*
  Romans 8:28

- ☐ *May the God of hope fill you with all joy and peace as you trust in him, so that you may overflow with hope by the power of the Holy Spirit.*
  Romans 15:13

- ☐ *Consider it pure joy, my brothers and sisters, whenever you face trials of many kinds, because you know that the testing of your faith produces perseverance. Let perseverance finish its work so that you may be mature and complete, not lacking anything.*
  James 1:2-4

- ☐ *Because of the Lord's great love we are not consumed, for his compassions never fail. They are new every morning; great is your faithfulness.*
  Lamentations 3:22-23

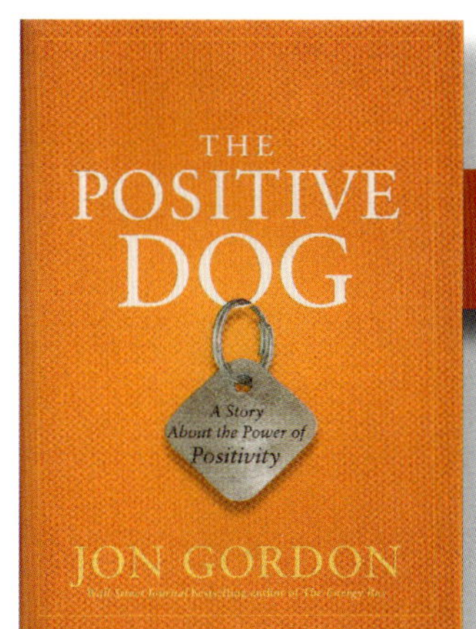

Today's Reading To Grow Your Faith

Read *The Positive Dog*
Chapters:
Tell Yourself Positive Stories – pg. 27
Get to instead of *Have to* – pg. 33
Blessed instead of Stressed – pg. 35

Answer these questions from today's reading:

1. On page 28, Matt had learned that "when he practiced ____________ throughout the day, instead of _______________ about everything, he saw the world through the eyes of gratitude and it changed his reality."[76]

2. What two-word "*word swap"* did Bubba explain to Matt?[77]

____

3. Fill in these blanks from page 36: "When you feel ______ you can't feel _______."[78]

4. When you feel blessed instead of stressed, you look for what instead of foes?[79]

____

5. What did Bubba recommend for Matt to think of when he feels stressed?[80]

____

Scripture Memory

Psalm 118:1 (NIV)

Give thanks to the Lord, for he is good; his love endures forever!

Quote this verse to a family member or friend and then place a check in the box. ❑

"I knew this was a great hiding place,
but have they given up looking for me?"

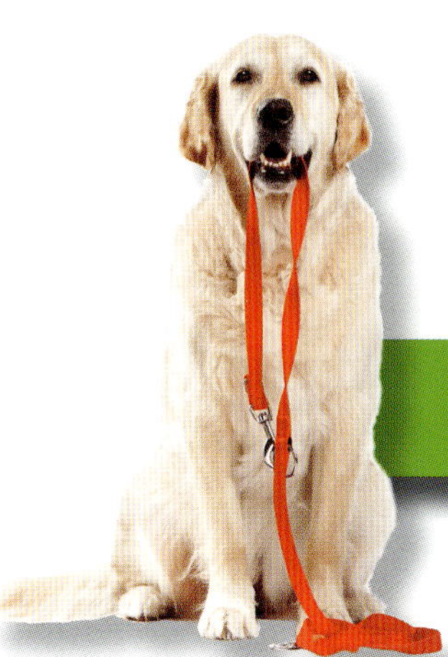

Week 6: Day 1

Lesson 16

No Whining Zone

None of us is perfect. We all have areas to grow in. When my husband speaks on Cat and Dog Theology, he points this out by saying, “Ask my wife if I’m a perfect Dog. She’ll laugh and say, ‘No, he definitely has his *cattitudes*!’” He whines sometimes.

We all wrestle with trying to be Dogs, because we all have an old nature inside of us fighting to be in control.

List the top three areas you feel you struggle in the most to be positive. Maybe it’s “obeying your parents” or “school” or “sports.”

1. ______________________________

2. ______________________________

3. ______________________________

WHINING

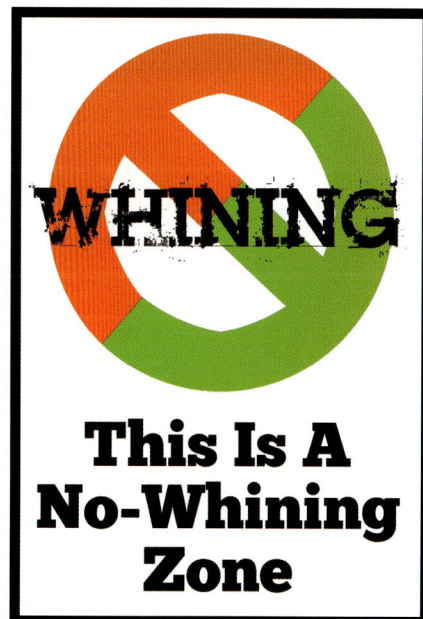

This Is A No-Whining Zone

Now, write “Cause Me” prayers for each of those three areas.

1. ______________________________

____

2. ______________________________

3. ______________________________

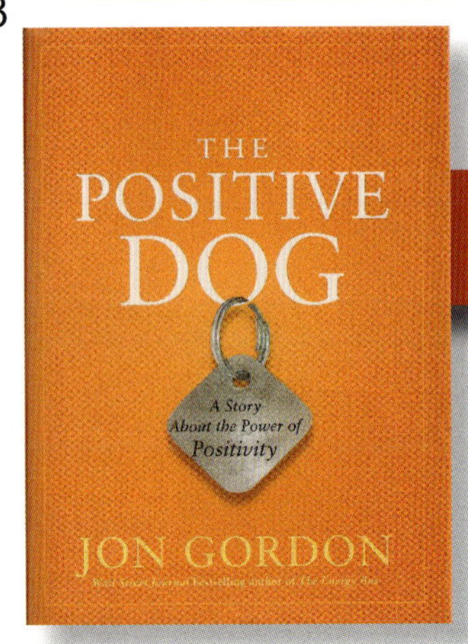

Today's Reading To Grow Your Faith

Read *The Positive Dog*
Chapters:
Turn Complaints into Solutions – pg. 39
Fear or Faith – pg. 43
Challenges or Opportunities – pg. 47

Answer these questions from today's reading:

1. On page 40, what was Jade's "No Complaining Rule?"[81]

___

2. On page 43, what did Bubba tell Matt was the most important decision to make?[82]

___

3. On page 44, Bubba told Matt that "both faith and fear believe in ...?"[83]

___

4. On page 45, "Best of all faith helps you turn challenges into ________________?"[84]

5. On page 47, Bubba says, "We can allow these challenges to destroy us or they can make us ________________?"[85]

Scripture Memory

I Thessalonians 5:11 (ESV)

Therefore encourage one another
and build one another up, just as you are doing.

Week 6: Day 2

Lesson 17

Open His Eyes

God has given us great examples of people who can see through the negative circumstances and view it from a positive perspective—God's perspective. One such man was the prophet Elisha.

He was surrounded by an army that had come just to get him! He was greatly outnumbered. His servant was scared. He cried, "What shall we do?"

But Elisha wasn't worried. He had a positive attitude. He knew God was taking care of him. So he prayed to the Lord, "Open my servant's eyes that he might see."

To find out what happened, read 2 Kings 6:8-19.

(Oops, we blew it! Turn to page 325 if you need help finding the answers for these three questions below.)

1. What did Elisha's servant see?[223]

____

2. What happened to the army?[224]

____

3. Has God promised to always take care of you?[225] Circle One: Yes No

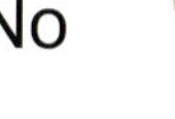

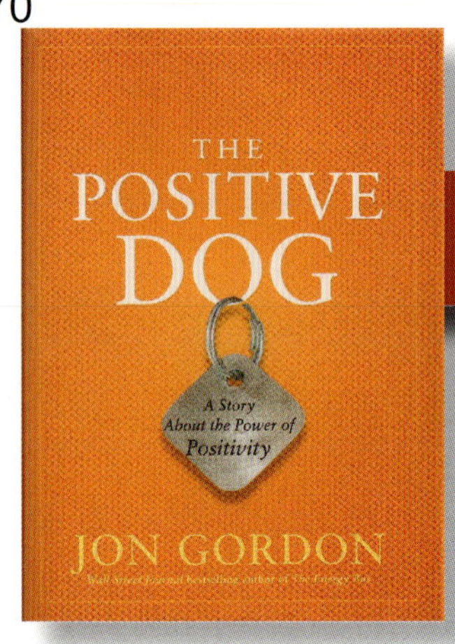

Today's Reading To Grow Your Faith

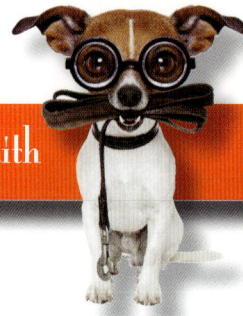

Read *The Positive Dog*
Chapters:
An Opportunity – pg. 49
The Positive Dog Grows – pg. 53
Positive Energy is Contagious – pg. 57

Answer these questions from today's reading:

1. What two things did Matt discover that built his positivity? (page 53)[86]

____

2. On page 55, where did Matt change his focus from being a complainer to...?[87]

____

3. What is one thing that is proven to reduce stress and boost positivity?[88]

____

4. Who benefits from your positivity? (page 56)[89]

____

5. Finish this quote from the last line on page 56: When you are positive,... [90]

____

Scripture Memory

I Thessalonians 5:11 (ESV)

Therefore encourage one another
and build one another up, just as you are doing.

Where Cats And Dogs Run When They're Afraid

What opportunity is the Cat missing? [91]

____

____

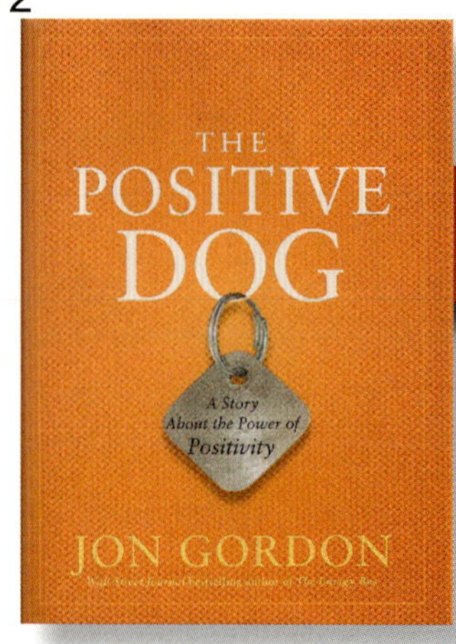

Today's Reading To Grow Your Faith

Read *The Positive Dog*
Chapters:
Positive Boomerang – pg. 59
Feeding Others – pg. 63
Love – pg. 65

Answer these questions from today's reading:

1. On page 63, what did Bubba say was a great place to start "feeding others"?[92]

____

2. What two new "dog bone" quotes did Matt learn?[93]

   1. ____

   2. ____

3. On page 65, why are many of us afraid to give love?[94]

____

4. What are the six qualities of love that Bubba describes?[95]

   1. ____

   2. ____

   3. ____

   4. ____

   5. ____

   6. ____

I Thessalonians 5:11 (ESV)

Therefore encourage one another
and build one another up, just as you are doing.

Quote this verse to a family member or friend and then put a check in the box after you have said it correctly. ☐

Some days I just have a hard time getting up.

Sometimes we can be real funny!
This was around Easter when
we went to the March For Jesus rally.
(No, I didn't wear the hat to the rally.)

Week 7: Day 1

Lesson 19

No Ordinary Day

Have you ever had a bad day—like a really, really bad day? What kind of an attitude did you have during that day? If you're like me, probably a very bad one, huh?

Well, there was one person who had a day worse than any I've ever had, and probably worse than any day you've had. His name was Paul. He is who many people call "The Apostle Paul."

His bad day was no ordinary day. He was arrested for talking about Jesus and then beaten with whips that had pieces of glass in it. That must have really hurt him on his back. And then after he had been severely whipped, he was thrown into jail. If there was any day for having a pity party, this was a perfect one for Paul.

But Paul didn't have a pity party. Neither did Silas, his friend who was with him. They did something that was amazing.

Read Acts 16:22-25.

Paul and Silas were physically hurting. Their backs had just been torn up. Yet they were singing hymns of praise to God. They must have felt that it was a privilege to suffer for Christ.

Do you realize what this teaches us? If we have the right perspective, God's **JOY** can permeate our lives—no matter what our circumstances are! Imagine, having joy anytime, anywhere, in any circumstance. This is what God wants for me. This is what God wants for you.

We just need the right perspective! This is what *The Positive Dog* is all about!

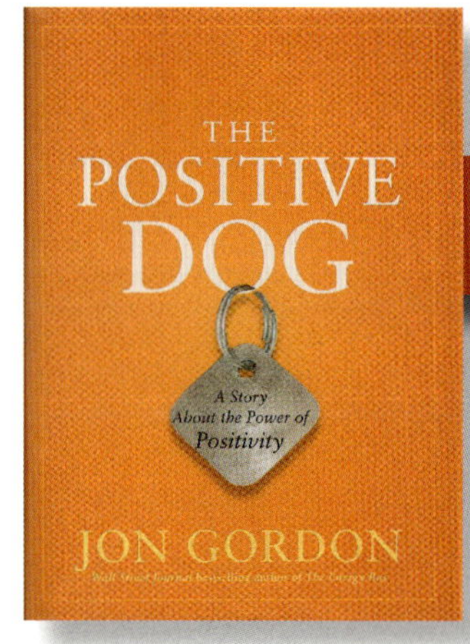

Today's Reading To Grow Your Faith

Read *The Positive Dog*
Chapters:
Encouragement – pg. 67
No Ordinary Day – pg. 71
Negativity Serves A Purpose – 73

Answer these questions from today's reading:

1. What final powerful way to feed other's positivity did Bubba share with Matt?[96]

____

2. What are the opposites of *pessimist*s and *realists*?[97]

____

3. What four words do most people need us to speak into their hearts?[98]

____

4. List three of the positive benefits Matt realized, ironically, to be gained from negativity? (page74)[99]

1. ____

2. ____

3. ____

Romans 8:28 (ESV)

And we know that for those who love God all things work together for good, for those who are called according to His purpose.

"Seriously? You got a dog?
What were you thinking? Now I have to hide all day.
I thought you loved me.

My husband loves to fish.
One day he had to throw away his old recliner
so he took a picture in his truck like he was fishing!

Week 7: Day 2

Lesson 20

Do Not Be Afraid

Wouldn't it be great to never be afraid? You'd never have to fear about the monster under your bed? (Ha!—You're a little too old for that one, right?) Nor would you have to fear about having a boyfriend or girlfriend, or tests or grades, or if you'll win the big game.

Life without fear would be great!

But we all have fear. Remember Paul in the last lesson? Even though there were times when he was singing in jail after having been badly beaten, there were other times when he was afraid. In fact, the Lord had to appear to Paul and say, "Paul, don't be afraid." Read it in Acts 18:9 and Acts 27:24.

In the Old Testament, even Abraham was fearful.

God told him to leave his house, his family, his friends, and to go to a new land to start a new life. That would be scary, wouldn't it? But God had an answer for his fear. It was a simple answer, and one that can give us a new perspective on life. Look at what God said to Abraham.

> *After this, the word of the Lord came to Abram in a vision:*
> *"Do not be afraid, Abram. I am your shield, your very great reward."*
> (Genesis 15:1, NIV)

God's answer for our fear is Himself. If we know that God is with us, that He is going to protect us, we don't have to fear—anything. Isn't that great!

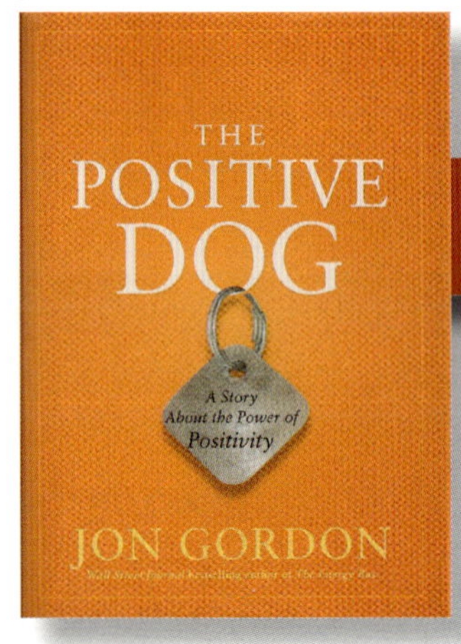

Today's Reading To Grow Your Faith

Read *The Positive Dog*
Chapters:
What Would Bubba Do? – pg. 77
A Special Day – pg. 81
Two Positive Dogs are Better than One – pg. 83

Answer these questions from today's reading:

1. List four ways Matt modeled what Bubba had taught him?[100]

1. ______________________________

2. ______________________________

3. ______________________________

4. ______________________________

2. On page 84, what two things did Matt discover that would diffuse negative thoughts and emotions, but also transform him from the inside out?[101]

____

3. Name one way that Matt was different with his new family than in the beginning of this book.[102]

____

4. Name one way your life or attitudes have changed since you started reading this book.[103]

____

(If you would like to share with me how God has used *The Positive Dog* book to change your attitudes or life, please feel free to email me at debby@mmpublishers.com)

Romans 8:28 (ESV)

And we know that for those who love God all things work together for good, for those who are called according to His purpose.

"You see, I figure they keep us dogs on a leash
because they want us.
That's why you never find a cat on a leash."

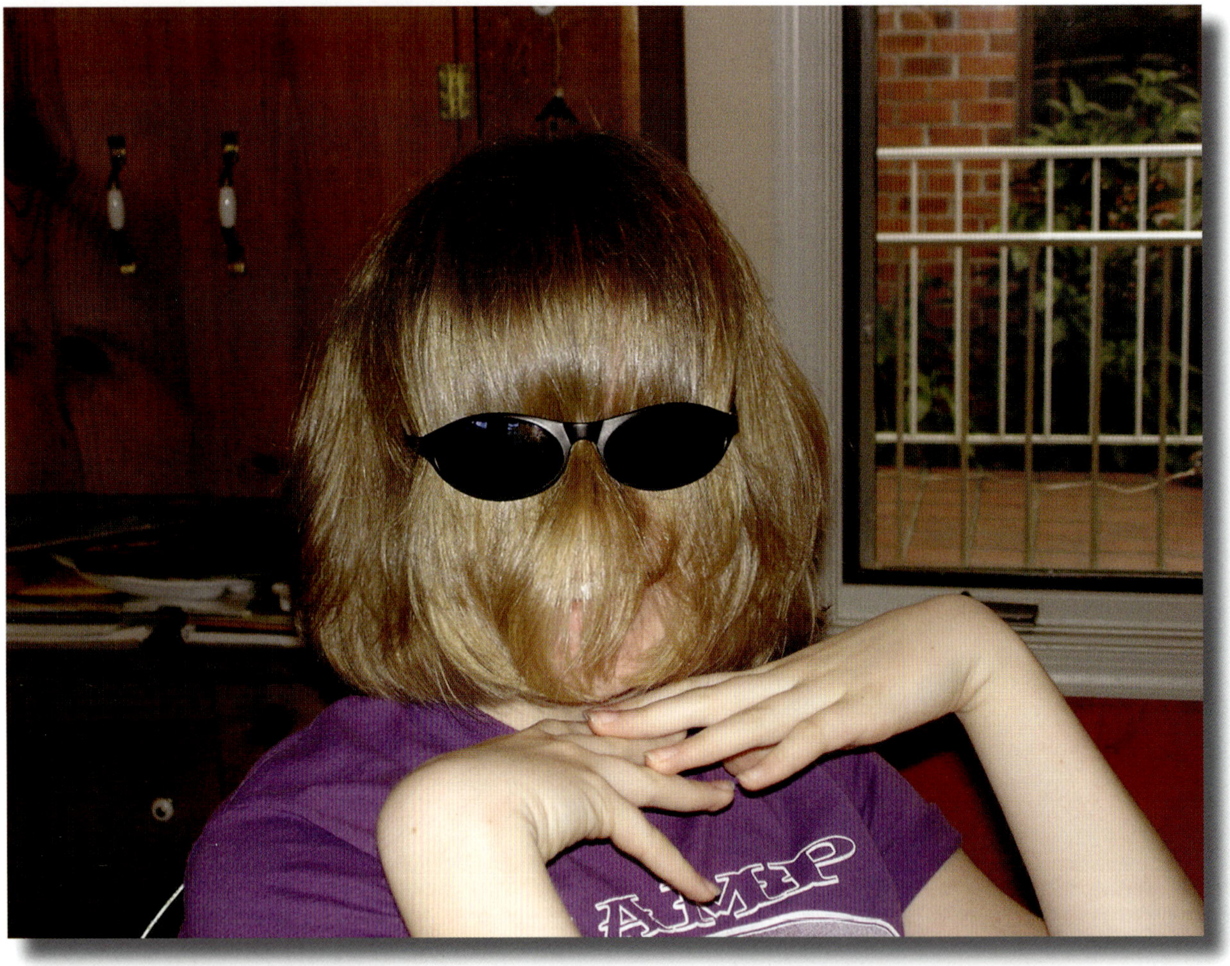

Here's Abby being crazy!
I'll bet you do things to make your
parents laugh too.

Cats And Dogs Prepare Differently For The "Game Of Life"

What is wrong with the Cat's attitude? [104]

___

___

God is in Control

Fear is a part of life that we all have to face. Everyone can be afraid. Even my husband and I get fearful at times.

In the last lesson, we found a solution: God will be with us. He will protect us. And He is our very great reward. This is what Dogs try to keep focused on. But God has given us another reason to realize that we don't have to be fearful.

God is completely in control. He is sovereign.

Many people think that God and Satan have been enemies forever and there will be an eternal battle between the two of them. Sometimes Satan wins (when bad things happen to us). Sometimes God wins (when good things happen to us). But this is not what the Bible teaches.

The Bible teaches that God created Satan. That's right! Satan hasn't existed forever in eternity past. He had a beginning and God gave it to him. We discover this in the book of Colossians.

> *For in him all things were created: things in heaven and on earth, visible and invisible, whether thrones or powers or rulers or authorities; all things have been created through him and for him. He is before all things, and in him all things hold together.* (Colossians 1:16,17, NIV)

Satan is a power, a ruler, an authority; therefore, he was created by God. And did you catch those two powerful little words: ***for him?*** God created Satan for His own purposes. God has a plan of how He wants to use Satan. Everything was created for God's purposes, even Satan.

If we realize this, we can have peace. Why? Because now we know that *God is completely in control!* And if He is in control, we can trust Him.

Knowing He's in control helps us have a positive attitude as well, doesn't it? No matter what life may throw at us, we can always say, "God knew this was coming. He allowed it. And God has always promised to take care of me and do good to me, so this must be for my good." Dogs know that and realize that this is a great way to live life!

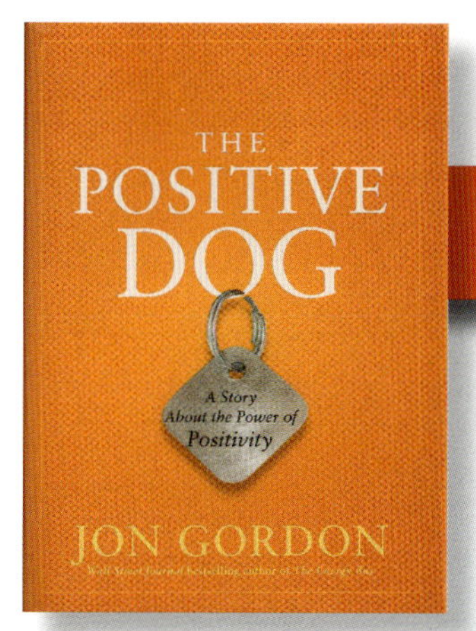

Today's Reading To Grow Your Faith

Final Project: *The Positive Dog*
Read *The Positive Dog*
Chapter:
Feed the Positive Dog:
Action Plan – pg. 87

Choose ***one*** of the author's 11 suggestions and live it out today. Write down which one you chose to do.

____

What effect do you think it will have on your Positivity?

____

____

____

Scripture Memory

Romans 8:28 (ESV)

And we know that for those who love God all things work together for good, for those who are called according to His purpose.

Quote this verse to a family member or friend and then put a check in the box. ❑

My husband and my son, Hunter,
were the last ones to read through the Bible in a year.
Hunter was very motivated as you can see below.

(Sorry, moms and dads, but we thought it was money well invested!)

Week 8: Day 1

Lesson 22

Devoted to The Master: Read, Need, Deed

Have you ever noticed that when a dog feels really loved by his master, he is totally loyal and devoted to him?

I remember our dog, Jasmine, that we rescued from a local dog pound when she was only eight weeks old. She was a white lab-husky mix that our family loved for almost 16 years. She was devoted totally to my husband; he was truly her master at our house! Whenever he said, "Go outside, Jasmine," she immediately went to the door. Whenever she heard his truck drive up to our house, she would run, with her tail wagging, to greet him. She loved her master. Jasmine loved taking walks with him and just spending time with him every day. He was her BFF in our family.

So what about us? As Dog Christians, we want to learn to love and obey, to truly follow Jesus Christ for a lifetime. So just like Jasmine, we can become truly devoted to our Master, Jesus, by spending time with Him every day.

The weeks ahead in *The Dog Walk* you will learn three different ways of spending time growing in your friendship with Jesus, and learning how to hear and obey His commands each day.

Today's plan is called: **Read, Need, Deed**

Each of these words will guide you to do one step that will cause you to listen to God's Voice speaking in your mind or heart. Then, like a dog obeys her master, hopefully, you will obey the voice of your BFF and Master, Jesus Christ.

READ: With this step, you will choose either one verse or a short passage of Scripture to ***read***, then write down the Scripture reference you read plus one sentence or phrase you sense in your heart or mind that God wants you to learn, think about, or do today.

NEED: Next, take a minute to think about one question or problem or ***need*** you have in your life or family today that you want to ask God to solve or answer or cause to work together for His Glory and your good. Write it down.

DEED: Next, take a quiet minute and ask God to put the face or name of someone you can bless today or this week with an act of kindness or a good ***deed*** for His Glory and their joy. Below, write their name down and what you plan to do and when.

Finish your Quiet Time or Devotion Time with Jesus by thanking Him for speaking to you and asking Him to give you the power, by His Holy Spirit, to obey what He spoke to you today.

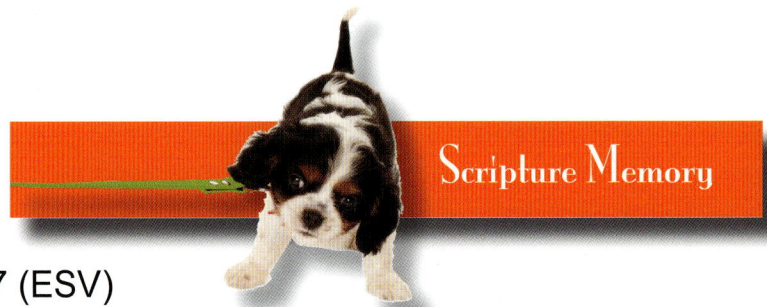

Scripture Memory

Colossians 2:6-7 (ESV)

Therefore, as you received Christ Jesus the Lord, so walk in Him,
rooted and built up in Him and established in the faith,
just as you were taught, abounding in thanksgiving.

Now, using the outline below, follow the ***Read, Need, Deed*** plan using your Scripture Memory Verses for this week: Colossians 2:6-7.

Read: ____

Need: ____

Deed: ____

End in prayer as directed above.

Week 8: Day 2

Lesson 23

Read, Need, Deed: Repeated

Today may seem easy, but to "walk in Him" for a lifetime takes growing deep roots in your relationship with Jesus, just like our Scripture Memory verses this week tell us. *Think of it like this:* would your BFF like it if you never spent time listening to her or him talk? Would you feel close to him or her if you never hung out together?

Your friendship wouldn't really be that close, would it? You truly have to spend TIME together to grow in a friendship. That's what happened to me that summer when I was 13 and the next year of my life. I would go into my bedroom at night and sit at a little cardboard table I had put into the corner of my room. I turned on a small lamp, had my Bible, a pen, and a notebook. Then I spent time with my new BFF, Jesus Christ, before I went to bed each night. I remember starting with the book of I Peter found in the New Testament, and I would just read a couple of verses each night and listen to Jesus speak to my heart about how to follow Him each day. I wrote in my notebook what He taught me. It was truly awesome!!!

Now, in order for a new activity in your life to become a habit, research says you have to do it consistently for 30 days. Yep, **30 DAYS**!!! So, we are going to repeat our *Read, Need, Deed* plan of growing in our friendship with Jesus today.

READ: With this step, you will choose either one verse or a short passage of Scripture to ***read***, then write down the Scripture reference you read plus one sentence or phrase you sense in your heart or mind that God wants you to learn, think about, or do today.

NEED: Next, take a minute to think about one question or problem or ***need*** you have in your life or family today that you want to ask God to solve or answer or cause to work together for His Glory and your good. Write it down.

DEED: Next, take a quiet minute and ask God to put the face or name of someone you can bless today or this week with an act of kindness or a good ***deed*** for His Glory and their joy. Write their name down and what you plan to do and when.

Finish your Quiet Time or Devotion Time with Jesus by thanking Him for speaking to you and asking Him to give you the power, by His Holy Spirit, to obey what He spoke to you today.

Now, using the outline below, follow the *Read, Need, Deed* plan using any book of the Bible you would like to study, or if you can't choose I recommend: I Peter 1:3-9

Read: ______________________________

Need: ______________________________

Deed: ______________________________

End in prayer as directed on page 88.

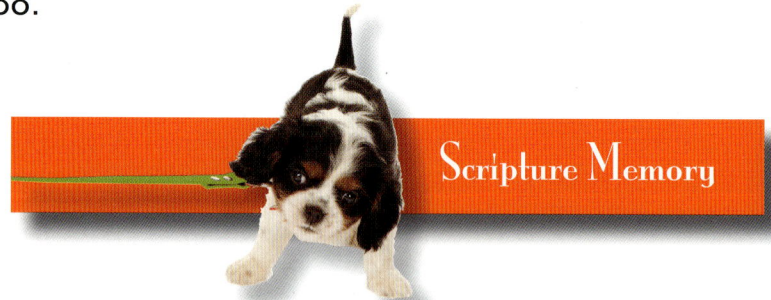

Scripture Memory

Colossians 2:6-7 (ESV)

Therefore, as you received Christ Jesus the Lord, so walk in Him,
Rooted and built up in Him and established in the faith,
just as you were taught, abounding in thanksgiving.

I'm rested and ready God. I'll obey whatever you show me!

Oh, I stayed up so late watching T.V. I am so tired, I can't even keep my eyes open.

Cats And Dogs Having Quiet Times

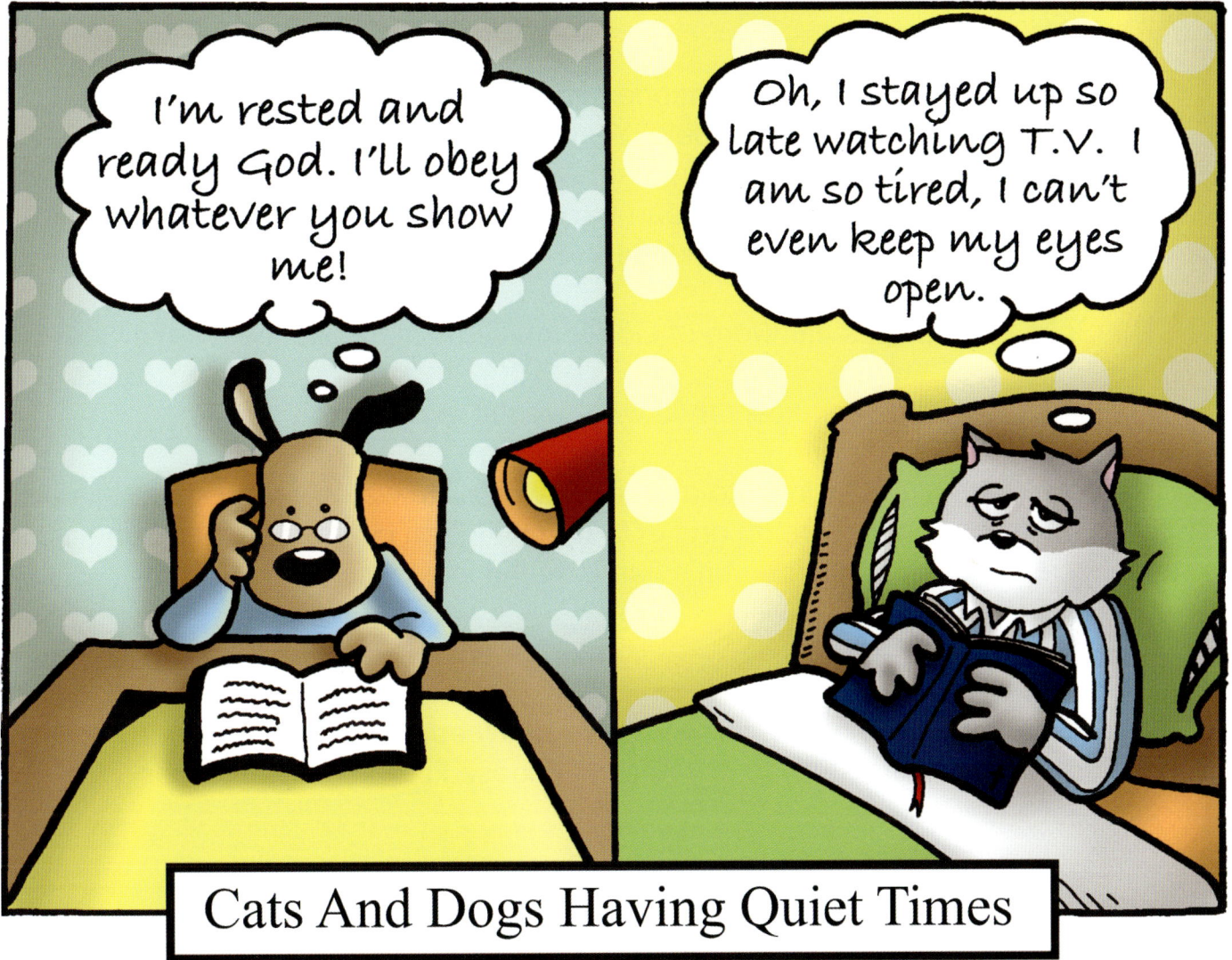

What did the Dog have to do to be ready to meet with God? [105]

____

____

Read, Need, Deed, Training Day!

Okay, in *The Positive Dog,* remember the lesson that Matt the Mutt learned when Bubba was adopted (by his former owner) before Matt found his family? Matt decided to "mentor other dogs the way that Bubba had mentored him". So, I bet you know what is coming next!

Today, I want you to "mentor" someone either in your family, your neighborhood, or a friend in what you learned this week. Yes, I want you to spend about 30 minutes teaching someone else how to use the *Read, Need, Deed* plan to meet with God and hear what He speaks to your mind or heart through His Word. I heard a great quote from Rick Warren in church a few weeks ago:

"The Spirit of God uses the Word of God to make us more like the Son of God."

Doesn't that explain in one sentence what we are learning this week?

Okay, now take a quiet minute to ask Jesus whom He wants you to share this plan with today, then take a deep breath and ***JUST DO IT***! (You can call on the phone or Skype if necessary.) Write the person's name on the line below.

____

Now, using the outline below, follow the ***Read, Need, Deed*** plan using any book of the Bible you would like to study, or if you can't choose I recommend: James 1:2-8

Read: ____

Need: ____

Deed: ____

End in prayer as directed on page 88.

Colossians 2:6-7 (ESV)

Therefore, as you received Christ Jesus the Lord, so walk in Him,
Rooted and built up in Him and established in the faith,
just as you were taught, abounding in thanksgiving.

Quote this verse to a family member or friend and then check the box. ❑

"Here Kitty, Kitty."

"Don't even think about it."

We love blessing our neighbors.
This is Mr. Johnnie and Mrs. Nita who live next door.
They are in their 80s.

Week 9: Day 1

Lesson 25

Walking Daily with The Master: "Cinco Devo"

Hola, Amigos! Como estas? Oh my, I'm getting so excited about our new plan for meeting with Jesus that I just started writing in Spanish!

Well, I hope you enjoyed learning the first way of having quiet times, ***Read, Need and Deed***. Hopefully, you began to grow closer to Jesus, your Master, on your Dog Walk last week.

And how was it teaching someone else to use the *Read, Need, Deed* plan? Isn't it exciting to watch God work through you to bring another person closer to Him? Training other Dogs will be an important part of your Dog Walk the rest of this year. That's how Jesus lived while on earth, right? He spent most of His time training His 12 disciples how to follow Him and make God famous like He did.

Today, we will dive into my *second plan* to help you begin to form that lifelong habit of meeting with your BFF, Jesus Christ, as a part of your daily life. We will learn one more plan, my new favorite, next week and then you will choose your favorite one to continue on your Dog Walk for the rest of this year.

This second plan I am calling "Cinco Devo"—"cinco" means ***five*** in Spanish and "devo" stands for ***devotion*** or growing to be more ***devoted*** to your Master! So, let's begin now...

CINCO DEVO: You will work through five parts on this plan, but don't be overwhelmed because each part is simple and short!

UNO (Part One): Choose a Psalm, any Psalm in the Bible. Read it until you find five words or phrases that describe our Master, the Lord God of the Bible or what He does. Write down those five words by the numbers below. Here is an example from Psalm 3:

1. my shield
2. my glory
3. lifter of my head
4. answers me
5. holy

Now go to Psalm 91 and write down the five words or phrases that describe our Master or what He does.

1. ______________________________

2. ______________________________

3. ______________________________

4. ______________________________

5. ______________________________

DOS (Part Two): Now take a minute to read back over the five words you wrote in the **UNO** Section, praising God for each of those character traits that make Him awesome!

TRES (Part Three): Now you are finished with Psalm 91. In this third section, I want you to stop and look into the "mirror" of your own heart and life. Write down any sins you need to confess, then ask forgiveness of your Master before your start your day. (I John 1:9) After you ask forgiveness for each one, then cross it out by writing ***FORGIVEN*** over it in all caps!!! (If you can't think of five, that's okay!)

1. ______________________________

2. ______________________________

3. ______________________________

4. ______________________________

5. ______________________________

CUATRO (Part Four): Next, you get to think for a minute then write down five things or people you are ***thankful to God*** for today:

1. ____________________
2. ____________________
3. ____________________
4. ____________________
5. ____________________

CINCO (Part Five): Finally, write down five short requests you would like to talk to your Master, your BFF, Jesus Christ, about this day. These could be your own personal needs or a friend's or family member's needs. It could also be a problem in another part of the world that you want to write down to ask God to give special attention to this day:

1. ____________________
2. ____________________
3. ____________________
4. ____________________
5. ____________________

Scripture Memory

Psalm 16:11 (NIV)

You make known to me the path of life;
you will fill me with joy in your presence,
with eternal pleasures at your right hand.

"Don't confess? Blame the dog? Okay Mommy, that's what I'll do."

Week 9: Day 2

Lesson 26

"Cinco Devo" Repeated

Good Morning, fellow Dogs! Woof Woof! Can you tell I'm excited about another day of "**Cinco Devo**"? Hope you are as well. Let's JUST DO IT!

***The Dog Walk's* "Cinco Devo" Plan to Meet with the Master Today**

UNO (Part One): In your second day in "**Cinco Devo**," I'm not going to give you a Psalm. You need to choose one. Go to your Bible and open to the Psalms (an easy way to find Psalms is to open your Bible right to the middle) and choose one. Write which one you chose here: ___________

Now, write down the five words or phrases that describe our Master or what He does.

1. ____

2. ____

3. ____

4. ____

5. ____

DOS (Part Two): Now take a minute to read back over the five words you wrote in the **UNO** Section, praising God for each of those character traits that make Him awesome!

TRES (Part Three): Now that you have finished your Psalm, stop and look into the "mirror" of your own heart and life. Write down any sins you need to confess, then ask forgiveness of your Master before your start your day. (I John 1:9) After you ask forgiveness for each one, then cross it out by writing ***FORGIVEN*** over it in all caps!!!

1. ______________________________

2. ______________________________

3. ______________________________

4. ______________________________

5. ______________________________

CUATRO (Part Four): Next, you get to think for a minute then write down five things or people you are ***thankful to God*** for today:

1. ______________________________

2. ______________________________

3. ______________________________

4. ______________________________

5. ______________________________

CINCO (Part Five): Finally, write down five short requests you would like to talk to your Master, your BFF, Jesus Christ about this day. These could be your own personal needs or a friend's or family member's needs. It could also be a problem in another part of the world that you want to write down to ask God to give special attention to this day:

1. ______________________________

2. ______________________________

3. ______________________________

4. ______________________________

5. ______________________________

Psalm 16:11 (NIV)

You make known to me the path of life;
you will fill me with joy in your presence,
with eternal pleasures at your right hand.

By Chienlit via Wikimedia Commons

"Master, look what I found outside! She's so cute. Can we keep her?
She can sleep with me here on the couch."

When Hunter was in 6th grade,
I homeschooled him and his friend, Adam,
together at the same time.

VA

GOALS FOR Meeting with GOD

- 2 OR 3 TIMES A ~~WEEK~~ MONTH
- 5-10 MINUTES EACH

GOALS FOR MEETING with GOD

- 5-6 DAYS A WEEK FOR 30-90 MINUTES
- ½ DAY OF PRAYER EACH QUARTER
- EPHESIANS 6:18 "PRAYING WITHOUT CEASING"

Which set of goals communicates that God is their highest priority and why? [106]

____

____

Final "Cinco Devo" Dog Training Day!

Hey Dog Walking Friends! I think you know what is coming next. Today, you need to "pass it on." Find a family member or friend you can walk through the "**Cinco Devo**" plan with today.

Who do you want to train today? ________________________________

A great way to train them is to walk through a devotion with them. So let's go! Choose a Psalm for them (or with them). Which is it? Write it here: ____________

UNO (Part One): In your third day in "**Cinco Devo**," I'm not going to give you a Psalm. You need to choose one. Go to your Bible and open to the Psalms (an easy way to find Psalms is to open your Bible right to the middle) and choose one. Write which one you chose here: __________

Now, write down the five words or phrases that describe our Master or what He does.

1. ____

2. ____

3. ____

4. ____

5. ____

DOS (Part Two): Now take a minute to read back over the five words you wrote in the **UNO** Section, praising God for each of those character traits that make Him awesome!

TRES (Part Three): Now that you have finished your Psalm, stop and look into the "mirror" of your own heart and life. Write down any sins you need to confess, then ask

forgiveness of your Master before you start your day. (I John 1:9) After you ask forgiveness for each one, then cross it out by writing ***FORGIVEN*** over it in all caps!!!

1. ______________________________

2. ______________________________

3. ______________________________

4. ______________________________

5. ______________________________

CUATRO (Part Four): Next, you get to think for a minute then write down 5 things or people you are ***thankful to God*** for today:

1. ______________________________

2. ______________________________

3. ______________________________

4. ______________________________

5. ______________________________

CINCO (Part Five): Finally, write down five short requests you would like to talk to your Master, your BFF, Jesus Christ about this day. These could be your own personal needs or a friend's or family member's or a problem in another part of the world that you want to write down to ask God to give special attention to this day:

1. ______________________________

2. ______________________________

3. ______________________________

4. ______________________________

5. ______________________________

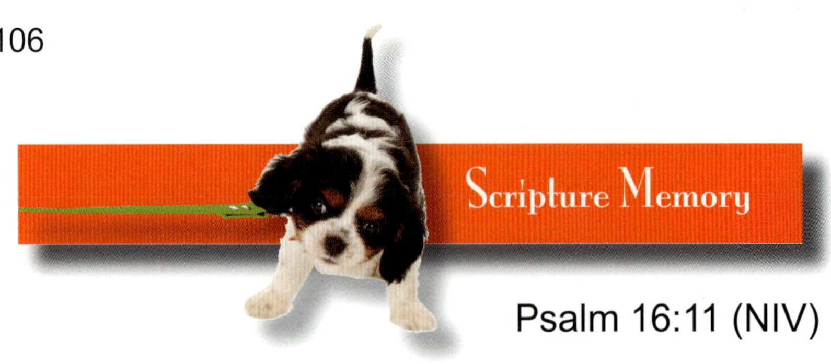

Psalm 16:11 (NIV)

You make known to me the path of life;
you will fill me with joy in your presence,
with eternal pleasures at your right hand.

Quote this verse to a family member and check the box when you have successfully done it! ☐

1. Circle which time with God you liked the most so far?

2. Write why you liked it on the lines below:

____

____

Week 10: Day 1

Lesson 28

SOAK: Finding Joy in God's Presence!

Well, how was your week using the "**Cinco Devo**" plan? It was a little longer than the ***Read, Need, Deed*** plan, but I hope you enjoyed discovering more amazing words to praise our Master, the Lord God, from the Psalms. And I think it's very freeing to take the time to write down our mistakes, but then immediately ask God's forgiveness, isn't it?

So, today I want to teach you our third and final Dog Walk plan to learn how to really have a time of friendship building each day with your BFF and Master, Jesus Christ. This plan is new even for me. So I am especially excited about teaching it to you!

I read a book last year that my daughter recommended called *Opening to God* by David Benner. It challenged me in my Quiet Time each day to really meet with God, not just read the Bible and have a prayer time. So, I took what I learned from the book and created this four-step plan that I like to call ***SOAK***.

The overall meaning is that since we "leak" as followers of Jesus therefore we need to "***soak***" in God's Presence every day to be refilled with His Spirit. (Ephesians 5:18–20)

The second meaning is that each letter of the word ***SOAK*** stands for one section of this new plan of being refreshed in God's Presence, and our time of sitting and listening/talking with our BFF, Jesus Christ!

This is going to be your third way for meeting with God! I hope you enjoy it as much as I do!

SOAK: Finding JOY in God's Presence!

This plan can actually take as little as 10 minutes or as long as you want. When I have a very busy day, I use a timer (stop watch, kitchen timer, timer on a smart phone, or even just a digital clock can work). For the 10-minute version, I set the timer for 2 minutes for each of the first 3 parts "S-O-A" and then 4 minutes for "K."

S = Sit in Silence

Some of you are saying, "Yes," especially if you have a noisy little brother or sister in the house! Others of you are saying, "NOOOOOO!" You like to do all the talking with friends and family or you love music and just noise being all around you. I am probably more like the "noise-loving" ones, but I have begun to learn the great benefit of having a little bit of "quiet" or "silence" in my life, mind, and heart each day.

But, honestly, this first step on the plan is very important. We all need to learn how to "Be still and know that He is God" (Psalm 46:10a) to keep walking like a Dog for the rest of your life!

I promise you it will not be easy at first. So many thoughts will come into your mind. But keep pushing them aside till later, by saying, "*Jesus, I want to welcome you here today so we can grow in our friendship and I can follow you today and bring you glory!*" Got it?

When you are ready to "sit in silence" for 2 minutes, start your timer.

S—SOAK: Sit in Silence while you welcome and wait for God's Presence.
"Wait for the LORD; be strong, and let your heart take courage;
Wait for the LORD!" Psalm 27:14 (ESV)

O = Observe Your Heart

During this section of ***SOAK***, I ask Jesus to show me what is on my heart or mind today. What is bothering me? What is making me really happy or really sad? What am I worried about today? What kind of things do you want to share with your BFF today? Then I just write down those thoughts and give them all to Him knowing He can take care of all of them.

"Casting all your anxieties on him (Jesus), because he cares for you."
I Peter 5:7 (ESV)

O—SOAK: Observe Your Heart: Let God speak to you.

In the lines below, write down any "anxieties" or burdens or happy thoughts or joys that you want to share with Jesus this day. If Jesus shows you a worry or sin you need to confess and ask His forgiveness, then do so now as well.

Cast your cares on the Lord and he will sustain you;
he will never let the righteous be shaken.
Psalm 55:22 (NIV)

When you are ready to "observe your heart" for two minutes, start your timer.

____

____

____

A = Adoration (Praise and Thanksgiving)

Adoration means "the act of paying honor." The root word of adoration is "adore." So what do you do when you "adore" someone or you want to pay them honor? Yes, you will say lots of good things to them! You will probably praise them and even maybe thank them for all the ways they bless you and make your life happier, right?

So that is what we will do now in this section of *SOAK*. Don't you think it is natural to give thanks and praise to God after He has listened to all your burdens and joys for a few minutes? Perhaps He has even quickly forgiven you for any sin you confessed. Now, this is the section of our *SOAK* plan where we joyfully praise and adore Him!

"Every day I will bless you and praise your name forever and ever."
Psalm 145:2 (ESV)

A—SOAK: Adoration: Worship your God!

On the next page, write down any words of praise or thanks you want to say to Jesus today. (If I don't think of many words of praise or thanks, sometimes I will just read a few verses from a Psalm to remind me of many reasons I can give God thanks on this day.)

Turn the page and start your timer for 2—3 minutes.

____

____

____

K= Know Jesus More

When I started my friendship with Jesus at age 13, I really wanted to get to know Him. Just like making a new friend, you want to spend time together and you want to learn what's important to them and what makes them happy or sad, right? So, I quickly learned that if I began reading in the New Testament, especially the first four books (*Matthew, Mark, Luke and John*) I could see how Jesus lived. I could also read what He said to people, and learn all about my new BFF, Jesus Christ!

That's what this "K" section of SOAK is all about! How can we follow our Master, Jesus Christ, on our Dog Walk, if we don't really know Him? Let's get to know Him a little more each day as we SOAK in God's Presence.

"And this is eternal life, that they know you the only true God,
and Jesus Christ whom you have sent."
John 17:3 (ESV)

K—SOAK: Know Jesus More: Get to know your BFF!

I want you to choose one of the first four books of the New Testament to start knowing Jesus more. So, choose Matthew, Mark, Luke or John. Which one did you choose? ____________________________

So start with the first chapter and the first verse. Now read until you have learned one new thing about Jesus that you want to remember or live out this day. On the pages below, write down the name of the book, then chapter and verse numbers you read today first. Like this: John 1:1-3. Then write down the one thing you learned today from those verses about Jesus or the one thing He said that you want to obey.

____

____

____

End this time of SOAK by thanking Jesus for spending time with you today!

Scripture Memory for Week 10:
No new verses: Review the first 9 weeks!

If you haven't already done so, I highly recommend you write down these first nine verses on 3" by 5" index cards or, even better, ask your mom or dad to buy you a small spiral-bound set of index cards that you can use for reviewing all your verses.

If you can't buy the index cards, a second best option would be to type out all nine verses on a Word Document today. Then review the verses using the index cards on which you hand wrote them or the printed document you have typed.

<u>Here is your list so far:</u>

Week 1: II Corinthians 5:17
Week 2: Mark 12:30-31
Week 3: Ezekiel 36:27
Week 4: John 10:10
Week 5: Psalm 118:1
Week 6: I Thessalonians 5:11
Week 7: Romans 8:28
Week 8: Colossians 2:6-7
Week 9: Psalm 16:11

We also love to host international students.
This is our daughter's Arabic teacher
from Tunisia.

Did you know that 80% of all international
students never make it into
an American home?

Week 10: Day 2

Lesson 29

SOAK Repeated

Okay, my Dog Walk buddies, how did you like the time of SOAK in your last lesson? It may be difficult at first; it was for me, too. But honestly, it is my favorite way to spend time with my Master and BFF these days! Let's do it again today, okay?

Remember to grab your Bible, a pen, a timer or clock (optional), *The Dog Walk* (Ha! You already have it! You are reading it right now.), and also an open mind and heart to meet with Jesus and learn from Him today.

Remember, this plan can actually take as little as 10 minutes or as long as you want. When I have a very busy day, I use a timer (stop watch, kitchen timer, timer on a smart phone, or even just a digital clock can work). For the 10-minute version, I set the timer for 2 minutes for each of the first 3 parts "S-O-A" and then 4 minutes for "K."

S = Sit in Silence

Don't forget, this first step on the plan is very important. We all need to learn how to "Be still and know that He is God" (Psalm 46:10a) to keep walking like a Dog for the rest of your life!

When you are ready to "sit in silence" for 2 minutes, start your timer.

S—SOAK: Sit in Silence while you welcome and wait for God's Presence.

"Wait for the LORD; be strong, and let your heart take courage;
Wait for the LORD!" Psalm 27:14 (ESV)

O = Observe Your Heart

Remember, in this section, I ask Jesus to show me what is on my heart or mind today. What is bothering me? What is making me really happy or really sad? What am I worried about today? What kind of things do you want to share with your BFF today? Then I just write down those thoughts and give them all to Him knowing He can take care of all of them.

Casting all your anxieties on him (Jesus), because he cares for you.
I Peter 5:7 (ESV)

O—SOAK: Observe Your Heart: Let God speak to you.

In the lines below, write down any "anxieties" or burdens or happy thoughts or joys that you want to share with Jesus this day. If Jesus shows you a worry or sin you need to confess and ask His forgiveness, then do so now as well.

Cast your cares on the Lord and he will sustain you;
he will never let the righteous be shaken.
Psalm 55:22 (NIV)

When you are ready to "observe your heart" for two minutes, start your timer.

____

____

____

A = Adoration (Praise and Thanksgiving)

Don't forget, adoration means "the act of paying honor." That is what we will do now in this section of *SOAK*. This is where we joyfully praise and adore Him!

Every day I will bless you and praise your name forever and ever.
Psalm 145:2 (ESV)

A—SOAK: Adoration: Worship your God!

On the next page, write down any words of praise or thanks you want to say to Jesus today. If you don't think of many words of praise or thanks, sometimes I will just read a few verses from a Psalm to remind me of many reasons I can give God thanks on this day.

Start your timer for 2-3 minutes.

____

____

____

K= Know Jesus More

Remember, in this section, you simply want to get to know Jesus more as your BFF by reading the Gospels. That's one of the best places to learn about Him! How can we follow our Master, Jesus Christ, on our Dog Walk, if we don't really know Him? Let's get to know Him a little more each day as we SOAK in God's Presence.

And this is eternal life, that they know you the only true God,
and Jesus Christ whom you have sent.
John 17:3 (ESV)

K—SOAK: Know Jesus More: Get to know your BFF!

You chose, in our last lesson, one of the first four books of the New Testament to start knowing Jesus more. Which one did you choose? ____________________

Start reading today where you ended reading the first day. Now read until you have learned one new thing about Jesus that you want to remember or live out this day. On the lines below, write down the name of the book, then chapter and verse numbers you read today first. Like this: John 1:1-3. Then write down the one thing you learned today from those verses about Jesus or the one thing He said that you want to obey.

____

____

____

End this time of SOAK by thanking Jesus for spending time with you today!

Scripture Memory for Week 10:
No new verses: Review the first 9 weeks!

<u>Here is your list so far:</u>

Week 1: II Corinthians 5:17
Week 2: Mark 12:30-31
Week 3: Ezekiel 36:27
Week 4: John 10:10
Week 5: Psalm 118:1
Week 6: I Thessalonians 5:11
Week 7: Romans 8:28
Week 8: Colossians 2:6-7
Week 9: Psalm 16:11

Hopefully, you wrote or typed out all of your verses so far in *The Dog Walk* during your last lesson on index cards or a Word Document on your computer. That will really help you review and learn them so you can live it out as you follow Jesus and share God's Word with others.

Review all nine verses today by saying them aloud to yourself in the mirror or to a family member or friend. You can also practice by recording your voice saying them into a computer or smart phone with a recording app. Review! Practice! Review!

Cartoon Day

Week 10: Day 3

Lesson 30

O.K. GOD. I'M HERE.
MY SOUL IS STILL BEFORE YOU.
I'LL WAIT FOR YOU AND YOU
ALONE—I JUST WANT YOU.

How Cats And Dogs Wait On God

Does the left or right side of the picture best represent your life and why? [107]

____

____

Learning Life Lessons with Mrs. Debby

SOAKing One Last Time!

Okay, my Dog Walk buddies, we're going to do a SOAK one more time. Why? Because the more you do it, the more it will become a part of your life.

If you simply do these quiet times during this curriculum, but then never do it again, I have failed you. ***These sections are here to encourage you to have a quiet time on a regular basis!*** For some, that means every day. For others, it might mean every other day. Whatever the case, you need to keep your friendship growing with Jesus or else you won't be as close to Him as you want. Also, I encourage you to buy a blank journal or composition book to use as you continue to meet with Jesus on your own the rest of this year.

So, here's a condensed version of SOAK. If you've forgotten what each section is, please go back to earlier lessons and review it.

Got your timer? Okay, go for it!

S = Sit in Silence (2 Minutes)

S—SOAK: Sit in Silence while you welcome and wait for God's Presence.

Wait for the LORD; be strong, and let your heart take courage;
Wait for the LORD! Psalm 27:14 (ESV)

O = Observe Your Heart (2 Minutes)

O—SOAK: Observe Your Heart: Let God speak to you.

Cast your cares on the Lord and he will sustain you;
he will never let the righteous be shaken.
Psalm 55:22 (NIV)

___

___

A = Adoration (Praise and Thanksgiving)

(2 Minutes)

A—SOAK: Adoration: Worship your God!

Every day I will bless you and praise your name forever and ever.
Psalm 145:2 (ESV)

____

____

____

K= Know Jesus More

(4 Minutes) Which book are you reading? _______________

K—SOAK: Know Jesus More: Get to know your BFF!

And this is eternal life, that they know you the only true God,
and Jesus Christ whom you have sent.
John 17:3 (ESV)

____

____

____

End this time of SOAK by thanking Jesus for spending time with you today!

Circle Which Of The Three Ways Of Meeting With God You Enjoyed The Most:

Read, Need, Deed

#2 **Cinco Devo**

SOAK

Scripture Memory

Review the first nine weeks by filling in the blanks!

Therefore, if ________________ is in Christ, he is a new ______________. The old has ___________ __________; behold, the ________ has come. 2 Corinthians 5:17

And you shall ____________ the Lord your God with all your ___________ and with all your ________ and with all your __________ and with all your strength. The second is this: You shall love your ____________ as _______________. There is no other commandment greater than these. Mark 12:30,31

And I will put my Spirit within you, and ____________ ________ to walk in my statutes and be careful to _________ my rules. Ezekiel 36:27

The ____________ comes only to _________ and kill and _____________. I came that they may have __________ and have it ________________. John 10:10

Oh give thanks to the Lord, for he is good; for his ____________ love endures forever! Psalm 118:1

Therefore ______________ one another and _________ one another up....
1 Thessalonians 5:11

And we know that for those who love God _____ things work together for ______, for those who are called according to his ______________. Romans 8:28

Therefore, as you received Christ Jesus the Lord, ____ ________ in him, rooted and built up in him and _____________ in the faith, just as you were taught, abounding in _______________. Colossians 2:6,7

You make known to me the _________ of _______; in your presence there is ______________ of joy; at your right hand are pleasures _________________.
Psalm 16:11

Week 11: Day 1

Lesson 31

Learning Life Lessons with Mrs. Debby

Walking in the Word: "The Word Hand"

Hopefully you've been sensing God speaking to you as you've been reading the Bible in your quiet times. Maybe you only took four minutes to read—maybe you read for 30 minutes. Whatever the case, I am praying you sensed God was wanting to communicate with you through His Word, and that you will continue using one of the plans you learned the past few weeks.

But it amazes me that even when I read a passage for the 10th (or 100th) time, I can still get new things out of it. There are always new insights to discover in God's Word.

And although reading it multiple times is great, we can even go deeper. That's what today's lesson is all about.

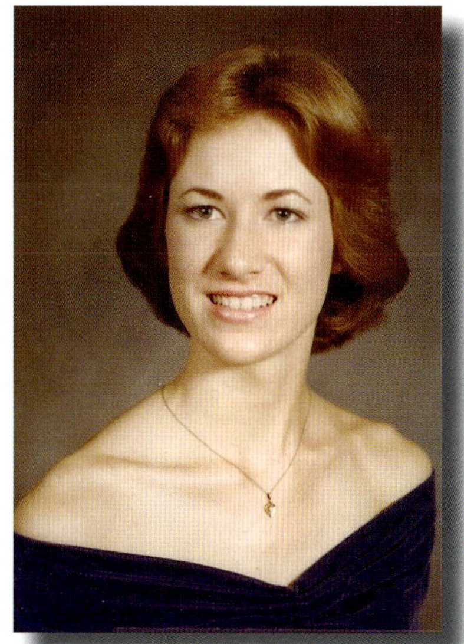

Here's my Senior picture from high school.

This week we will discover a really easy-to-remember illustration that describes five different ways to dive into the Word of God. I learned this illustration when I was in high school, but it makes so much sense that I knew you could handle it! A worldwide, Christian discipleship ministry called *The Navigators,* created this illustration.

To help us really learn "The Word Hand," as it is now called, we will draw one of The Navigators' favorite illustrations that help us remember five ways we can learn and grow from the Bible, God's Word. So here we go!

On the next page, place your left or right hand, whichever one you don't write with, right in the middle of the page. Now trace around it with a pen or pencil.

Your Hand

From the Navigators, we see this hand which helps us describe the five ways we go deeper in God's Word.

Now you will label your four fingers, then your thumb. But first write "The Word of God" in the palm of your hand area. Then starting with your pinkie finger, write these words:

Pinkie finger: **HEAR**
Ring finger: **READ**
Middle finger: **STUDY**
Pointer or index finger: **MEMORIZE**
Then on the thumb: **MEDITATE**

These five words represent "five very important methods of learning from the Bible." We will take time over the next few weeks to dive into all of them!

But let's not forget one important thing! *We've got to obey what we hear from God.* My pastor growing up always said, ***"Light obeyed increases light, but light dismayed brings forth the night."*** As Dogs walk in the "light" by obeying the commands of our Master, He will give us more "light" or truth so that we will keep growing in our Dog Walk! If we "dismay the light," or choose not to do what He tells us, we may feel like we are stumbling in the dark like a lost puppy in our Walk. Let's choose to obey what our Master, Jesus, tells us to do today and everyday!

Scripture Memory

Romans 10:17 (ESV)

So faith comes from hearing, and hearing through the word of Christ.

Write this verse on a 3" x 5" index card and start memorizing it today.

Check here when you have done it: ❑

Today I am super stoked to introduce you to the next book we will be reading 3 stories from each week till the end of *The Dog Walk*. If you have completed our elementary curriculum, you will be familiar with Charissa Roberson's book: *I Heard Good News Today 2: Big Life.* A homeschooled teenager herself, Charissa wrote it when she was 14 years-old! Amazing isn't it! She lives with her family in Maryland. God has given her the gift of writing for His Glory!

Because the first one was so well done, we at UnveilinGLORY have commissioned her to write our newest worldwide book of adventures displaying God's glory: *I Heard Good News Today 3: Faith Adventures with God!*

All these stories are true and are going to help your faith grow so you too can share your faith with those around you! So let's begin watching God use the courage and boldness of one man to share and multiply the good news of Jesus Christ all over this planet!

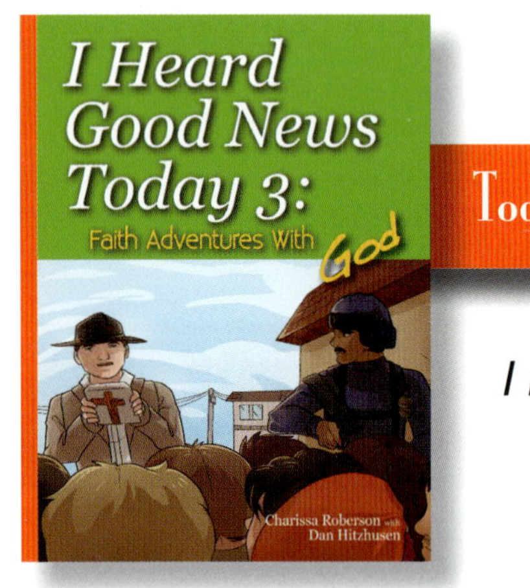

Today's Reading To Grow Your Faith

I Heard Good News Today 3
Read: The Introduction and Chapter 1—Below the Dogs

Even though people don't think they are worthy of God's love, does God still love them and why? [108]

Find the country mentioned on the map on page ix of *I Heard Good News Today 3* and pray for new believers there.

Week 11: Day 2

Lesson 32

Walking in the Word: Hearing the Word

We are so blessed to be able to ***hear*** God's Word these days in so many forms and fashions! You can find Christian teaching on the radio. You can go to YouTube and watch entire sermons from some of the greatest preachers around. You can have sermons automatically downloaded on your iPad or iPhone and listen to them. You can get Christian books in audio form.

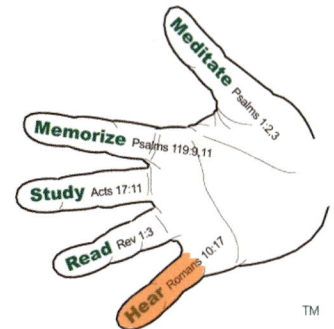

So the question we Dogs need to ask ourselves is this: How much time each week do we take advantage of these opportunities to listen to God's Word either on our smart phones or on the internet?

Especially, when you add up the amount of hours you spend reading a fiction novel, or playing video games, or watching funny YouTube videos, or just looking at photos on your computer or perhaps Instagram or Facebook. If you were to compare that to the amount of time you spend listening to God's Word, which would add up to more? If you are like me, the difference can be astounding—and sometimes embarrassing.

So what do we do about it? As Dog Christians we know that we are here on this planet to live for the Glory of God and not just our *own* fame or even our *own* little daily desires. We also know that as we choose to spend our time in ways that will cause our hearts to want to bring Glory to His name, He blesses us with the greatest joy we can ever imagine.

So where do you start? Where do you go to find a place or multiple places to listen to God's word?

May I suggest doing a search either on Google or YouTube such as, "Sermons by ???" and see what pops up. I would recommend sermons by:

Andy Stanley
Matt Chandler
Rick Warren
Tim Keller

So, this week, I challenge you, my fellow Dogs, give 15 minutes to listening to God's Word (or studying it on your own) three times, three different days this week when you are thinking about doing something else with those 15 minutes. Start today, right now. Write it down below:

Date	Activity I gave up	Whom did I listen to?	How much time?
1.			
2.			
3.			

Scripture Memory

Romans 10:17 (ESV)

So faith comes from hearing, and hearing through the word of Christ.

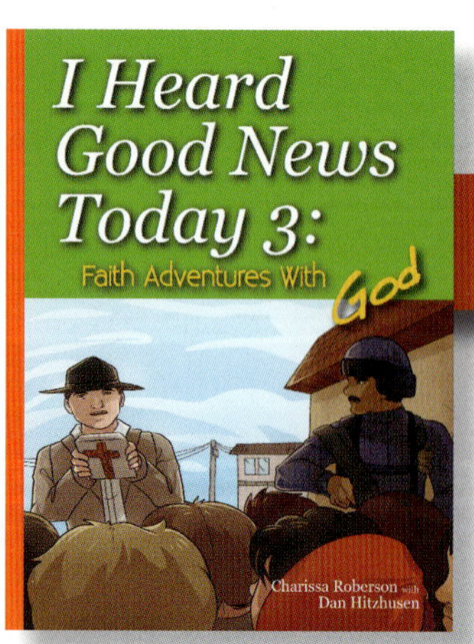

Today's Reading To Grow Your Faith

I Heard Good News Today 3
Read: Chapter 2—No Contacts? No Problem

Which contact amazed you the most? [109]

____

I HOPE I GET BLESSED TODAY.

LORD, I'll OBEY WHATEVER YOU REVEAL TO ME. I JUST WANT TO KNOW YOU MORE.

What Cats And Dogs Are Thinking Right Before The Sermon Starts

Do you want to be more like the Cat or the Dog in this cartoon and why? [110]

____

____

Meditate Psalms 1:2-3
Memorize Psalms 119:9,11
Study Acts 17:11
Read Rev 1:3
Hear Romans 10:17
TM

Hearing God's Word (Part 2)

You may have noticed that some of the sermons you found on YouTube were over 30 minutes in length. Some were even 45 minutes! Wow, that's a lot of time isn't it! (Yet I find I can spend 45 minutes on Facebook and it seems to fly by!)

If you want to listen to one of those sermons, you can start it and listen for 15 to 20 minutes and then push "Pause" on the video player on your screen. Then come back the next day and pick it back up. It may take you two or three different times to finish a sermon, but it will have been well worth it!

Go back to page 126, and fill out #2. Spend more time listening to God's Word and less time in something that isn't pointing you to God.

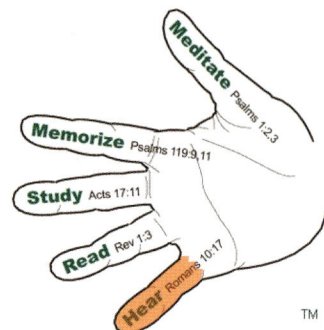

Scripture Memory

Romans 10:17 (ESV)

So faith comes from hearing, and hearing through the word of Christ.

Quote this verse to a family member and check the box when finished. ☐

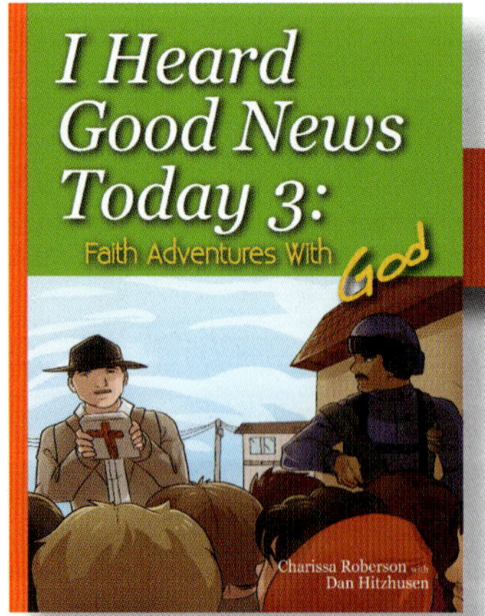

Today's Reading To Grow Your Faith

I Heard Good News Today 3
Read: Chapter 3—From Faith to Faith
Find the country mentioned on the map on page ix of *IHGNT 3* and pray for new believers there.

Why was Diana so key in Dan's first trip to Israel? [111]

Walking in the Word: Reading the Word

Hey fellow *Dog Walkers*, did you know that the whole Bible can be read in as little as 80 hours by the average reader? Think about that—just 80 hours! If you read the Bible straight through all day, you could be finished in under three and a half days! (Though you'd be a zombie because you wouldn't have had any sleep!)

But many times it is very helpful to read all the way through the Bible. Doing this gives you an overall picture of what God has been doing. Many people find it helpful to use a daily reading program which takes them systematically through the Bible.

If you started this curriculum in September, you may be nearing Thanksgiving or Christmas at this time. Am I right? If so, this week will be a great time to make a plan for attempting to read through a long portion of Scripture during the next calendar year.

What do I mean by calendar year? Well, that means January through December. Got it? So, when my own kids were your age, I challenged them during their middle school years to take the plunge and choose to read through the whole Bible in ONE YEAR! And guess what? They all did. (It didn't hurt that I promised them a "Ben Franklin" if they completed that goal. What do I mean by a "Ben Franklin"—in US dollars that means—$100 bill!)

However, I know we all have strengths and we all have weaknesses in the area of reading. So, you can decide with your parents or teacher, what will be your long portion of Scripture challenge for the next calendar year, or maybe just during the next calendar month! You could choose to read through all four of the gospels: Matthew, Mark, Luke or John. Or maybe you could choose to read through the complete New Testament! That would be an awesome goal! Or take the big challenge the next time January rolls around and challenge yourself to read the whole Bible in 12 months!

(Maybe your parent will give you a "Ben Franklin" too, right?)

If you want to read through the Bible in an entire year, the Blue Letter Bible gives you many options. Go to www.BlueLetterBible.org and at the very bottom you'll find something that looks like this:

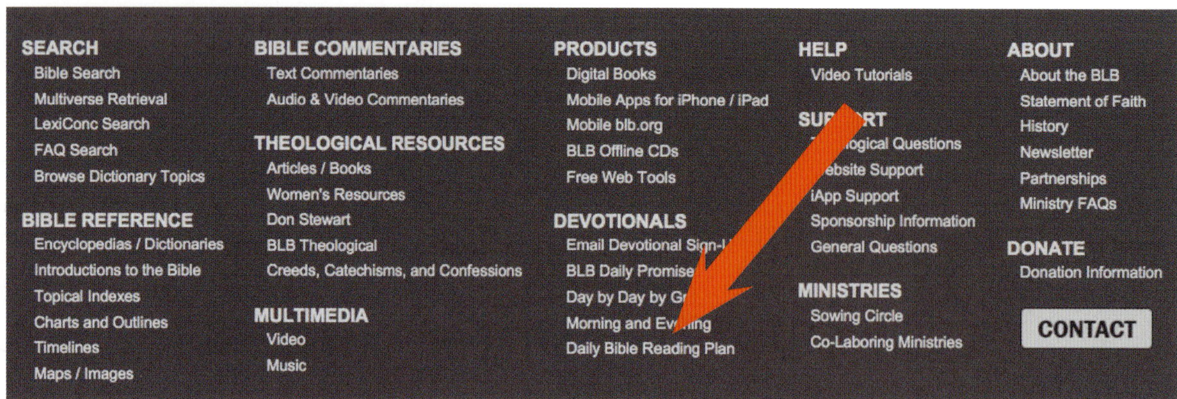

Click on the words "Daily Bible Read Plan." There you'll find multiple plans that you can download and follow. It looks like this:

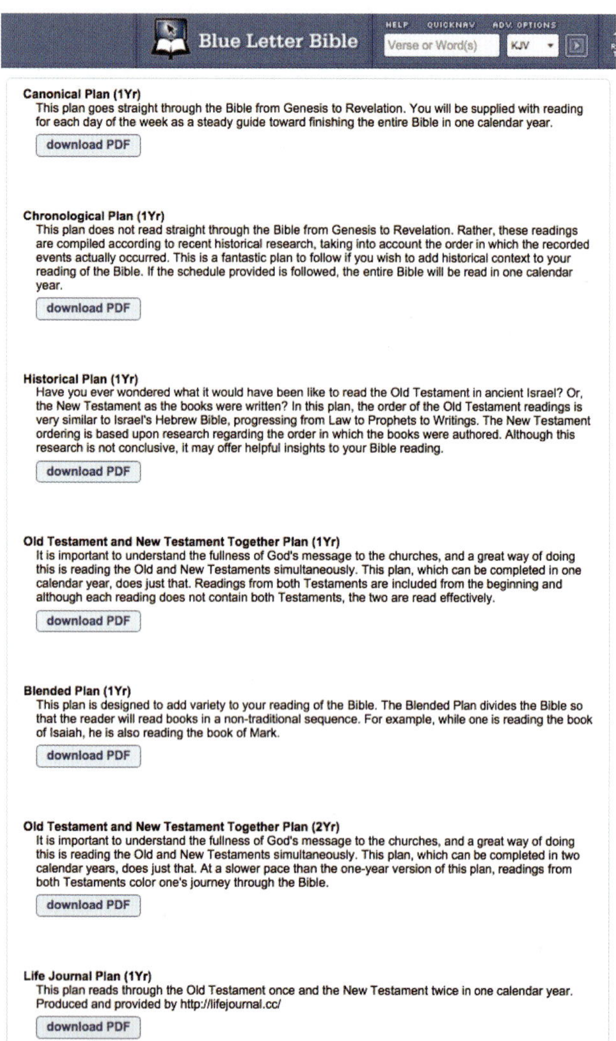

Blue Letter Bible

Canonical Plan (1Yr)
This plan goes straight through the Bible from Genesis to Revelation. You will be supplied with reading for each day of the week as a steady guide toward finishing the entire Bible in one calendar year.
download PDF

Chronological Plan (1Yr)
This plan does not read straight through the Bible from Genesis to Revelation. Rather, these readings are compiled according to recent historical research, taking into account the order in which the recorded events actually occurred. This is a fantastic plan to follow if you wish to add historical context to your reading of the Bible. If the schedule provided is followed, the entire Bible will be read in one calendar year.
download PDF

Historical Plan (1Yr)
Have you ever wondered what it would have been like to read the Old Testament in ancient Israel? Or, the New Testament as the books were written? In this plan, the order of the Old Testament readings is very similar to Israel's Hebrew Bible, progressing from Law to Prophets to Writings. The New Testament ordering is based upon research regarding the order in which the books were authored. Although this research is not conclusive, it may offer helpful insights to your Bible reading.
download PDF

Old Testament and New Testament Together Plan (1Yr)
It is important to understand the fullness of God's message to the churches, and a great way of doing this is reading the Old and New Testaments simultaneously. This plan, which can be completed in one calendar year, does just that. Readings from both Testaments are included from the beginning and although each reading does not contain both Testaments, the two are read effectively.
download PDF

Blended Plan (1Yr)
This plan is designed to add variety to your reading of the Bible. The Blended Plan divides the Bible so that the reader will read books in a non-traditional sequence. For example, while one is reading the book of Isaiah, he is also reading the book of Mark.
download PDF

Old Testament and New Testament Together Plan (2Yr)
It is important to understand the fullness of God's message to the churches, and a great way of doing this is reading the Old and New Testaments simultaneously. This plan, which can be completed in two calendar years, does just that. At a slower pace than the one-year version of this plan, readings from both Testaments color one's journey through the Bible.
download PDF

Life Journal Plan (1Yr)
This plan reads through the Old Testament once and the New Testament twice in one calendar year. Produced and provided by http://lifejournal.cc/
download PDF

Making a commitment like this isn't something you do quickly. You are going to want to pray about it and talk with your mom and dad about it.

And then once you make the decision, you are going to need to stick to it! This will be the hardest part, because it requires time—time each day when you may want to be doing other things.

I remember lots of times when my kids would remember at the end of the day, "Oops, I forgot to read." And so they would spend the last 30 minutes of their day reading their Bible.

My youngest took the challenge up with my husband. Both of them read through the Bible in a year. Maybe you could ask your mom or dad if they want to do it with you!

On the next page you are going to be asked to circle an option. Don't do it right now. Take time and pray through it and talk to your parents. But do make a decision!

Circle the one you want to do:

One Book of the Bible

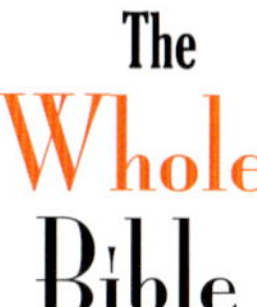

After you choose which you want to do, set some goals. Fill in the following blanks.

When will you begin your reading plan? ______________________________

When is your ending goal? ______________________________________

Who will be your supervisor for this challenge? _________________________

Will you have a reward to gain when you finish? List here:

____

When my husband was away from home,
I would help Hunter (my youngest)
with reading through his Bible in a year.

Revelation 1:3 (GNT)

Happy is the one who reads this book, and happy are those who listen to the words of this prophetic message and obey what is written in this book!

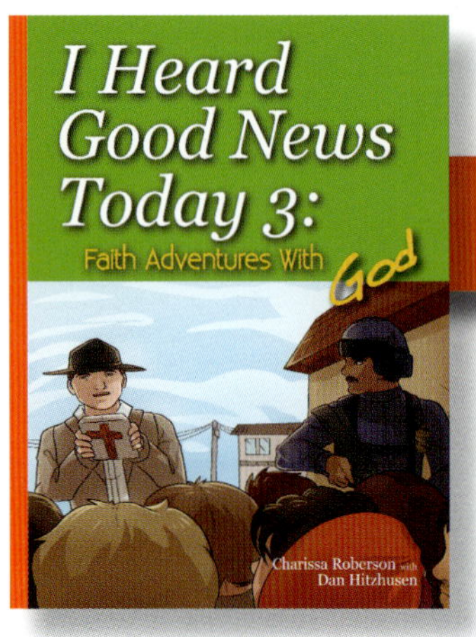

Today's Reading To Grow Your Faith

I Heard Good News Today 3
Read: Chapter 4—It's a Miracle

Sometimes God uses people we're not expecting to bring about miracles in our lives. Whom did God use with Dan? [112]

Find the country mentioned on the map on page ix of *I Heard Good News Today 3* and pray for new believers there.

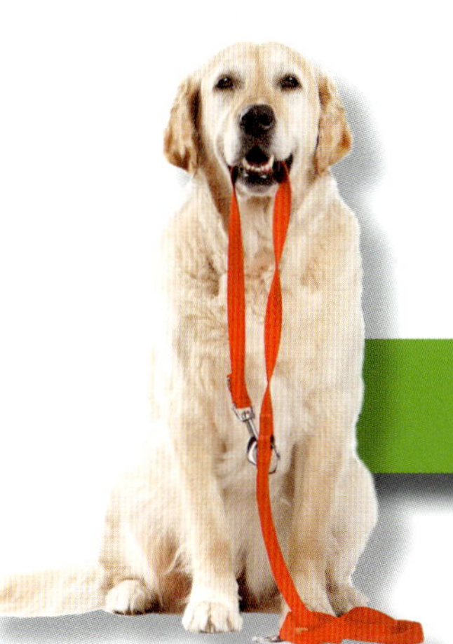

Week 12: Day 2

Lesson 35

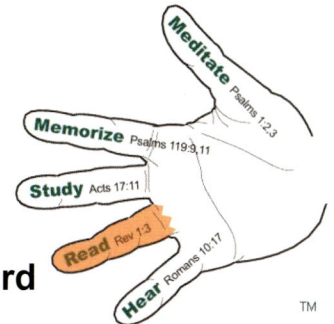

Learning Life Lessons with Mrs. Debby

Meditate Psalms 1:2-3
Memorize Psalms 119:9,11
Study Acts 17:11
Read Rev 1:3
Hear Romans 10:17
TM

The Benefits of Reading God's Word

Some of you who don't like to read may be asking yourself one question, "Why read a longer portion of God's Word? Why not just read a verse a day to keep the doctor away?" (Ha-Ha! Just kidding!)

Remember our Scripture Memory Verse from Week 11? That was just last week! Can you say it with me now:

"So faith comes from hearing, and hearing through the _______________ of _____________________."[113]

Yep! That is one major reason you want to be reading the Scripture on a daily basis: ***to increase your faith***. Why is that important? Well, look up Hebrews 11:6 (ESV) and fill in these blanks:

"And without _______________ it is impossible to ____________________ him,
for whoever would draw near to _______________
must believe that he exists
and that he _________________ those who seek him."[114]

After reading Hebrews 11:6, doesn't it make sense why we who are seeking to walk like a Dog Christian, would want to read our Bibles and grow in our faith? As Dogs, our overall goal in life is to glorify God—to please Him. The verse above from Hebrews 11 tells us that it is impossible to please God without faith. Then our Scripture memory from last week (Week 11) tells us that faith grows as we hear and read the word of Christ. Can you tell I'm excited? Let's just do it, Dog Walkers!!!

Now if you haven't decided what reading plan you are going to do for the new year, go back to page 131 and circle one if you and your parents are ready. If not, keep on praying about it. But don't wait forever! The new year will be here before you know it!

Revelation 1:3 (Good News Translation)

Happy is the one who reads this book,
and happy are those who listen to the words of this prophetic message
and obey what is written in this book!

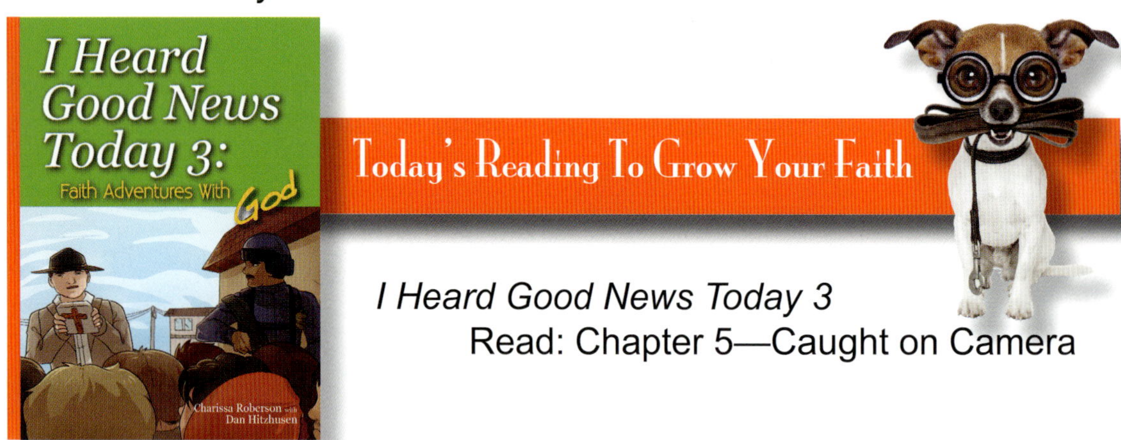

I Heard Good News Today 3
Read: Chapter 5—Caught on Camera

What had Dan and his team communicated to Jamal and Latifa about Christianity?[115]

Find the country mentioned on the map on page ix of *I Heard Good News Today 3* and pray for new believers there.

WOW! A SALE ON LAWN MOWERS. PRAISE GOD!

YUM OH

LETS LOOK AT JOSHUA CHAPTER 1.

BIBLE

What Cats And Dogs First Read Each Morning

Based on Revelation 1:3, who do you think has a greater happiness and why? [118]

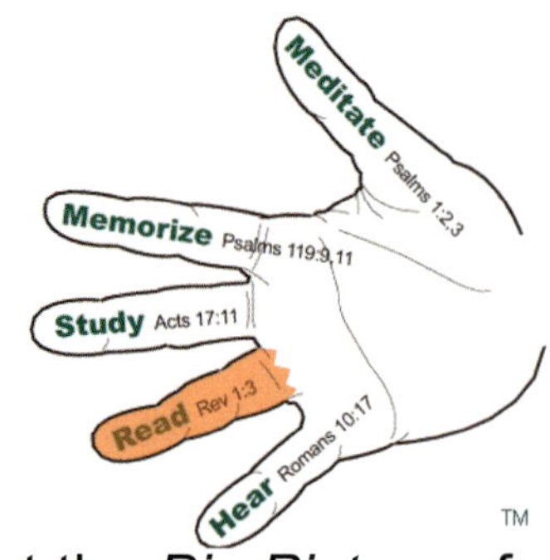

The Big Picture of God's Word

Do you know what it means when someone says, "Let's look at the *Big Picture* of what happened in a book or a movie?" Well, the *Big Picture* of a story or movie is not all the little details that happened, but the main theme or story that took place.

Did you ever watch the movie *Inside Out*? It was a hilarious movie that tried to communicate a key thought or idea. What did it communicate? The overall big picture was that we need to express our feelings—even feelings of sadness—if we are to be emotionally healthy. Maybe you just enjoyed the movie and missed that whole theme. That's okay. But when movies are made, many are trying to communicate a key thought rather than just entertain.

The same is true with God's written Word, the Bible. There are many, many stories in our Bible, and there are even 66 total books: ________ [116] books are in the Old Testament and _______ [117] books are in the New Testament. But how do you really learn the *Big Picture* from God's written words to us? By ***reading*** the whole story! Right?

I have an older woman in my life who really encourages me. I call her "Miss Carolyn"! She always seemed like the Church Mother to me at our local church so I wanted to get to know her and learn from her all I could about loving Jesus and knowing God more. She really challenged me a few years ago! She told me about a book or plan called *The Bible in 90 Days*. Why do you think that was the title? You probably won't believe it, but it's true. This plan has you read the whole Bible in three months or 90 days! At first I thought, why would I even try to do this crazy plan???

But then I took her challenge, and I completed it for the first time in January—March of 2013. I had to spend about one hour each day reading to complete my Bible portion for each day, but I discovered one thing to be true: I saw much more clearly the *Big Picture* of what God is like and what He was doing in the Bible and even today: God wants all of us to know Him and love Him and tell the whole world about Him!

Now I'm not really suggesting you take the challenge that Miss Carolyn gave to me, but if you are an avid reader, here is the link:

http://www.thebrooknetwork.org/wp-content/uploads/2011/12/BibleIn90Days.pdf

To finish our week on Reading the Bible (second finger of the Word Hand), I want you to choose one book of the Bible to read in its entirety ***today***. Even better, read the book you have chosen aloud to one of your siblings or to a friend.

Which book did you choose? ________________________________

Check here when finished. ☐

Scripture Memory

Revelation 1:3 (Good News Translation)

Happy is the one who reads this book,
and happy are those who listen to the words of this prophetic message
and obey what is written in this book!

Quote this verse to a family member or friend and place a check in the box after you have successfully done it. ☐

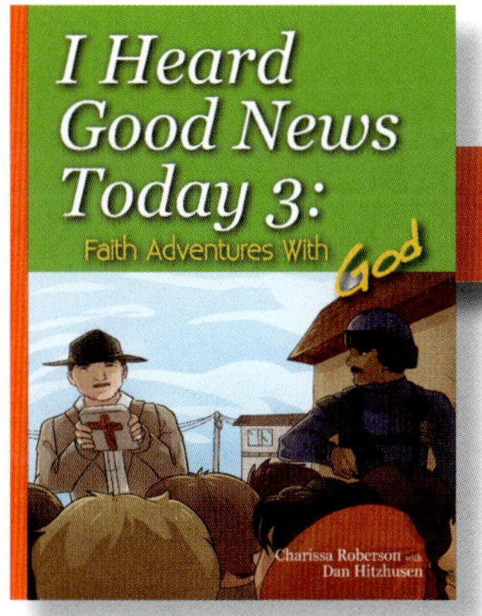

Today's Reading To Grow Your Faith

I Heard Good News Today 3
Read: Chapter 6—I See Love

What was so amazing about Dan's step of faith? [119]

____

Find the country mentioned on the map on page ix of I Heard Good News Today 3 and pray for new believers there.

Our daughter, Elise, is very creative. She loves to hold parties for her friends.

This was during the Christmas holiday season on her college break.

Walking in the Word: Studying the Word

Another week has begun in *The Dog Walk*! Are you ready for another life lesson in how to learn and grow as a Dog Christian? This week we move to the next finger of the Word Hand: Studying the Word. Your Scripture memory verse for this week explains one reason we take time in our lives as Dogs to study the Word of God.

Read this verse three times slowly and then answer the question below: *"They listened to the message with great eagerness, and every day they studied the Scriptures to see if what Paul said was really true." (Acts 17:11b, GNT)*

What is the reason that the Jews in Berea in Acts 17 were "studying the Scriptures every day?" ____[120]

The same must be true of us, fellow Dogs. When we hear another person teach about the Word of God, we must take time to study the Bible ourselves to make sure what the preacher or teacher taught is truly in God's Word.

So what are some practical tools to help you ***Study*** the Word of God? This week we will learn about three of them: ***Cross-Referencing***, ***Concordances*** and ***Commentaries.*** Each day we will also practice using them in a simple study of a passage of Scripture. These tools will be something you can use the rest of your life!

Today's focus will be on Cross-Referencing the Scriptures! This tool is allowing the Word of God to give you more understanding and insight into the Word of God itself.

Cross-Referencing

What is it? A *cross-reference* is when you go to read another verse somewhere else in the Bible to help you better understand the meaning of the verse you are studying presently. Sometimes a *cross-reference* will also show you where a quote from another part of the Bible will be found. There are four easy ways to find and use them.

#1 If you have a Bible that has little tiny letters of the alphabet after some verses, those tiny letters are "cross-reference" guides. Those tiny letters will also be found either at the bottom or the middle of the page in your Bible. After each tiny letter, you will see either one or more Bible verses written behind the tiny letters. You can then turn to read the verse listed so that you can gain more insight or understanding of this passage. See the one below here for Titus, chapter 1.

TITUS 1:1 1278 TO KNOW GOD & MAKE HIM KNOWN

1 Paul, a servant of God[a] and an apostle of Jesus Christ for the faith of
God's elect and the knowledge of the
truth[b] that leads to godliness— 2 a faith
and knowledge resting on the hope of
eternal life,[c] which God, who does not
lie, promised before the beginning of
time,[d] 3 and at his appointed season[e] he
brought his word to light[f] through the
preaching entrusted to me[g] by the command of God our Savior,[h]

4 To Titus,[i] my true son in our com-
mon faith:

Grace and peace from God the Father
and Christ Jesus our Savior.

1:1 [a]Ro 1:1
[b]1Ti 2:4
1:2 [c]2Ti 1:1
[d]2Ti 1:9
1:3 [e]1Ti 2:6
[f]2Ti 1:10
[g]1Ti 1:11
[h]Lk 1:47
1:4 [i]2Co 2:13
1:5 [j]Ac 27:7
[k]Ac 11:30
1:6 [l]1Ti 3:2
1:7 [m]1Ti 3:1
[n]1Co 4:1
[o]1Ti 3:3,8
1:8 [p]1Ti 3:2
[q]2Ti 3:3
1:9 [r]1Ti 1:19
[s]1Ti 1:10
1:10 [t]1Ti 1:6
[u]11:2
1:11 [v]2Ti 3:6

12 Even one of their own prophets[w] has
said, "Cretans[x] are always liars, evil
brutes, lazy gluttons." 13 This testimony
is true. Therefore, rebuke[y] them sharply,
so that they will be sound in the faith[z]
14 and will pay no attention to Jewish
myths[a] or to the commands[b] of those
who reject the truth. 15 To the pure, all
things are pure, but to those who are corrupted and do not believe, nothing is
pure.[c] In fact, both their minds and con-
sciences are corrupted. 16 They claim to
know God, but by their actions they deny
him.[d] They are detestable, disobedient
and unfit for doing anything good.

In the above example you'll find a small letter "a" to the right of the word "God." In the middle of the page, you'll see "1:1" signifying "chapter 1, verse 1." The you'll see the small letter "a" again. After it come the verse "Romans 1:1." It is wanting you to read Romans 1:1 to cross reference what is being written in verse 1 when speaking about God. Verse 1 also has a "b" reference.

#2 If you are using a Bible APP like *Blue Letter Bible,* it will guide you to just "tap" a verse if you want to discover a bunch of *cross-references*. Some verses may have 30 cross references!

#3 If you have access to a computer, you can find Blue Letter Bible there as well. Go to www.BlueLetterBible.org and go to any verse. There you can click on "Tools" to the left of the verse and then go to "Cross Ref" section.

#4 Another way is simply to go to www.TKS-Online.com. There type in a verse and all of the cross-references are right there!

Activity For Today

Activity for Today:
Cross-referencing John 3:16

Look up John 3:16 in any of the four ways listed on the left page.

Turn to one or more verses referenced and read them carefully. Write down any new insight or knowledge you gain from the other verses that help\ you understand the original verse (John 3:16) better.

____

____

____

____

Scripture Memory

Acts 17:11b (Good News Translation)

They listened to the message with great eagerness,
and every day they studied the Scriptures
to see if what Paul said was really true.

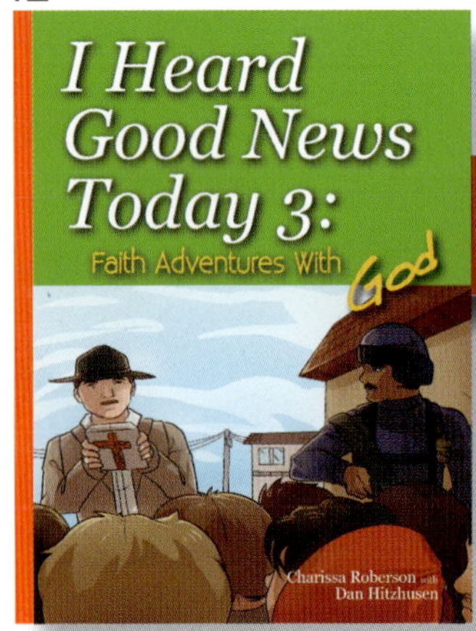

Today's Reading To Grow Your Faith

I Heard Good News Today 3
Read: Chapter 7—Two Fish

What did Vern feel the first time he shared his faith? [121]

Find the country mentioned on the map on page ix of *I Heard Good News Today 3* and pray for new believers there.

Hunter's Golden Retriever, Jenne Jewel, had two litters. The first litter had 10 puppies, the second had 11 puppies!

Week 13: Day 2

Lesson 38

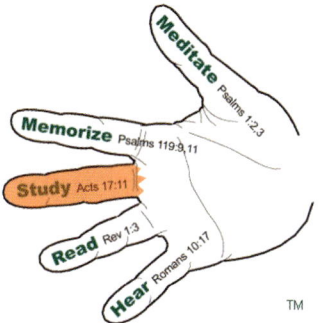

Meditate Psalms 1:2,3
Memorize Psalms 119:9,11
Study Acts 17:11
Read Rev 1:3
Hear Romans 10:17
TM

Studying the Word: Concordance

In our last lesson, we gave you a new challenge to learn how to go deeper into the verses or passages of Scripture that you have just been hearing or reading in the past. Today we will learn another way to study our Bibles on our *Dog Walk* so that we can be ready to find whatever *spiritual food* we need to grow as Dog Christians seeking to follow our Master, the Lord Jesus, the rest of our lives!

Concordance

What is it? The dictionary defines a concordance as "an alphabetical index of the principal words of a book, as of the Bible, with a reference to the passage in which each occurs."

How to use it? A *concordance* is a great tool if you want to study a topic or a specific word in your Bible. For example: if you are trying to understand the meaning of the word "grace" that you have read in Ephesians 2:8-9, "For by *grace* you have been saved through faith..." You can often look in the back of your Bible, especially if it is a Study Bible, and you will see an alphabetical listing of the main words used most often in the Scriptures. (An example is seen to the right.) To find more understanding of the word *grace*, just go to the "g" section and after the word *grace* you will see several other Bible references

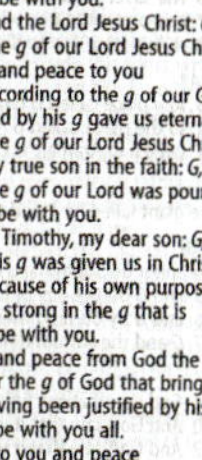

GOVERN 1462

GOVERN (GOVERNMENT)
Ge 1: 16 the greater light to g the day
Job 34: 17 Can he who hates justice g?
Ro 12: 8 it is leadership, let him g diligently;

GOVERNMENT (GOVERN)
Isa 9: 6 and the g will be on his shoulders.

GRACE* (GRACIOUS)
Ps 45: 2 lips have been anointed with g,
Pr 1: 9 will be a garland to g your head
3: 22 an ornament to g your neck.
3: 34 but gives g to the humble.
4: 9 She will set a garland of g
Isa 26: 10 Though g is shown to the wicked,
Jnh 2: 8 forfeit the g that could be theirs.
Zec 12: 10 of Jerusalem a spirit of g
Lk 2: 40 and the g of God was upon him.
Jn 1: 14 who came from the Father, full of g
1: 16 of his g we have all received one
1: 17 g and truth came through Jesus
Ac 4: 33 and much g was upon them all.
6: 8 a man full of God's g and power,
11: 23 saw the evidence of the g of God,
13: 43 them to continue in the g of God.
14: 3 message of his g by enabling them
14: 26 they had been committed to the g
15: 11 We believe it is through the g
15: 40 by the brothers to the g of the Lord
18: 27 to those who by g had believed.
20: 24 testifying to the gospel of God's g.
20: 32 to God and to the word of his g,
Ro 1: 5 we received g and apostleship
1: 7 G and peace to you
3: 24 and are justified freely by his g
4: 16 be by g and may be guaranteed
5: 2 access by faith into this g
5: 15 came by the g of the one man,
5: 15 how much more did God's g
5: 17 God's abundant provision of g
5: 20 where sin increased, g increased all
5: 21 also g might reign
6: 1 on sinning so that g may increase?
6: 14 you are not under law, but under g.
6: 15 we are not under law but under g?
11: 5 there is a remnant chosen by g.
11: 6 if by g, then it is no longer by works
11: 6 if it were, g would no longer be g.
12: 3 For by the g given me I say
12: 6 according to the g given us.
15: 15 because of the g God gave me
16: 20 The g of our Lord Jesus be
1Co 1: 3 G and peace to you
1: 4 of his g given you in Christ Jesus.
3: 10 By the g God has given me,
15: 10 But by the g of God I am what I am
15: 10 but the g of God that was with me.
15: 10 his g to me was not without effect.
16: 23 The g of the Lord Jesus be with you
2Co 1: 2 G and peace to you
1: 12 wisdom but according to God's g.
4: 15 so that the g that is reaching more
6: 1 not to receive God's g in vain.
8: 1 to know about the g that God has
8: 6 also to completion this act of g
8: 7 also excel in this g of giving.
8: 9 For you know the g
9: 8 able to make all g abound to you,
9: 14 of the surpassing g God has given
12: 9 "My g is sufficient for you,
13: 14 May the g of the Lord Jesus Christ,
Gal 1: 3 G and peace to you
1: 6 the one who called you by the g
1: 15 from birth and called me by his g,
2: 9 when they recognized the g given
2: 21 I do not set aside the g of God,
3: 18 God in his g gave it to Abraham
5: 4 you have fallen away from g.
6: 18 The g of our Lord Jesus Christ be
Eph 1: 2 G and peace to you
1: 6 to the praise of his glorious g,
1: 7 riches of God's g that he lavished
2: 5 it is by g you have been saved.
2: 7 the incomparable riches of his g,
2: 8 For it is by g you have been saved,
3: 2 of God's g that was given to me
3: 7 by the gift of God's g given me
3: 8 God's people, this g was given me:
4: 7 to each one of us g has been given
6: 24 G to all who love our Lord Jesus
Php 1: 2 G and peace to you
1: 7 all of you share in God's g with me.
4: 23 The g of the Lord Jesus Christ be
Col 1: 2 G and peace to you
1: 6 understood God's g in all its truth.
4: 6 conversation be always full of g,
4: 18 G be with you.
1Th 1: 1 and the Lord Jesus Christ: G
5: 28 The g of our Lord Jesus Christ be
2Th 1: 2 G and peace to you
1: 12 according to the g of our God
2: 16 and by his g gave us eternal
3: 18 The g of our Lord Jesus Christ be
1Ti 1: 2 my true son in the faith: G,
1: 14 The g of our Lord was poured out
6: 21 G be with you.
2Ti 1: 2 To Timothy, my dear son: G,
1: 9 This g was given us in Christ Jesus
1: 9 because of his own purpose and g.
2: 1 be strong in the g that is
4: 22 G be with you.
Tit 1: 4 G and peace from God the Father
2: 11 For the g of God that brings
3: 7 having been justified by his g,
3: 15 G be with you all.
Phm : 3 G to you and peace
: 25 The g of the Lord Jesus Christ be
Heb 2: 9 that by the g of God he might taste
4: 16 find g to help us in our time of need
4: 16 the throne of g with confidence,
10: 29 and who has insulted the Spirit of g
12: 15 See to it that no one misses the g
13: 9 hearts to be strengthened by g,
13: 25 G be with you all.
Jas 4: 6 but gives g to the humble."
4: 6 But he gives us more g. That is why
1Pe 1: 2 G and peace be yours in abundance
1: 10 who spoke of the g that was
1: 13 fully on the g to be given you
4: 10 faithfully administering God's g
5: 5 but gives g to the humble."
5: 10 the God of all g, who called you
5: 12 and testifying that this is the true g
2Pe 1: 2 G and peace be yours in abundance
3: 18 But grow in the g and knowledge
2Jn : 3 and will be with us forever: G,
Jude : 4 who change the g of our God
Rev 1: 4 G and peace to you
22: 21 The g of the Lord Jesus be

GRACIOUS (GRACE)
Ex 34: 6 the compassionate and g God,
Nu 6: 25 and be g to you;
Ne 9: 17 But you are a forgiving God, g
Ps 67: 1 May God be g to us and bless us
Pr 22: 11 a pure heart and whose speech is g
Isa 30: 18 Yet the LORD longs to be g to you

GRAIN
Lev 2: 1 When someone brings a g offering
Lk 17: 35 women will be grinding g together;
1Co 9: 9 ox while it is treading out the g."

GRANDCHILDREN (CHILD)
1Ti 5: 4 But if a widow has children or g,

GRANDMOTHER (MOTHER)
2Ti 1: 5 which first lived in your g Lois

GRANT (GRANTED)
Ps 20: 5 May the LORD g all your requests
51: 12 g me a willing spirit, to sustain me.

GRANTED (GRANT)
Pr 10: 24 what the righteous desire will be g.
Mt 15: 28 great faith! Your request is g."
Php 1: 29 For it has been g to you on behalf

GRAPES
Nu 13: 23 branch bearing a single cluster of g.
Jer 31: 29 'The fathers have eaten sour g,
Eze 18: 2 " 'The fathers eat sour g,
Mt 7: 16 Do people pick g from thornbushes
Rev 14: 18 and gather the clusters of g

GRASPED
Php 2: 6 with God something to be g,

GRASS
Ps 103: 15 As for man, his days are like g,
Isa 40: 6 "All men are like g,
Mt 6: 30 If that is how God clothes the g
1Pe 1: 24 "All men are like g,

GRASSHOPPERS
Nu 13: 33 We seemed like g in our own eyes,

besides the one you are reading in Ephesians. Look up these other verses and ask God to give you more understanding of the word *grace*.

If you are using a Bible website (www.biblegateway.com) or Bible APP, you can click on the Concordance section and look up the word or topic you want to learn more about.

Activity for Today: Using a Concordance to Study God's Word

We will practice using the *concordance* today.

Decide if you will use a Study Bible or website: www.biblegateway.com.

If using a Study Bible, turn to the back and look at the alphabetical words until you find: **"word,"** then choose to read three verses that are listed, finish by reading II Timothy 2:15.

List the verses you looked up and read here:

a. ______________________________

b. ______________________________

c. ______________________________

d. II Timothy 2:15

Or If using the website: www.biblegateway.com , type the words: WORD OF TRUTH where it has a box near the top of the page that says: *Enter keyword, passage or topic.*

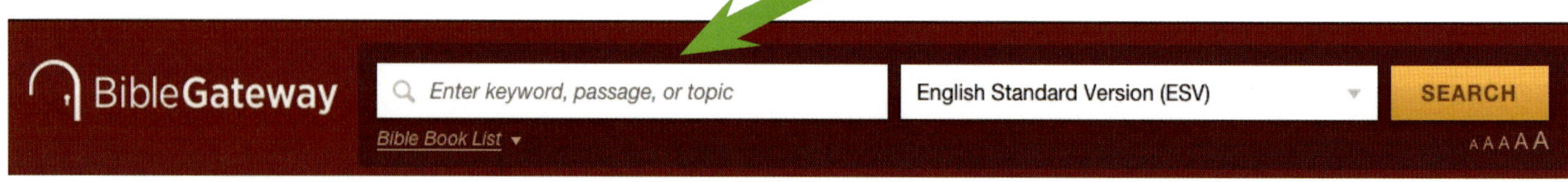

Then choose which version of the Bible you want to read in the next box to the right. Then click "Search." You will see a list of verses with "WORD OF TRUTH" highlighted in them. Read three of the verses listed ending with II Timothy 2:15.

List the verses you read here:

a. ________________________________

b. ________________________________

c. ________________________________

d. II Timothy 2:15

Now, read II Timothy 2:15 again. According to this verse, what are some ways that studying the Bible on our Dog Walk brings glory to God?

____ [122]

Acts 17:11b (Good News Translation)

They listened to the message with great eagerness,
and every day they studied the Scriptures
to see if what Paul said was really true.

I Heard Good News Today 3
Read: Chapter 8—To India by Faith

Sometimes God answers our prayers after we take steps of faith. When did Dan and his team get their permits? [123]

____

Find the country mentioned on the map on page ix of *I Heard Good News Today 3* and pray for new believers there.

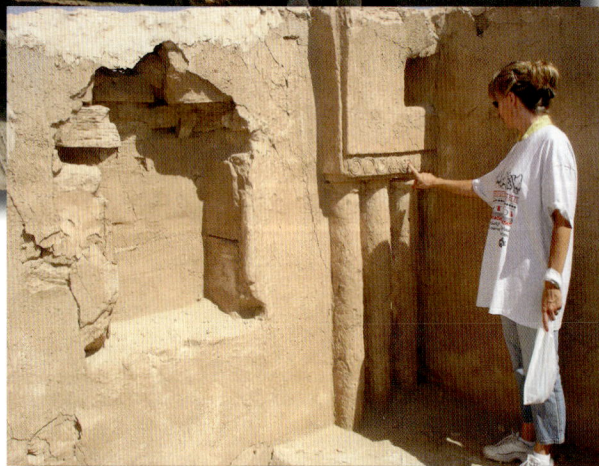

My husband was asked to speak in Saudi Arabia.
While there, we went out and visited a church
that was built in the 4th century
and also saw these cute camels on the way!

I BELIEVE EVERYTHING MY PASTOR SAYS!

THIS SOUNDS GOOD, BUT HOW DOES THAT MATCH UP WITH MATTHEW 18?

How Cats And Dogs Respond To Their Pastor's Teaching

Do you think it is okay to question a pastor's words and why? [124]

____

____

Studying God's Word: Commentaries

Okay, fellow Dogs, I know...I know...I know. Go ahead and say it: this has been an intense week, right? But I was your age when I started learning how to really study the Bible, God's Word of Truth. So I know you can do it!

Today I will introduce you to something quite different than *cross-referencing* the Bible and using a *concordance* to study the Scriptures. You see, in both of those study tools, we were using Scripture to study and understand Scripture better.

Today's tool for Bible Study called a *commentary* is actually reading and learning from older, more educated men and women who have spent hours, days, months and years deeply studying the Bible. Because of the time spent, they have a lot of good wisdom to share with us. You may want to ask your parent(s) or teacher if they recommend or have a favorite commentator for you to study online.

Commentaries

What is it? A *commentary* is another person's knowledge gained from an intense and prolonged study of a topic or a passage of Scripture. In other words, godly men and women have studied the Bible their whole lives and have written down some amazing things about the passage for people like you and me to read! We get to benefit from their life-long learning.

How do you find what they've written? There are a couple of ways to find them. Some Study Bibles have them written at the bottom of the page. It will sometimes be called "comments" for a certain verse. You will find the comment listed after the verse number. This is usually a short commentary.

If you are using a Bible website or Bible APP, you can find many different choices of *commentaries* to read for more understanding or insight. In the Blue Letter Bible, go to any passage, click on "Tools," then click on "Commentaries." Here is a sample commentary of Genesis 1:1.

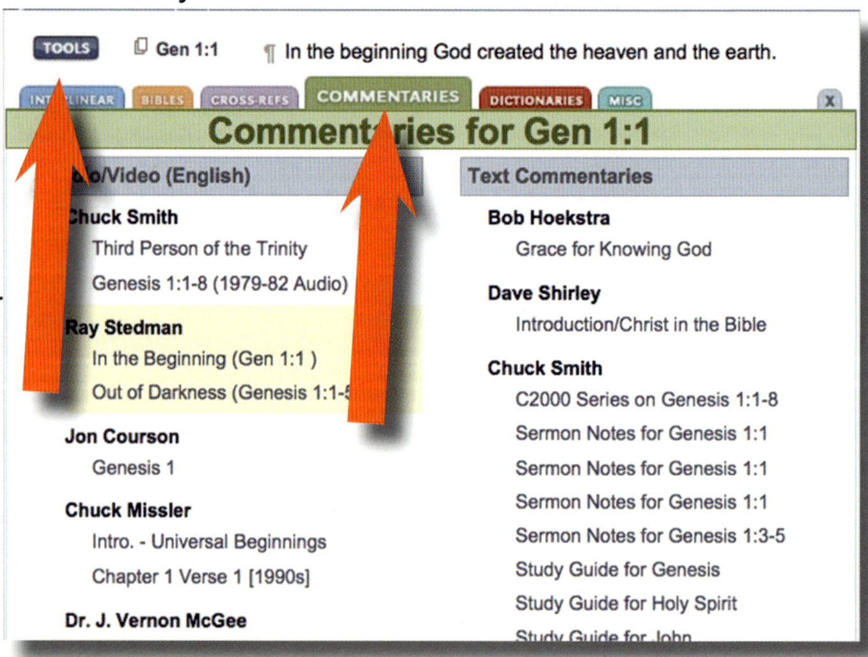

My favorite commentator is Matthew Henry (not shown, he

is further down the list, but wasn't copied.) Though he uses "Old English" and is sometimes difficult to understand, God has given him amazing insights into God's Word and they have really helped my husband and me.

Activity for Today: Choose a Commentary to Gain Understanding

Find this passage in your Bible: II Timothy 3:16-17 Read these two verses slowly three times. Look up any *cross-references*. Write down one thing you learned.

____

____

Now look at the bottom of the page if you have a Study Bible and read what the commentator (or author of these endnotes) has to say about this verse. Or if you are using a Bible website or APP, read one of the recommended commentators' insight on these verses. Write something new or interesting you learned from the *commentary*.

____

____

Acts 17:11b (Good News Translation)

*They listened to the message with great eagerness,
and every day they studied the Scriptures
to see if what Paul said was really true.*

Quote this verse to a family member or friend and then put a check in the box after you have successfully done it. ☐

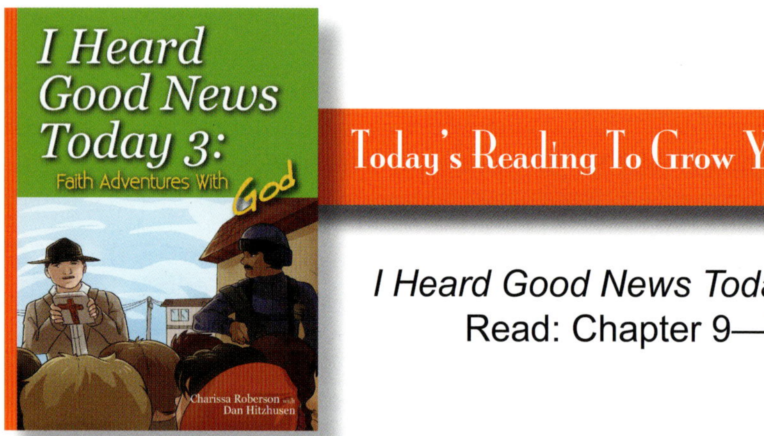

I Heard Good News Today 3
Read: Chapter 9—The Terrorist Village

What was so shocking about going to the terrorist village? [125]

Find the country mentioned on the map on page ix of *I Heard Good News Today 3* and pray for new believers there.

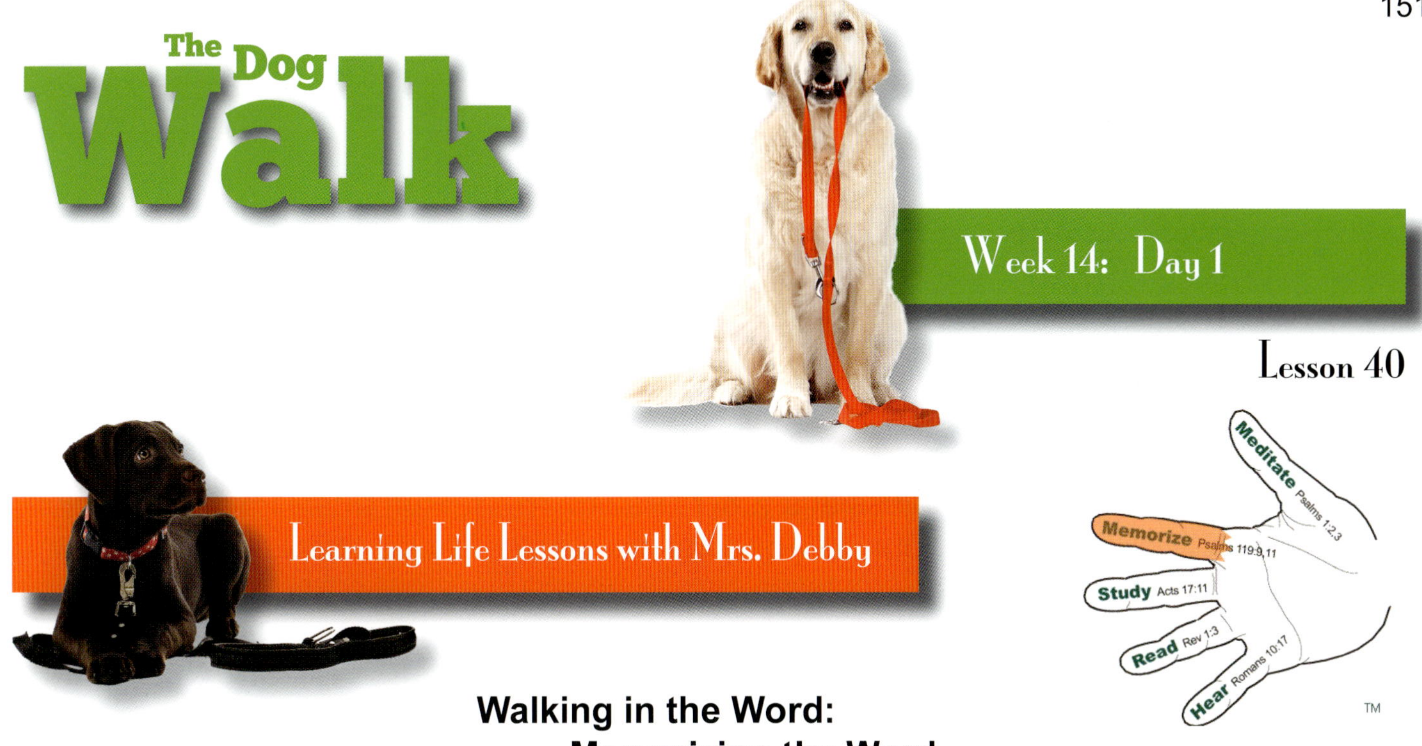

Walking in the Word: Memorizing the Word

Well, guess what? We are almost halfway through *The Dog Walk*! Can you believe it? Me neither.

This week we will focus on the last finger of our Word Hand: Memorize.

You have already been doing this all year long, so this week will be a little easier than the past several weeks. I want to encourage you this week to press into your Scripture Memory and Review, Review, Review!!!

The Navigators' website (www.navigators.org) gives us three good reasons why we should memorize God's Word. They are:

1. To help us in our personal growth.
2. To help us share God's word with others.
3. To help us overcome Satan and other temptations.

When I first started memorizing the Word of God, someone told me that if you memorize but never review those verses, ***you quickly forget them***. So, that's why I encouraged you in the beginning of our *Dog Walk* to get some 3" by 5" index cards or spiral-bound index cards. If you have not done that yet, I want you to ask your parent to buy that for you this week, okay? If you get the loose-leaf index cards, you will also need a small plastic recipe-type box to organize your verse cards.

Activity for Today:
Organizing your Scripture Memory Verses

Using index cards (or spiral-index cards), write each one of your Scripture Memory Verses you have learned so far in *The Dog Walk*. Here is the list again if you need it: 2 Corinthians 5:17, Mark 12:30–31, Ezekiel 36:27, John 10:10, Psalm 118:1, I Thessalonians 5:11, Romans 8:28, Colossians 2:6-7, Psalm 16:11, Romans 11:17, Revelation 1:3, Acts 17:11 and write out your new one for this week: Psalm 119:9,11 (see below)

Use this format on each index card: Reference, Verse, Reference **For example:**

2 Corinthians 5:17

Therefore, if anyone is in Christ, he is a new creation. The old has passed away; behold, the new has come.

2 Corinthians 5:17

Now create little dividers to separate the index cards into three sections. (If you are using the spiral-bound index cards, you will need some colorful paper clips to separate your verse cards.)

Label the dividers: ***New, Learning, Review***

Now organize your cards. Put your new verse for this week (right below this activity) behind the "New" divider. Put any verses you are still learning behind the "Learning" divider. Put all the verses you know really well behind the "Review" divider. (If you are

using the spiral-bound index cards, choose one color of paper clip to represent each divider: ***New, Learning, Review.*** Then, clip the appropriate color paper clip on the side of each verse card.)

Whew! You are finished for today's activity!!!

Scripture Memory

Psalm 119:9,11 (Good News Translation)

9 *How can young people keep their lives pure? By obeying your commands.*
11 *I keep your law in my heart, so that I will not sin against You.*

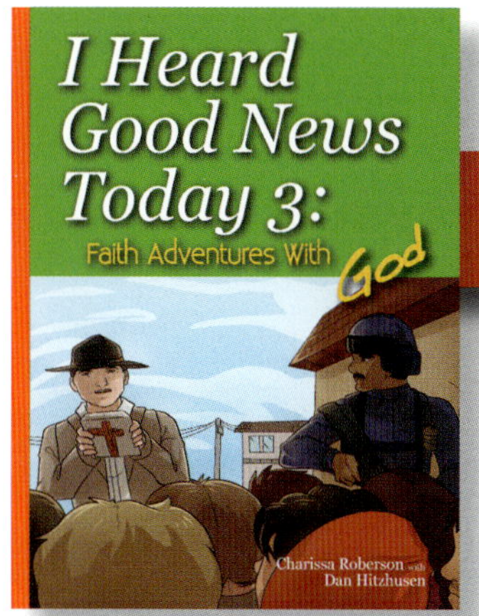

Today's Reading To Grow Your Faith

I Heard Good News Today 3
Read: Chapter 10—No Matter What the Cost

What price did Nilikaanta have to pray for accepting Christ? [126]

Find the country mentioned on the map on page ix of *I Heard Good News Today 3* and pray for new believers there.

After Bob's dad died, his mom came and lived with us for 16 years.
It was an honor to take care of her all that time.
She died when she was 96 years-old.

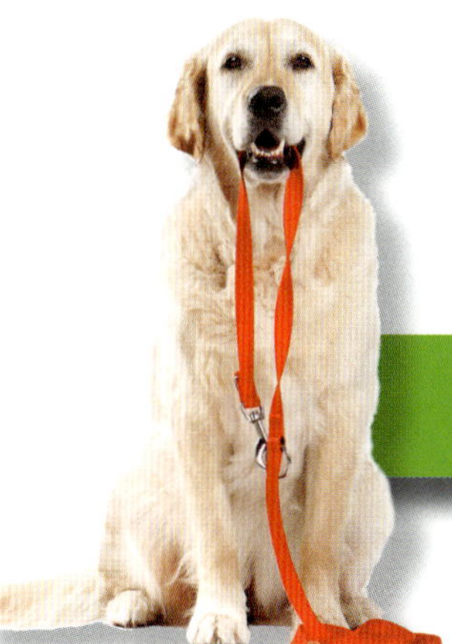

Week 14: Day 2

Lesson 41

Learning Life Lessons with Mrs. Debby

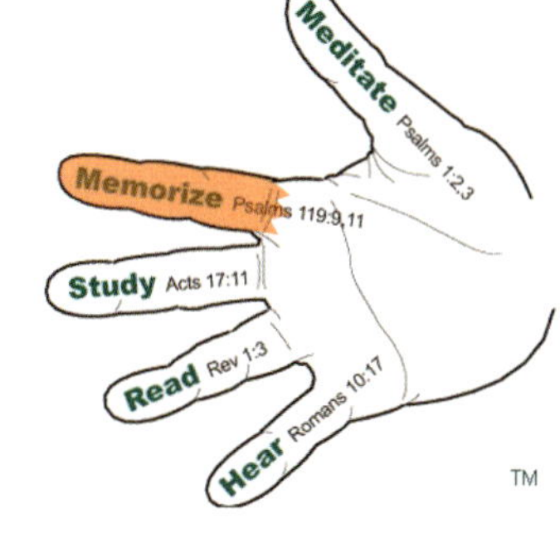

How to Use Your Scripture Memory Organizer

How many of my fellow Dog Walkers enjoy being organized like I do? Well if you do, you will love this week's lesson then! And the rest of you, please bear with us...I promise you will enjoy the benefit of joining us in our "organizing-craze" for the rest of your Dog-days!!!

Activity For Today

Activity for Today:
Learning to Use Your New System of Scripture Memory

Hold your newly organized Scripture Memory Box or spiral-bound "paper-clip-coded" index cards in front of you.

Start with your "New" section and begin memorizing your verse for this week: Psalm 119:9,11. Remember to say the reference first, then the verse, then the reference. Repeat at least three times. Close your eyes the last time.

Next, do the same with your "Learning" section of memory verse index cards. Repeat each one three times. If you really feel you know it well today, you can then move that card (or change the paper clip color) behind the divider that says "Review."

Finally, quickly say each of the verses in your "Review" section out loud, but with your eyes closed, after you have said the reference at the beginning of the verse card.

Hooray! You have just begun a spiritual habit that will change your life if you

continue to do this just once a day. I recommend doing it at bedtime before you fall asleep...you will find out why next week!

Psalm 119:9,11 (Good News Translation)

9 *How can young people keep their lives pure? By obeying your commands.*
11 *I keep your law in my heart, so that I will not sin against You.*

I Heard Good News Today 3
Read: Chapter 11—A Wild Ride

True or False? God's work is always safe. [127]

Find the country mentioned on the map on page ix of *I Heard Good News Today 3* and pray for new believers there.

The Dog
Walk

Cartoon Day

Week 14: Day 3

Lesson 42

The Lord is my...
Hey, I wonder if I can go over to Billy's house and play today. Oh wait, The Lord... If not today, maybe I can go tomorrow...
THE Lord is my Shepherd
The LORD is my Shepherd
The Lord IS my Shepherd
The Lord is MY Shepherd
The Lord is my SHEPHERD

How Cats and Dogs Memorize Scripture

Tell why memorizing Scripture takes a lot of hard work. [133]

____

____

Training Others in Memorizing Scripture

Well, we haven't had to be "Dog Trainers" in several weeks, have we? So find your "leash" and your "treats" for another puppy-in-training, okay?

Seriously, I'd like you to show your Scripture Memory Organizer to one other person today. Not your parent (if they have been doing it with you), but find another friend or sibling or grandparent to demonstrate what you have learned.

Before we do our activity for today, let's talk about "why" God's Word says it is important to memorize Scripture\:

Fill in one reason after reading each verse:

Psalm 119:11: ______________________________ [128]

Proverbs 7:1-3: ______________________________ [129]

2 Timothy 3:16-17: ______________________________ [130]

Psalm 1:2-3: ______________________________ [131]

I Peter 3:15: ______________________________ [132]

Make the appointment to share your Scripture Memory Organizer with someone else. When you meet, explain your Scripture Memory Organizer (or spiral-bound) and the dividers (or paper clips) to them. Ask them to quiz you on the cards in the Review section (you know these really well!).

Then, after they have seen it and have heard you, ask them to learn together with you one of the "Learning" verses. Demonstrate how you learn by saying the reference, verse, and reference again. Encourage them to make a box so they may become equipped for God's work.

Psalm 119:9,11 (Good News Translation)

9 *How can young people keep their lives pure? By obeying your commands.*
11 *I keep your law in my heart, so that I will not sin against You.*

Quote this verse to a family member or friend and then put a check in the box after you have successfully completed it. ☐

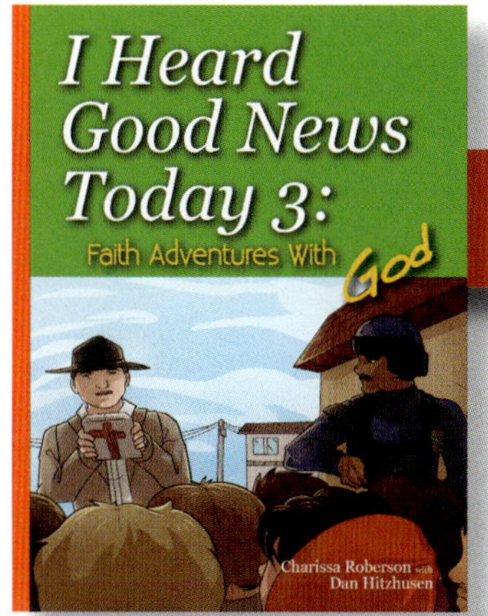

I Heard Good News Today 3
Read: Chapter 12—In a Place Without God

What was the irony of Dan's team worshiping God in the birthplace of the dictator?[134]

Find the country mentioned on the map on page ix of *I Heard Good News Today 3* and pray for new believers there.

After Bob's mom lived with us for 5 years, she got a call from her old boyfriend! They hadn't talked in 63 years. He asked if he could come out and see her. He came and they found out they were still in love. They were married a year later. They lived together at our house for 5 years until he died. (He was a pilot during World War II.)

Week 15: Day 1

Lesson 43

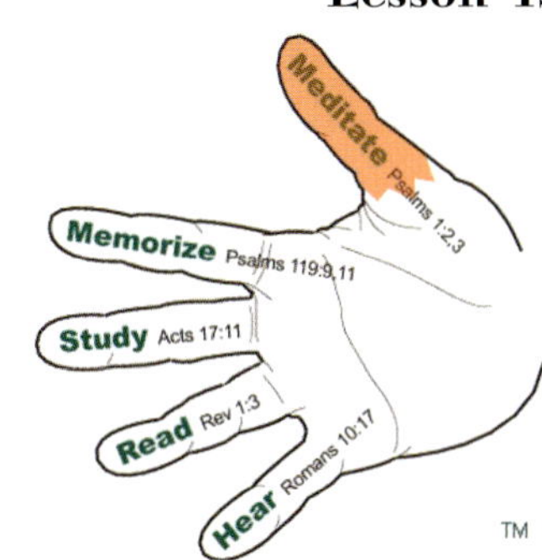

Learning Life Lessons with Mrs. Debby

Walking in the Word:
Meditating on the Word

> *"Meditation is the thumb of The Navigators' Word Hand, for 'it is able to touch each of the other fingers'. Only as you meditate on God's Word— thinking of its meaning and application in your life— will you discover its transforming power at work within you."*
> www.thenavigators.com

Sometimes in today's world we hear the word "meditate" and we think it is not for those of us following Jesus, but only for people who are following Buddha or the Hindu religion. Hopefully, by the end of this week, my fellow Dogs, you will see that God has a lot to say about meditating on Him and His Word for those of us living to know Him and glorify Him!

Meditation applies to all of the other areas you've learned. Hold up your thumb and say out loud "Meditate on the Word." Then take that hand and have your thumb touch each of your other fingers as you describe out loud *The Word Hand*. For example: have your thumb touch your pinkie finger and say "Hear the Word," then ring finger while saying "Read the Word," middle finger saying "Study the Word" and finally your pointer finger saying "Memorize the Word." Check here when you have done this. ❑

But just what is meditation? Maybe you have a wrong idea or maybe an incomplete idea. Go get a dictionary (or go online) and write in your own words a simple definition of "meditate" on the next page.

____ [135]

Sometimes the world has a different definition than what God has. In His Word, He has given us reasons to meditate on His Word. There are blessings on our Dog Walk when we *meditate* on the Word of God? List one benefit from each of these verses:

Psalm 1:2-3: ____ [136]

Joshua 1:8: ____ [137]

Psalm 19:14: ____ [138]

Psalm 119:97: ____ [139]

John 15:7-8: ____ [140]

Hopefully you are learning that "to meditate" means to "think deeply or carefully about something." And as Dog Christians—who are devoted to our Master and BFF, Jesus—we want to spend time getting to know Him better by thinking deeply or carefully about His Word so we can glorify Him each day.

So just how does a person meditate on God's word? Here are some simple steps to learning how to meditate using John 3:16 as an example:

1. Begin with asking the Holy Spirit to open your mind and heart to hear what God wants to say to you today.
2. Choose a verse or passage of Scripture you want to read.
3. Read it once normally.
4. Next, read it again, very slowly, thinking carefully about each word or phrase.
5. Now read it multiple times, emphasizing a key word each time you read it.
   a. For GOD so loved the world...
   b. For God so LOVED the world...
   c. For God so loved the WORLD...
6. Now, ask yourself two questions:
   a. What is God saying to me in this verse?
      Write it down here:
      ____
   b. Is there anything God wants me to do or tell someone else today?
      ____
7. Thank God for speaking to your heart and mind today.
8. Live out whatever He told you to do on your Dog Walk today!

Psalm 1:2,3c (ESV)

2 *But his delight is in the law of the LORD,*
and on His law he meditates day and night. ......
3c *In all that he does, he prospers.*

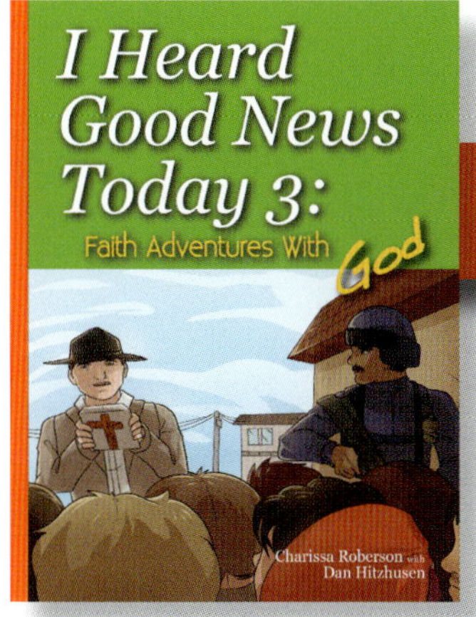

Today's Reading To Grow Your Faith

I Heard Good News Today 3
Read: Chapter 13—Into the Lion's Den

Why was the trip to Manipur, India, so dangerous? [141]

Find the country mentioned on the map on page ix of *I Heard Good News Today 3* and pray for new believers there.

"If he squeezes me any tighter
I swear I'm going to kill him."

This is my younger sister, Kelly. I am five years older than she is.
At one point we had a hard time being friends,
but God has healed our relationship and now we're good friends.

When to Begin our Meditation each Day?

When I was a little older than you, I was given a very small book called *Meditation* by Jim Downing (Navpress, 2011). This book taught me one amazing truth from Psalm 1:2-3. That's your memory verse for this week, right? Read the one page explanation of "How to Meditate on God's Word Day and Night."

How to Meditate Day and Night

By Jim Downing - Mar 13, 2006

One of the greatest promises in the Bible is found in Psalm 1:2-3. This passage teaches that if we meditate on God's Word day and night we will be "like a tree firmly planted by streams of water" (NAS). Here is the secret to the consistent Christian life.

But how does a person meditate day and night? One obvious way is to stay awake 24 hours a day. However, there is a less strenuous way to accomplish this.

Have you ever awakened in the night feeling rigid and tense? Have you ever gone to bed with a problem in your mind, and awakened the next morning exhausted-as though you had worked through the night? Have you ever noticed that your last thought of the day is usually your first thought of the next morning? Many people believe that these phenomena indicate that our subconscious minds keep on working while we are asleep.

When a person sleeps, his conscious mind rests while his subconscious

mind continues to function in order to keep the body's organ's working. But the conscious and the subconscious are in a closed-circuit relationship, so whatever the conscious was working on prior to his falling asleep will be transmitted to the subconscious.

Too often we are wrestling with a problem just before we go to sleep. So rather than allowing the subconscious to work on our problems and worries, we can meditate on the Word of God while we sleep.

A simple application of this theory is to read the passage intended for the next morning's quiet time just before you go to sleep. Take about three minutes to scan through the passage and ask God to give you a thought that will help you live for Him the next day. Take this thought with you to bed.

Your subconscious mind will work on the thought while you sleep, and you will probably have the same thought in your mind the next morning. The writer of the Proverbs may be alluding to this when he writes, "When you walk about, they will guide you; When you sleep, they will watch over you; And when you awake, they will talk to you" (Proverbs 6:22, NAS).

Make God's Word your last word every day, and with the help of the subconscious mind you will be able to meditate on the Word "day and night."[142]

Were you like Jim Downing and me? Were you wondering how to truly "meditate" on God's Word both day and night? Or were you thinking, "Come on, God, how can I think about your Word when I am sleeping?" If you were able to read the article above, you now know the answer.

In your own words, write how Dogs can ponder God's Word while we sleep:

____

Activity for Today:
Practice "HWLW" Tonight

Dawson Trotman, the Founder of The Navigators, coined the term, "HWLW" which stands for "His Word Last Word." Basically, Daws wanted to live out what Jim Downing taught about "meditating on God's Word day and night." So, before bed each night, he would say to his wife, "HWLW." At that moment, one of them would quote a verse of Scripture, and the other would reply with their own verse.

After I read this story, I was so excited that I decided to do this with my roommate when I was sharing an apartment with a good friend after college. More recently, when my own children were younger and sharing a bedroom, I taught "HWLW" to them. For many years, my sons, Luke and Hunter, said good night by saying "HWLW" and then quoting a Scripture Memory verse to each other! What a great way to end your day, thinking on that verse subconsciously all night, and then waking up to live it out the next day! You can do this, too, my fellow Dog Walkers!

Tonight, when you are going to sleep, say "HWLW" to your parent or sibling. Then quote one of your *Dog Walk* verses or any Bible verse. Ask them if they want to reply with their own verse. Then, fall asleep thinking on God's Word.

Check here if you did practice "HWLW" last night: ❑

Scripture Memory

Psalm 1:2,3c (ESV)

2 But his delight is in the law of the LORD,
and on His law he meditates day and night. ......
3c In all that he does, he prospers.

Today's Reading To Grow Your Faith

I Heard Good News Today 3
Read: Chapter 14—A Time to Dance

Why did Dan dance and would you have danced too? [143]

Find the country mentioned on the map on page ix of *I Heard Good News Today 3* and pray for new believers there.

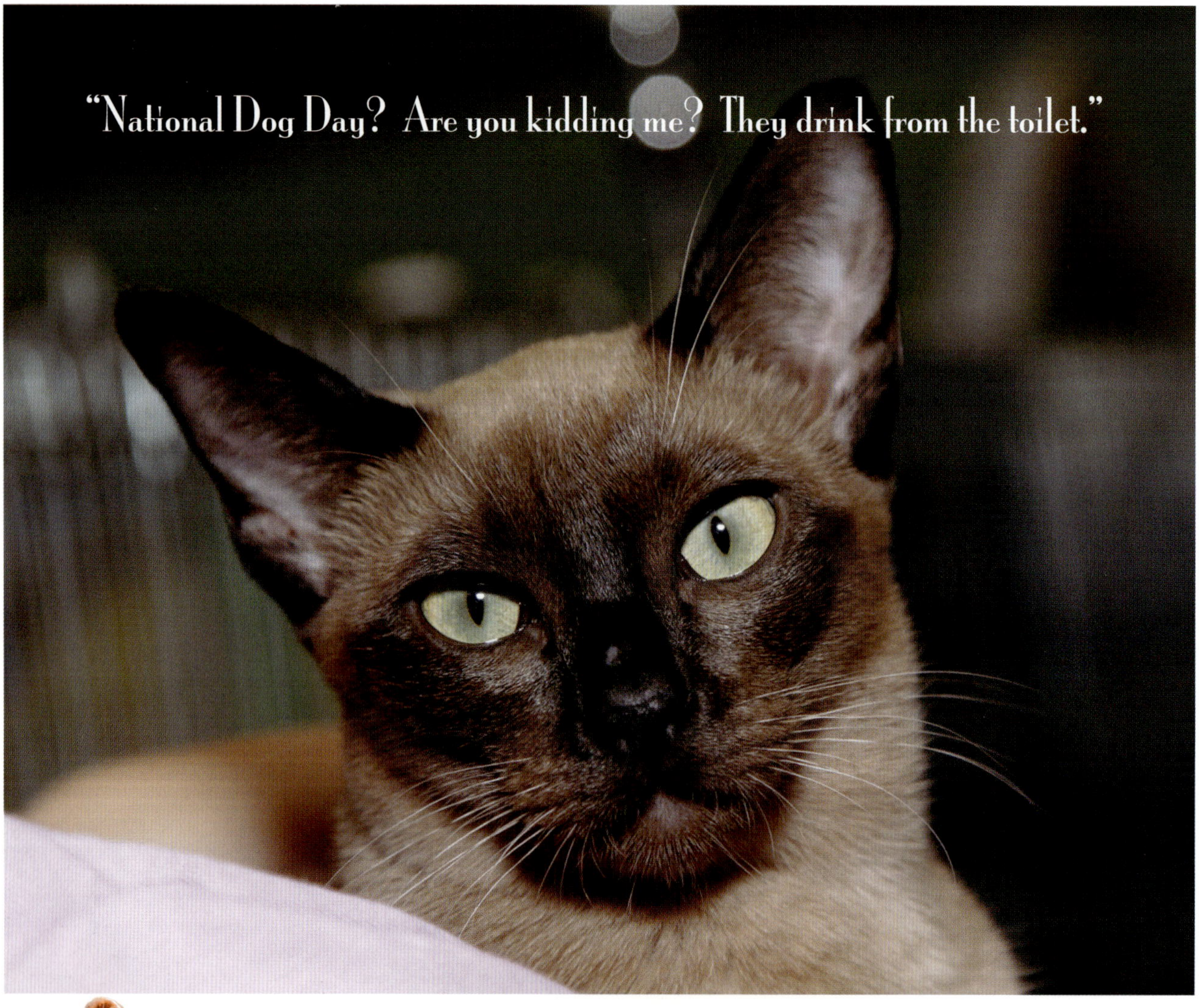

"National Dog Day? Are you kidding me? They drink from the toilet."

By Kamée via WikiCommons

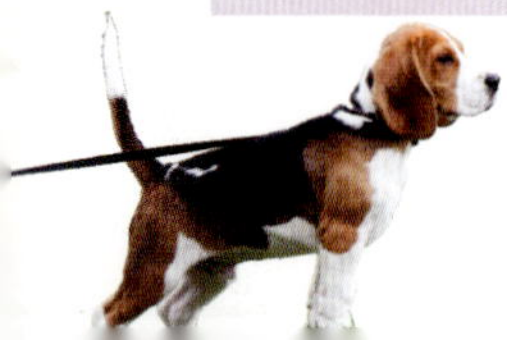

Cats Try To Fit God Into Their Busy Life.
Dogs Fit A Busy Life Around Their Time With God.

What shows a Dog's highest priority is God? [144]

Dog Training Day: HWLW!

Well, friends, I hope you have enjoyed this week as much as I have enjoyed writing about it!

Honestly, fellow Dogs, I feel like my life has been transformed by learning the importance of memorizing and especially *meditating on God's Word day and night* by using "HWLW" for many years now. Even if you don't have a parent or roommate to say your Scripture to out loud, by choosing to read or quote a Scripture before you go to sleep, God's Word is working in your heart and mind all night long!

So, today is your "Dog Training Day!" By now, I think you know what that means. Yes, you get to find a friend or sibling or relative to train in what you learned this week about the "thumb" of our Word Hand: Meditating on God's Word!

Activity for Today: Dog Training with Psalm 1:1-3

Ask a family member or call a friend to set up a time. When you meet with your Dog-in-Training , tell them about *The Word Hand* and what all the fingers plus thumb represent.

Explain that this week you have been learning about the "thumb" or meditation on God's Word. Explain how the hand doesn't really work well without the thumb, just like hearing, reading, studying or memorizing God's Word doesn't really "work well" in your life if you don't take some time each day to meditate on it. Then, ask them to practice meditating on Psalm 1:1-3 with you right now using these steps.

1. Begin with asking the Holy Spirit to open your mind and heart to hear what God wants to say to you today.
2. Choose a verse or passage of Scripture you want to read.
3. Read it once normally.
4. Next, read it again, very slowly, thinking carefully about each word or phrase.
5. Now read it multiple times, emphasizing a key word each time you read it.
    a. BLESSED is the man who does not walk...
    b. Blessed is the MAN who does not walk...
    c. Blessed is the man who does NOT walk...

6. Now, ask yourself two questions:
   a. What is God saying to me in this verse? Write it down here:

   ____

   b. Is there anything God wants me to do or tell someone else today?

   ____

7. Thank God for speaking to your heart and mind today.
8. Live out whatever He told you to do on your Dog Walk today!

Put a check here when you have completed your Dog Training. ☐

Psalm 1:2,3c (ESV)

[2] *But his delight is in the law of the LORD,*
and on His law he meditates day and night. ......
[3c] *In all that he does, he prospers.*

Quote this verse to a family member and then place a check in the box after you have successfully quoted the verse. ☐

Today's Reading To Grow Your Faith

I Heard Good News Today 3
Read: Chapter 15—My Best Friend Jesus

What did Dan tell the two men Jesus wanted with them? [145]

Find the country mentioned on the map on page ix of *I Heard Good News Today 3* and pray for new believers there.

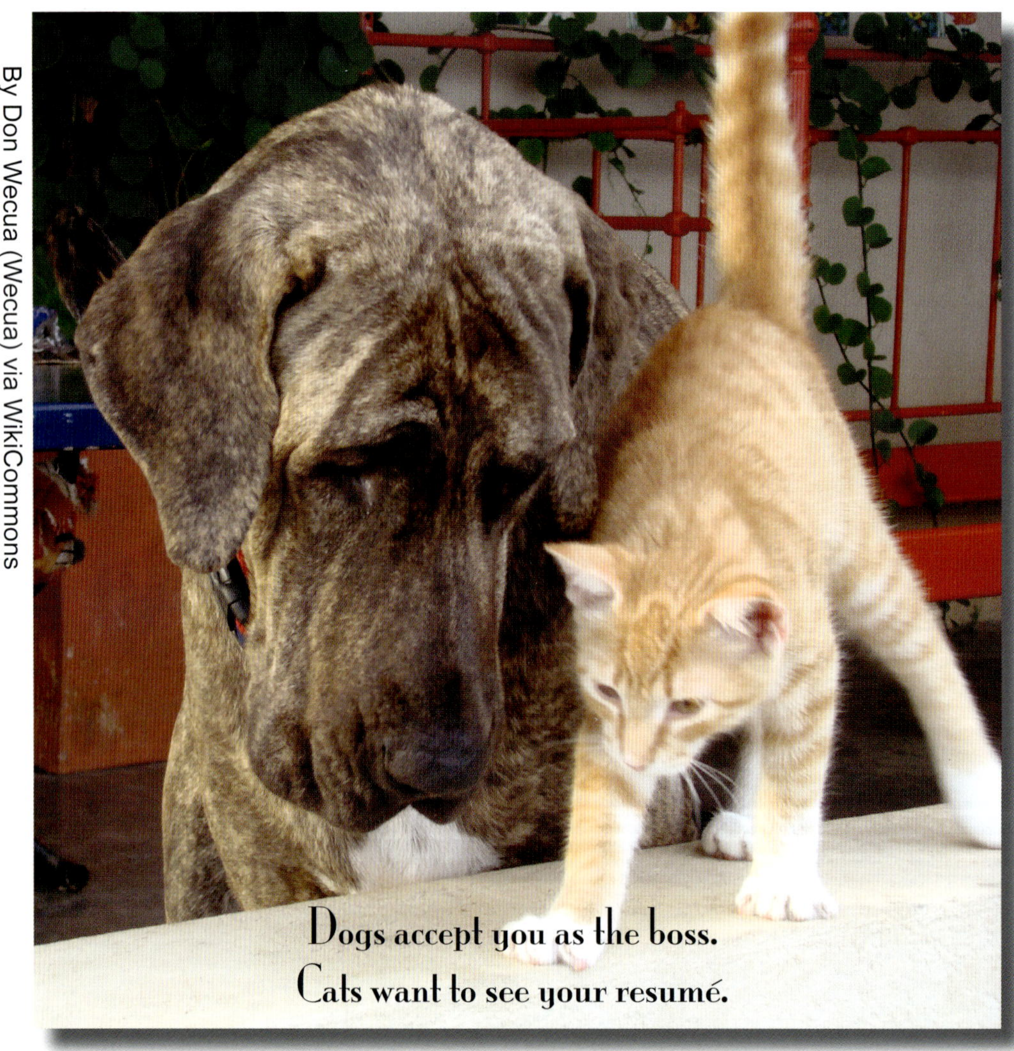

Dogs accept you as the boss.
Cats want to see your resumé.

By Don Wecua (Wecua) via WikiCommons

Week 16: Day 1

Lesson 46

Learning Life Lessons with Mrs. Debby

The Dog Walk: Following Your Master

Congratulations!!! You are now starting the second half of *The Dog Walk*! The first half has been devoted to training you to be truly devoted to your Master and BFF, Jesus Christ, plus learning the importance of living life with a positive attitude!

You have learned life lessons like how to make Jesus your BFF and the most important command of our Master: To love God and love others. We also learned the true daily path to JOY: Jesus, Others, and Yourself. We learned about "Cause Me" prayers that show true dependence on our Master. You have learned three different ways to connect with God in a 10-15 minutes daily devotion: ***Read, Need, Deed*** and ***Cinco Devo*** and ***SOAK*** (my favorite these days!).

Our furry friends, Buddy and Matt, taught us the importance of being thankful every day and the power of having a positive attitude whenever your circumstances may seem to put you down-in-the-dumps. Buddy's words of encouragement to Matt are just what God teaches us in the book of I Thessalonians and Philippians, too!

Finally, you have learned the utter importance of glorifying God by spending time in His Word in various ways explained by *The Word Hand*: Hearing, Reading, Studying, Memorizing and Meditating. Remember "HWLW?" I'm very proud of how you have been memorizing God's Word so you can live it out and share it with others.

Let's not forget how you have been training other Dogs in what you are learning. That is so KEY to living like a Dog the rest of your life! Everything God teaches you should never be kept just in your own Dog House. We are still here on this earth to share the Good News of our Master with others on our planet!

So let's jump into doing just that! This next section of *The Dog Walk* will focus on what it means to truly **Follow Our Master**. Remember, what Jesus said to his first disciples? Look up the following verses and write what Jesus asked each person to do (hint: woof woof ...two words!):

Matthew 4:19-______________________[146]

Matthew 8:22-______________________[147]

Matthew 9:9-________________________[148]

Mark 1:17-___________________________[149]

So I want to ask you one last question before you start learning your Scripture Memory for this week and read your missionary story:

Which phrase below is most important for us to live out on our Dog Walk?[150]
(Circle the correct answer based on the verses you read above)

Learning Stories ABOUT Jesus Or Following Jesus EVERY DAY

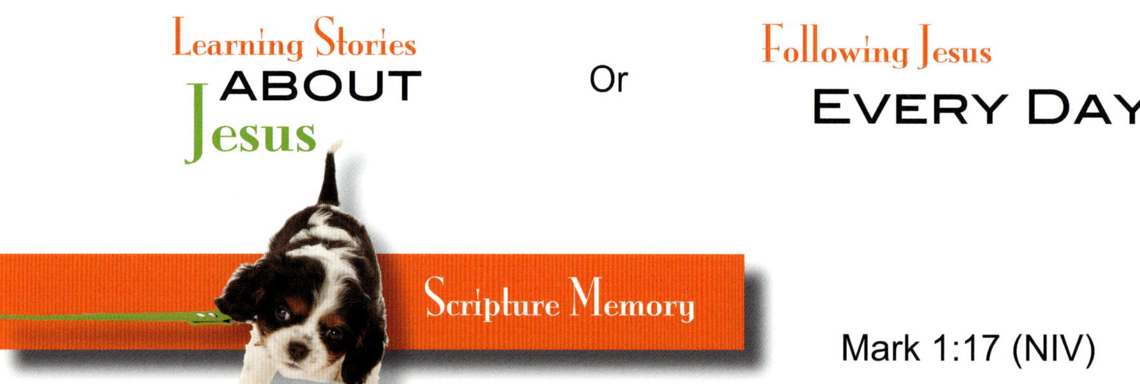

Mark 1:17 (NIV)

"Come follow Me," Jesus said, "and I will send you out to fish for people."

I Heard Good News Today 3
Read: Chapter 16—The 28 Day Journey

What do you think motivated them to travel seven days to hear Dan's team? [151]

____

Find the country mentioned and pray for new believers there.

Week 16: Day 2

Lesson 47

Fishing for People?

So, maybe you are now asking these questions: What does it mean for me to follow Jesus today, 2000 years after He died and rose again? And what does it mean to "fish for people"? (Mark 1:17)

Have you ever played the game called "Follow the Leader"? Do you remember lining up with your friends or siblings and the first person in line walked a certain way then the rest of the line had to hop, skip, walk backwards, etc. just like the first person in line dubbed the "leader"? Well, the same principle applies here to following Jesus.

Now you are thinking, "But He's not here anymore!" You are correct, but we have the first four books of the New Testament that show us how He lived and what He told us to do to follow Him. So, now do you see why we spent the first half of this year learning how to spend time in God's Word? Yes, so we could learn every day what it takes to follow Him.

How about our second question: how do we "fish for people" or some translations write "become a fisher of men"? My husband, Bob Sjogren, loves to go fishing at a local pond or in the flowing James River in his boat. He says it takes a lot of patience waiting for fish to bite sometimes, but other times he can catch fifteen fish in one hour! He also loves to take other people fishing to teach them how to fish as well. Fishing can be messy and smelly, too, and you have to have the right equipment or you will never catch anything, will you?

Let's relate "fishing for people" to going fishing at the pond. You need a place where there are fish to catch, you need the right equipment, and you need some bait. Let's look up these verses to find these same items related to "catching people" for Jesus:

Answer These Questions:

1. Where do we fish for people? Mark 16:15 ______________________________ [152]
2. Who or what aids us in catching people? Acts 1:8 ________________________ [153]

   I Thessalonians 2:13 ____ [154]
3. What bait do we use to catch people?

   Matthew 5:16____ [155]

   John 13:34-35 ____ [156]

Scripture Memory

Mark 1:17 (NIV)

"Come follow Me," Jesus said, "I will send you out to fish for people."

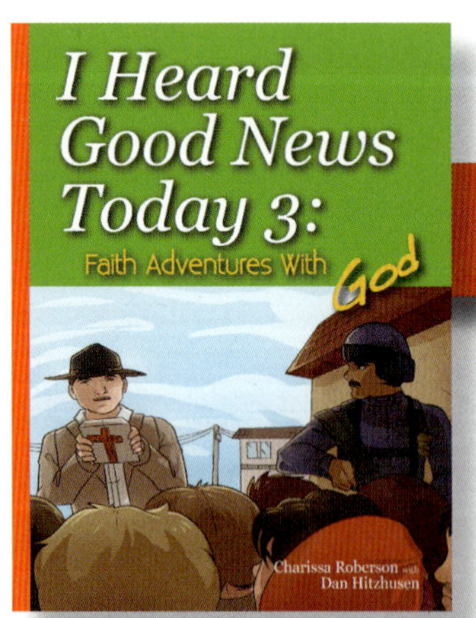

Today's Reading To Grow Your Faith

I Heard Good News Today 3
Read: Chapter 17—Unexplainable

What was the worst that could have happened to Dan and Debbie from the local authorities and what was the worst that coud have happened to the local believers? [157]

Find the country mentioned on the map and pray for new believers there.

AAH...MY STAFF

AAH...MY MASTER

How Cats And Dogs View God

Why would someone think that a Cat is not interested in being a "fisher of men?" [158]

____

____

Learning Life Lessons with Mrs. Debby

St. Francis of Assisi

This week we are talking about following Jesus by fishing for people, right?

I hope you were encouraged yesterday to realize that our "pond" is the whole world, and our "equipment" is God's Word and the Holy Spirit, and our "bait" is our love and good deeds. I am especially thankful that it is God the Holy Spirit who truly "catches the people" for Jesus as we share the Good News found in God's Word. We just need to start loving the people in our world and serving them by doing good deeds of kindness like He did on earth.

Today, fellow Dogs, I am super-duper excited to introduce you to someone who lived a long time ago, but his attitudes and actions still have a great impact today!

He had a different name given at his birth, Giovanni di Bernardone, but we know him today as St. Francis of Assisi. He lived from AD 1182—1226 and most of his life was spent in Italy. When he was 27 years old, he heard a sermon on Matthew 10:9 that led him to totally change his life, as he sought to follow the words of Jesus completely. He soon had 11 followers and started a religious order, now called "Franciscans." His one *Primitive Rule* for his followers was this: "To follow the teachings of our Lord Jesus Christ and to walk in his footsteps." (en.wikipedia.org/wiki/Francis_of_Assisi)

Why am I telling you all about St. Francis? Because one of his most famous quotes really speaks to me about how to live as a Dog Christian. And I try to live it out every day:

"Preach the gospel at all times and when necessary use words."

To me this quote says that my actions show Christ much more than my words ever can. Hopefully, the meaning will become clearer to you as you read and think about these words. When I try to hear from the Lord to understand someone's quote, I read it carefully (often out loud) at least three times. Then I pause... asking God for wisdom as I *meditate* on the words.

So I want you to do that with a few of these quotes from St. Francis below. Read all six of these quotes. Next, choose ***one*** of the quotes below to ***meditate*** on today and write 1-3 sentences about what his quote means to you.

1) *If you have men who will exclude any of God's creatures from the shelter of compassion and pity, you will have men who will deal likewise with their fellow men.*

2) *While you are proclaiming peace with your lips, be careful to have it even more fully in your heart.*

3) *Preach the Gospel at all times and when necessary use words.*

4) *It is no use walking anywhere to preach unless our walking is our preaching.*

5) *Lord, grant that I might not so much seek to be loved as to love.*

6) *All the darkness in the world cannot extinguish the light of a single candle.*

Here's what quote # _____ means to me:

____

____

____

Scripture Memory

Mark 1:17 (NIV)

"Come follow Me," Jesus said, "and I will send you out to fish for people."

Quote this verse to a family member and place a check in the box when you have successfully quoted it. ☐

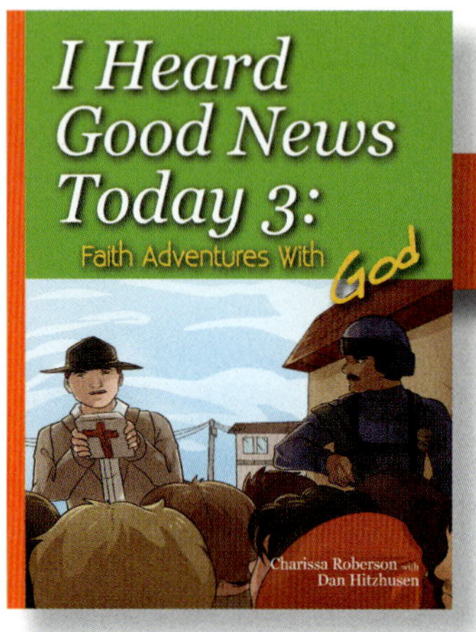

Today's Reading To Grow Your Faith

I Heard Good News Today 3

Read: Chapter 18—The Greatest Miracle

What was the greatest miracle? [159]

Find the country mentioned on the map on page ix of *I Heard Good News Today 3* and pray for new believers there.

Week 17: Day 1

Lesson 49

Learning Life Lessons with Mrs. Debby

Following Your Master: "Deny Yourself"

Did you know that both attitudes and actions matter in following Jesus?

We have talked about your *PMA* (Positive Mental Attitude) in the first half of our Dog Walk, and we will soon start talking more about our actions as Dogs following our Master, Jesus. However, today we are going to discuss a very deep attitude change that many of us need to work on every day in order to let our BFF, Jesus, shine so much brighter through us.

"Deny yourself" means to live a God-centered, others-focused life. Jesus was the only person to do this perfectly, but we are to follow in His steps on our Dog Walk.

If this doesn't make a lot of sense yet, I want to tell you a story I heard many years ago that I have never forgotten. The story happened to Dr. Helen Roseveare, a single missionary doctor in the Belgian Congo (Africa), when she was just beginning to serve the Lord in a new place and a new culture. Whenever I think about this phrase, "deny yourself," fellow Dog Christians, I often think of this story.

Story of Helen Roseveare: Cross Out the "I"

Pastor Ndugu, a godly African church elder, first made this truth real to me, some four years after I started my missionary service in Congo. Things had gone wrong at Nebobongo. I was very conscious that my life was not what it should have been. I was losing my temper with nurses, being impatient with the sick, getting irritated with workmen. Everything had got on top of me. I was overwhelmingly tired, with an impossible workload and endless responsibilities. Suddenly I knew that I had to get away from it all and sort myself out and seek God's forgiveness and restoration, if I was to continue in the work.

The pastor had seen my spiritual need and made all the arrangements for me to go

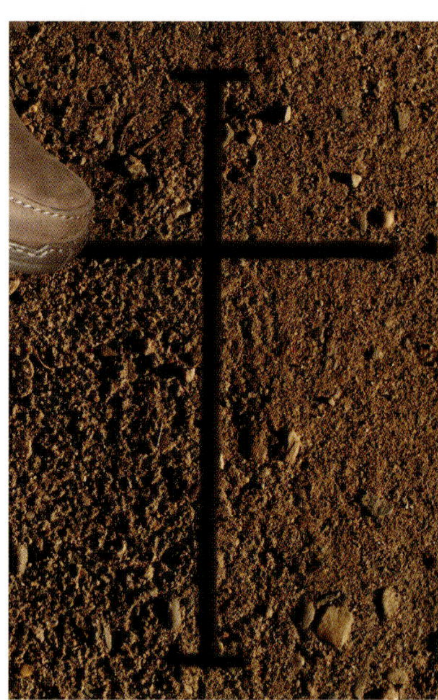

to stay in his village for a long weekend. I felt crushed by my own wretchedness and oft repeated failures. I knew I was quite unworthy of the title "missionary," and I yearned to know the secret of a closer walk with God and of a new in-filling by the Holy Spirit. On the Sunday evening, I went to the pastor and his wife, as they sat together in the palaver hut by the embers of the fire, and asked him to help me. I did not have to explain what I meant; he knew.

Opening his Bible at Galatians 2:20, Pastor drew a straight line in the dirt floor with his heel. "I," he said, "the capital I in our lives, Self, is the great enemy."

Stillness reigned.

"Helen," he said quietly after a long pause, "the trouble with you is that we can see so much Helen that we cannot see Jesus."

Again he paused, and my eyes filled with tears.

"I notice that you drink much coffee," he continued presently, apparently going off on a tangent. "When they bring a mug to you, wherever you are, whatever you're doing, you stand there holding it, until it is cool enough to drink. May I suggest that every time, as you stand and wait, you should just lift your heart to God and pray..." and as he spoke, he moved his shoe in the dirt across the I he had previously drawn, "...Please, God, cross out the I."

There in the dirt was his lesson of simplified theology–the Cross–the Crossed-Out "I" Life.

Crucifixion—death to self—the Cross in the life of a Christian, or as Paul worded it, "I have been crucified with Christ and I no longer live, but Christ lives in me" (Galatians 2:20).

Credit: Roseveare, Helen. *Living Holiness,* ISBN 0 340 38348 8, p. 67-68.

"The trouble with you is that we can see so much of you that we cannot see Jesus."

Luke 9:23 (NET)

Then He said to them all, 'If anyone wants to become my follower,
he must deny himself,
take up his cross daily,
and follow Me."

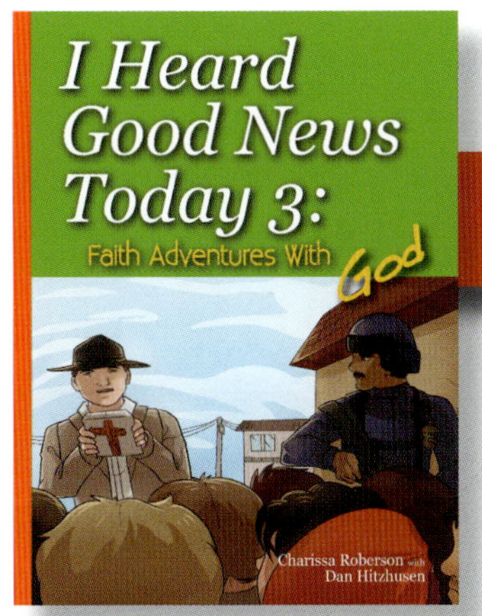

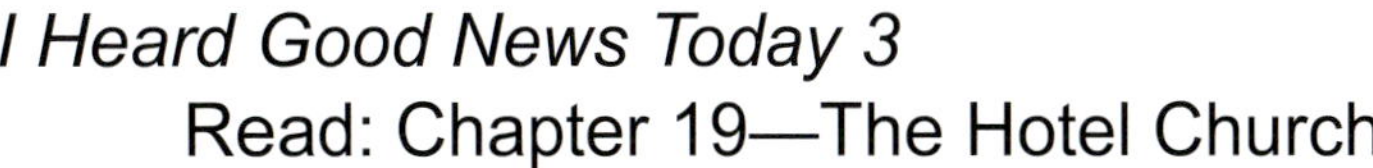

I Heard Good News Today 3
Read: Chapter 19—The Hotel Church

What plans did God have for Dan that Dan wasn't expecting? [160]

Find the country mentioned on the map on page ix of *I Heard Good News Today 3* and pray for new believers there.

I went to the
University of Alabama.

Roll Tide Roll!

IN THIS HOUSE WE
LOVE HUG
LAUGH A LOT
DREAM BIG
are grateful
HAVE FUN
CHEER FOR
ALABAMA

My good friend gave me
this sign and I love it!

It is in my kitchen where
I can see it everyday.

Week 17: Day 2

Lesson 50

"Take Up Your Cross Daily"

Yesterday we learned what is means to "deny yourself" from the life of Dr. Helen Roseveare. "Cross out the 'I' " is something I pray for myself (and others) when I see too much of me (or them) covering up the glory of God or the light of Jesus shining. How about you? Do you struggle with *denying* your wants and wishes for the good of others or the glory of God?

The second phrase in our memory verse for this week keeps showing us more and more how to live like Jesus on our Dog Walk. Jesus says to become His follower we must "take up our cross daily." What does that mean?

To "take up" means to lift up or raise up something...and the "cross" represents an instrument of death in the Ancient world. So when Jesus said "take up your cross" to His disciples 2000 years ago, they absolutely knew what He meant. Following Jesus meant death. But since He added the word "daily" at the end of the phrase, it changed the meaning slightly.

He wasn't saying to them or us, "If you want to follow Me, pick up a wooden cross and go and die today." Because He said the word "daily," we are to keep repeating this every day. It wasn't a one-time death, it was a daily death. Does that make sense?

To better understand it, He was talking about your attitude as well as your actions. Our attitude needs to be "Jesus first, others second, then me." Sound familiar? Remember, that's what JOY represents!

It's like He was repeating the phrase "deny yourself" but with a stronger emphasis. I think He was reminding us that becoming His follower was not a ***one time*** "deny yourself" experience. No, He says that to be one of His followers, we need to daily die to ourselves. We need to daily put others ahead of ourselves. We need to put God's plan over our plans *daily.* We need to put the needs of others before our needs *daily.*

To do that, we must choose to "cross out the 'I' " *daily*. Wow! That's difficult, isn't it? Yep, that's why Jesus called it a "cross."

Today, I want to highlight a missionary couple who truly learned what it meant to "take up your cross *daily*." Have you heard the story of Jim and Elisabeth Elliot?

Passion and Purity:
Romance of Jim and Elisabeth Elliot

Jim and Elisabeth fell in love when they met at Wheaton College. He was a handsome "BMOC" (Big Man on Campus) as a collegiate varsity wrestler. She was a talented writer and fun-loving lady. They both had a passion for missions. Even though they were "in love," they were willing to put God's plans before their own desires. Truly, the degree Jim most desired was what he called the A.U.G. degree—Approved Unto God. He continued to write letters to Elisabeth after they graduated, and they committed their romance to God.

Surely, deep in their hearts, they wanted to get married and raise a family like everyone else in the towns they were from. However, they were willing to "take up the cross daily" and wait for God's timing for their marriage to happen or not. Well, Jim continued to pursue a life of missions and felt called by God to Ecuador to work amongst the Auca Indians. Called by God herself, Elisabeth also left for South America to study Spanish and check out mission work in that area. After ***7 years of waiting*** *for God to give them the "green light," they finally knew God wanted them to serve Him together and were married. Their example of waiting on God and putting His Kingdom work among the tribes of South America before their own desires is truly an amazing example of "taking up the cross daily." (Their story is beautifully written in the book, Passion and Purity, by Elisabeth Elliot.)*

Luke 9:23 (NET)

Then He said to them all, "If anyone wants to become my follower,
he must deny himself,
take up his cross daily,
and follow Me."

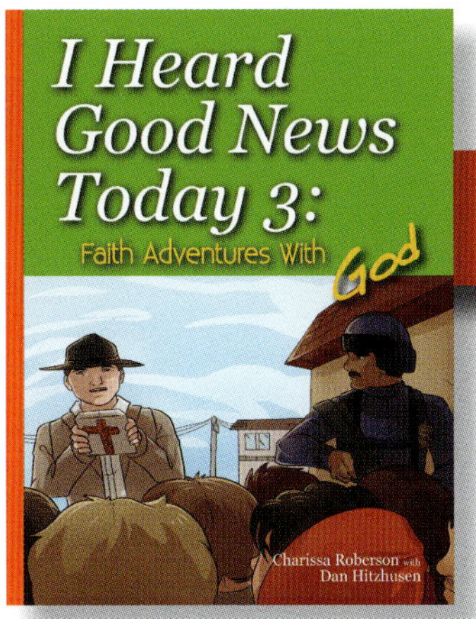

Today's Reading To Grow Your Faith

I Heard Good News Today 3
Read: Chapter 20—The Power to Save

For Kendall, a teenager, it took a lot of guts to pray. What would have happened if she hadn't prayed? [161]

Find the country mentioned on the map on page ix of *I Heard Good News Today 3* and pray for new believers there.

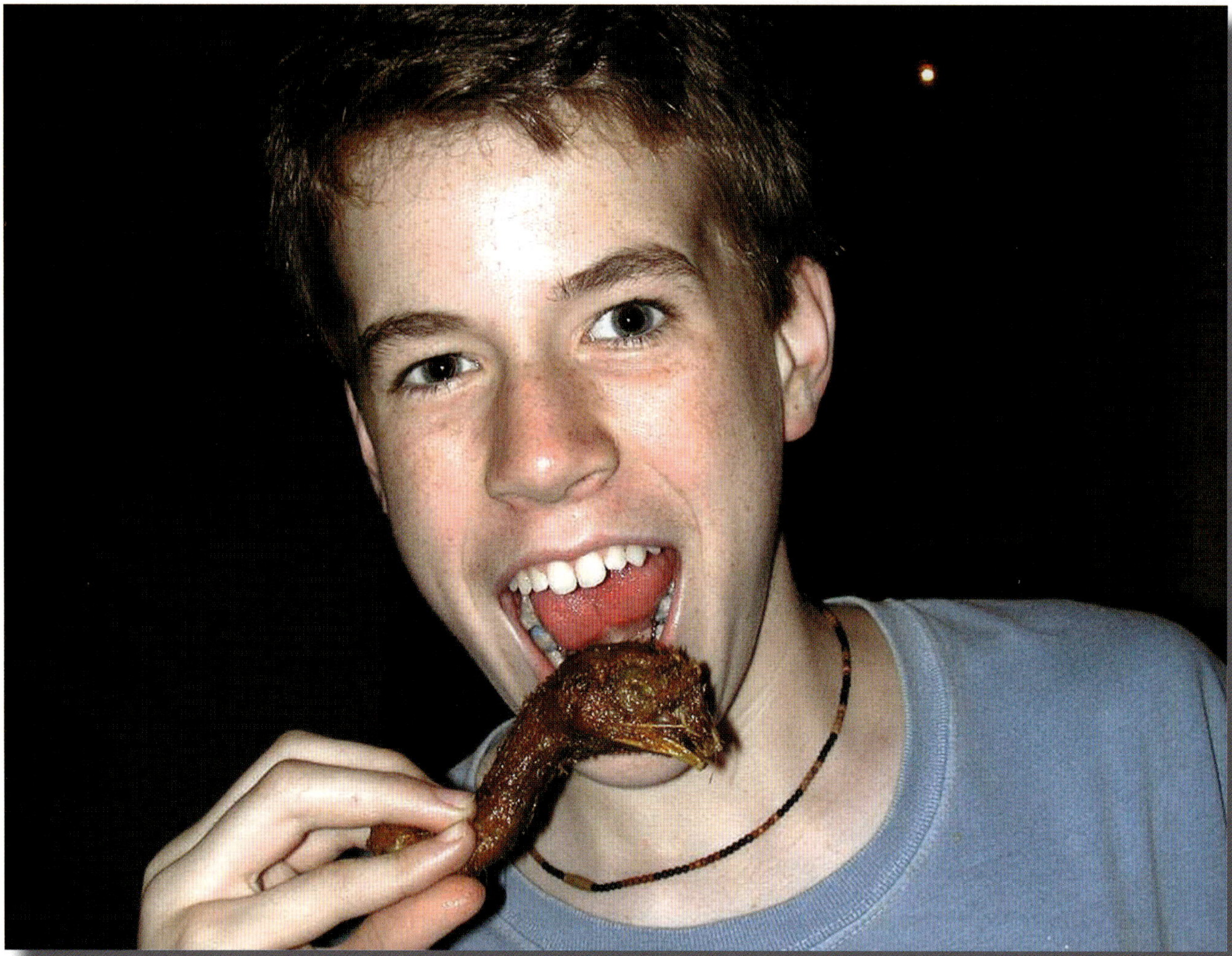

This is our son, Luke, eating a barbequed chicken head.
We have always encouraged our kids to try different foods.
We felt this prepared them to go overseas if the Lord led them that way.
Would you eat it?

I had this place first! He should know better.

Cats And Dogs Know Their Rightful Place

How is the Cat not “picking up his cross daily?” 162

____

____

"And Follow Me"

Hopefully, you almost have your verse for this week memorized. It is easier to memorize than to live out every day, right? But by the power of the Holy Spirit living inside of us, we can become followers of Jesus and live it out, right, Dogs?

The Journey of a Fellow Homeschooler: Elise

Today, we will look into the life of a homeschooled young lady whom I know very well. Her name is Elise Sjogren. Yes, she is my daughter! I have known her for over 20 years!!! And if you have gone through our elementary curriculum, Cat and Dog Attitudes, you may know her as the main author of that curriculum!

I want you to see through her life that following Jesus is not always easy and is not a "one time event," but a series of decisions in life that continually cause us to follow His commands and His plans.

When Elise was about your age, we went on our first family mission trip to Africa! After that trip, Elise bought several small flags of other countries that she felt God wanted her to pray for every night at bedtime. She had those five flags in a little flag stand on her bedside table. Also almost every morning, Elise would read from the Bible, talk to the Lord about her day and journal her prayers.

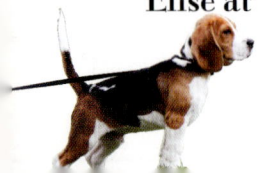

Elise at 17 years old

Several years later, she had heard about taking a "gap year" between high school and college to serve a missionary family as a nanny. She decided to graduate early, at age 16, so she could do just that! To make that happen, she had to double up her classes in high school and worked very hard to complete all her classes in three years instead of four. Next, she contacted a mission agency called Frontiers and applied to become a nanny. She was accepted.

At age 17, Elise got on a plane to the Middle East to live with a family and take care of a little baby girl so the mother could learn Arabic and reach out to her neighbors with the love of Jesus. Life was not always easy and not always fun that year. Elise learned a lot about "taking up her cross daily" and "denying herself" as she followed Jesus to another country.

But if you ask her today, she would say, "Yes, for me following Jesus started when I was young. I started reading my Bible and praying every day, including praying for other countries. Then the steps I took in high school to follow Jesus to serve a family in the Middle East have truly changed the course of my life. Even though some days are very difficult when we choose to follow Jesus, the deep joy I have in knowing my choices have honored the Lord and His purposes far out weighs the burdens I have had to bear."

After the one year of being a nanny, Elise came home to complete her university degree for four years. Then she followed Jesus back to the Middle East to teach 3rd grade students academics plus how to follow the straight path of Jesus!

1. Circle which mini-biography this week spoke the "loudest" to your heart:

Dr. Helen Roseveare　　Jim and Elisabeth Elliott　　Elise Sjogren

2. How will your life be different after reading these stories of fellow Dog Christians?

____

____

Scripture Memory

Luke 9:23 (NET)

Then He said to them all, "If anyone wants to become my follower, he must deny himself, take up his cross daily, and follow Me."

Quote this verse to a family member and place a check in the box after you have quoted it successfully. ☐

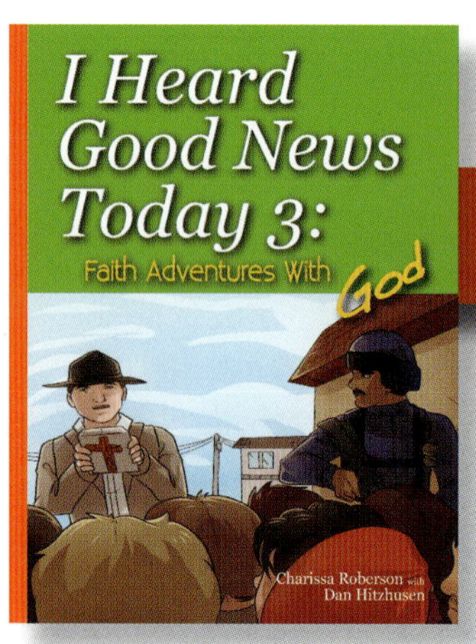

I Heard Good News Today 3

Read: Chapter 21—The Face of Jesus

What do you think was the most amazing thing about this story? [163]

Find the country mentioned on the map on page ix of *I Heard Good News Today 3* and pray for new believers there.

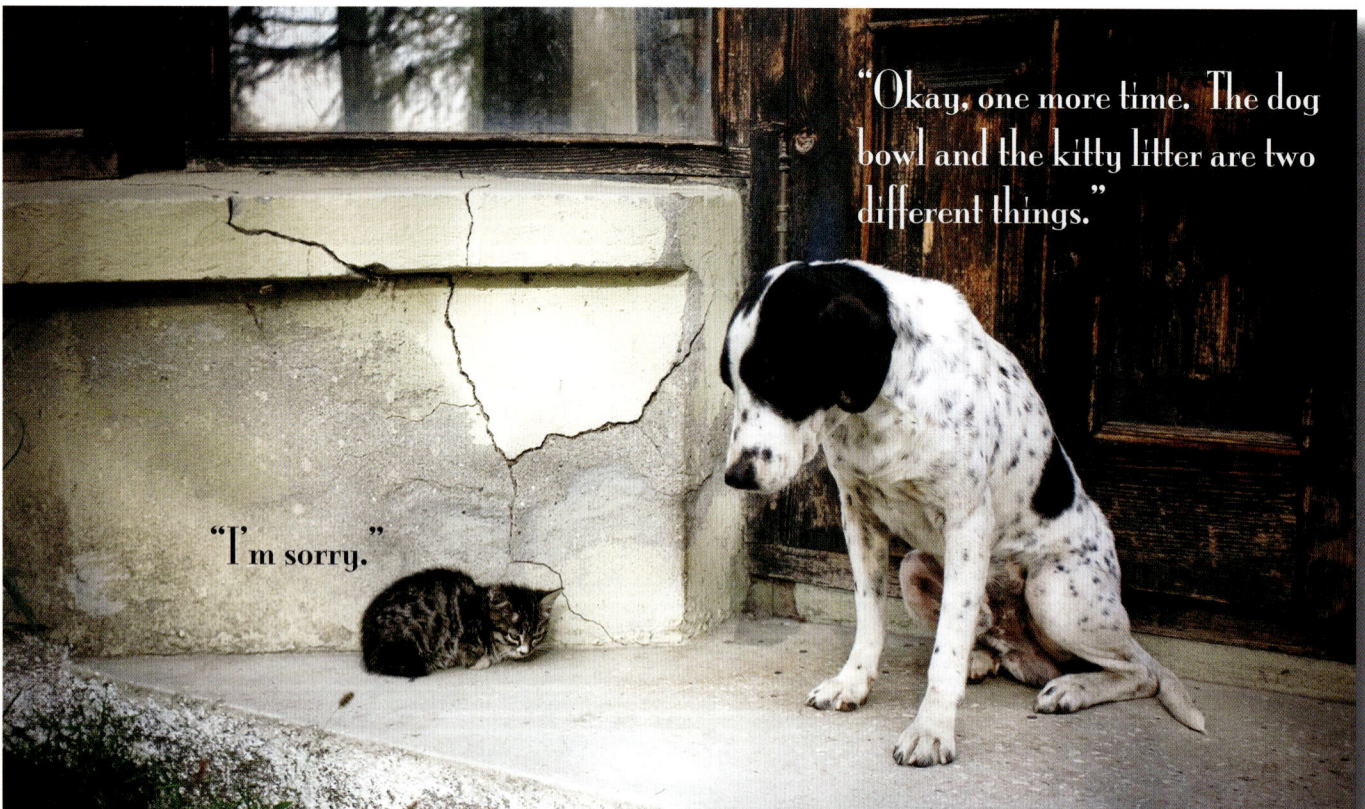

"Okay, one more time. The dog bowl and the kitty litter are two different things."

"I'm sorry."

By WomEOS via WikiCommons

Week 18: Day 1

Lesson 52

Learning Life Lessons with Mrs. Debby

Servant Evangelism (Mark 10:45)

Our Scripture memory from last week is a tough one to live out: Luke 9:23.

Which one of the three parts of that verse is most difficult for you to live out? (Circle your answer below.)

DENY Yourself OR Take Up Your Cross DAILY OR Follow Jesus

Honestly, for me, my fellow Dogs, it is probably the first one. Because I have learned that if I choose on any given day to "deny myself" or "cross out the 'I'" and put Jesus first and others second, then the other two choices above aren't so hard anymore. You know what I mean?

Well, this week we will look at how Jesus chose to live while on this earth in order to:

#1 bring His Father God glory

#2 be an example to all of us on *The Dog Walk*!

We can see the heart motivation and the work of Jesus' life in two verses: John 17:4 and Mark 10:45. Let's read these now:

John 17:4, *"I glorified You (Father God) on earth, having accomplished the work that You gave me to do."*

Mark 10:45, *"For even the Son of Man came not to be served but to serve, and to give His life as a ransom for many."*

So what was His heart motivation in John 17:4?[164] ______________________________

And what was His work in Mark 10:45?[165]

____

My husband, Bob Sjogren (who thought up the *Cat and Dog Theology*), has taught me that it is very, **Very, *VERY*** important that you keep the right order of priority with what Christ did on the cross.

Jesus died **primarily** (or first) for the glory of His Father, and **secondarily** (or second ☺) for us—to be the "payment" for our sins.

This changes **everything** in your Christianity. But many times we get them reversed. We think Jesus died **first** and **foremost** for us (solely for our sins.) If that is the case, we will live a me-centered or people-centered life. We expect God (and everyone else) to serve us.

But if you live like He lived—**for the glory of His Father**—then you will be willing to do anything God calls you to do for His Glory as well. We will live to serve God and serve others. The is the essence of the heart of a Dog Christian.

So, even though you are not going to follow Jesus to the cross literally and you are not going to die to pay for all the sins of all the peoples of the world, you **can** live a life that brings God great glory. You can also follow Jesus' example as He stated in Mark 10:45, He "came not to be served, but to serve..."

In learning to serve others, you are going to learn something called "servant evangelism." So you're going to finish today's lesson by watching this very short video clip on ***Servant Evangelism.*** Go to:

http://www.servantevangelism.com/videos/introduction-to-servant-evangelism/#.Vj0hqRCrSRs

Check this box when you have watched this video. ❑

Mark 10:45 (ESV)

For even the Son of Man came not to be served but to serve, and to give His life as a ransom for many.

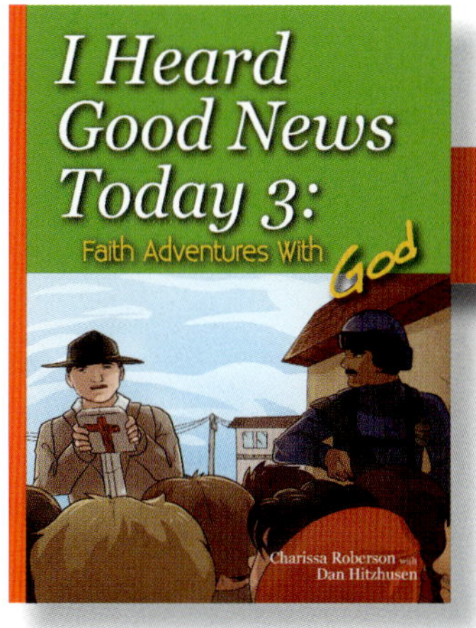

Today's Reading To Grow Your Faith

I Heard Good News Today 3
Read: Chapter 22—Somebody Town

What did Bekele do that most people today wouldn't do? [166]

Find the country mentioned on the map on page ix of *I Heard Good News Today 3* and pray for new believers there.

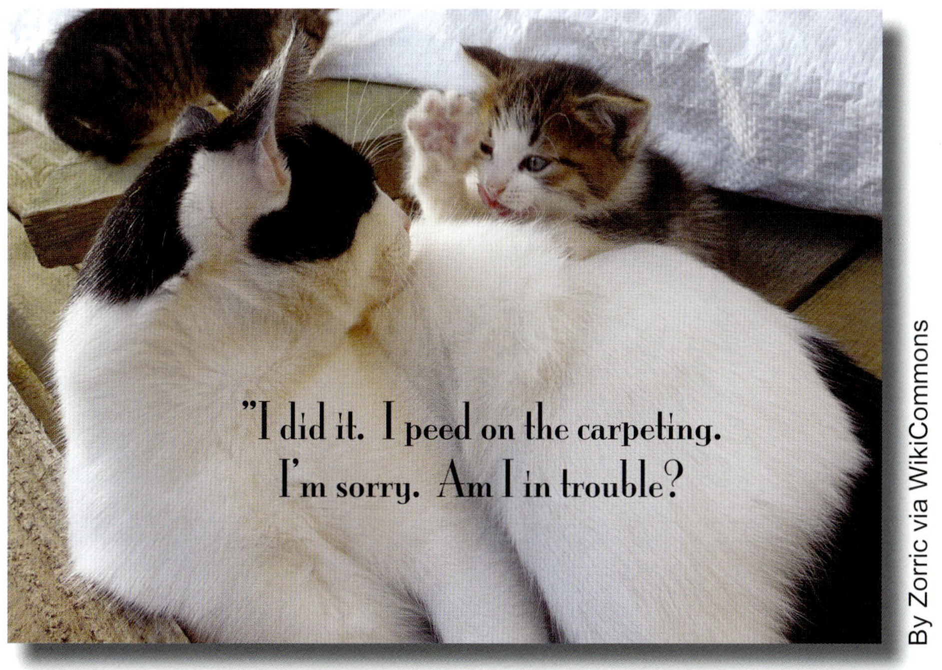

"I did it. I peed on the carpeting.
I'm sorry. Am I in trouble?

By Zorric via WikiCommons

Here I am with my wonderful mother, Jody. Not only is she a loving, godly example for me, but she also helped to edit this workbook!

Three generations celebrating Abby's college graduation!

Week 18: Day 2

Lesson 53

Learning Life Lessons with Mrs. Debby

Examples of Servant Evangelism

We learned yesterday that Jesus came to this earth to serve, not just to be served. He has left us an amazing example to follow as Dog Christians who want to live like He did: for the glory of God!

One man in recent decades has been called "the father of Servant Evangelism" for the modern day church. (You may be surprised at his last name, but he is not a close relative to our family.) His name is Steve Sjogren! Anyway, he has been a pastor of several churches across America and written several books, but he is best known for starting a movement called "Servant Evangelism" in churches across the United States. Our family learned about this idea when we were living in Arizona.

Here is my husband with Steve and Janie Sjogren

This quote from their website (www.servantevangelism.com) describes how Steve and Janie Sjogren connect serving people, who may not know Jesus yet, with the gospel message:

> *Our consistent message has been connected with the message of Romans 2:4, that "the kindness of God leads to repentance." We have found that as we serve not-yet Believers in simple but profound ways, along with verbalizing the Gospel message, in time they desire to repent and follow Jesus. We have seen many thousands go through the process of repentance and salvation.*

Below is a list of some of his creative ideas for Servant Evangelism: As you read through the list, put a check mark or star by the ones you might be interested in trying with your family or friends in the future—because that will eventually be a homework assignment! ☺.

House to House

Fruit give away

I was surprised at the popularity of this one. People really like fresh fruit and they will readily take it. I have tried this one across the US and it has gone over great guns. An orange, an apple and a banana is enough along with a connection card in a clear plastic bag. It works well door to door.

Sunday Morning Paper and Coffee Giveaways

Purchase a number of Sunday papers, brew excellent coffee and visit your neighbors. Look for the houses that don't have a paper in the driveway but be sure you don't knock on the door too early.

Leaf Raking

"We came, we saw, we raked!" Several people in a small group can rake an entire neighborhood on a single Saturday morning. Maybe you don't like raking your own yard; but when you're with a group of friends serving in the name of Christ, a chore becomes a joy. Many yards take only fifteen to twenty minutes to polish off. Note: If possible go to neighborhoods where the city vacuums leaves left on the curb (some do). If you bag them, leave the bags by the curb for later pick up.

Lawn Mowing

Several mowers make mowing the lawn short work. Look for long grass, knock on the door, and go for it.

Grass Edging

If you don't have time to mow an entire lawn, edge the driveway and sidewalks. Most homeowners don't edge very often, so they are in need of it and are grateful.

Screen Cleaning

Screens will have to be removed. Apply a bit of soapy water and use a soft brush. Hose them off and reinstall. Most homeowners never do this, though it is an easy way to improve the view.

Rain Gutter Cleaning

You will need some ladders, trash bags and gloves. Messy work but very appreciated by homeowners—especially in the fall.

Garbage Can Return from Street

This is one you could do for your entire street each week. Usually garbage pick up is done early in the morning. Be the first one out. Return them near their garage but do it quietly.

Food Delivery to Shut-ins

Find legitimate shut-ins in your neighborhood. Start a system with interested neighbors for a weekly hot food delivery. Keep in mind, many pre-Christians are very interested in helping others even though they don't yet know Christ. A project such as this could easily be an entry point to their hearts.

Kitchen Cleanup

Some who have been sick or depressed might need a good kitchen cleaning. Don't try this one by yourself. Two or three can clean up a super dirty kitchen on a Saturday morning.

General Yard Cleanup

After the winter weather is over, all sorts of debris become obvious. Go door to door with gloves, rakes, and trash bags.

Door-to-Door Carnation Giveaway

Carnations are affordable, and everyone likes them. This project could be done anytime, but Mother's Day is a particularly good excuse.

Tulip Bulbs

A handful of bulbs is affordable. When they come up in years to come, that person will reflect on your act of generosity.

Potted Plant Giveaways

Marigolds and Impatiens can be purchased affordably in numbers. Mums are great in the fall. Small poinsettias are a great touch at Christmas.

Flower Seed Packet Giveaways

Give out flower seeds to celebrate Spring. Some companies offer the option of having your church name printed on the outside of the packet.

Sidewalk Sweeping

In urban areas this is a huge hit. In some communities in Europe, residents are required by law to sweep the area in front of their apartment. Why not sweep your area as well as your neighbors'?

Windshield Washing

Some years ago when we started serving, this was one of our first projects. We still do it just about every weekend. The materials list is short and inexpensive: a good squeegee, a wiping rag, a connection card, and windshield cleaner (We recommend you not use Windex style cleaner—ask your car parts store what they recommend). If it's too hot (above 85°F) or too cold (below freezing) you might end up making a dirty windshield even worse. Ask your neighbor's permission before attempting this one.

Window Washing

Picture windows aren't that difficult to clean once you get the hang of using a wide squeegee. (See "Windshield Washing" for more details.)

Snow Removal from Walks and Drives

Men's groups take on their neighborhood with snow shovels and snow blowers. We go door to door explaining our project. The snow blowers aren't necessary but very helpful. Most drives and sidewalks can be finished in a matter of minutes. Be sure to bring coffee and hot chocolate for the workers.

Minor House Repairs

We usually focus this outreach on single parents and the elderly. It is important that you clarify what you are able to do in terms of repairs. There will always be more need than you can realistically meet. We do projects that can be done with our existing tools and

supplies and that can be finished in two hours.

General Interior Cleaning

Not everyone will let you come in at random and clean his or her house. It's best to stop by a prospective house to schedule a day before the cleaning team comes.

Community Dinner

Throw a dinner for the block. One family in a rough part of London has been doing grill outs for the past few years. The couple provides the grill and the hamburgers. Everyone else brings a part of the dinner. The result: Neighbors are talking to one another for the first time, they are watching out for each other and, naturally, the crime rate has gone down.

Doggie Yard Cleanup

It's an unsavory job, but someone has to do it. Jesus said, "If you want to be great in God's kingdom, be the servant of all." Does that include all breeds? Actually, it's not that tough with the right equipment. (You can find scooper equipment at a local pet store.) Give a connection card to pet owners and park officials in the area.

Weed Spraying

Spray for weeds in cracks in the sidewalk and areas where weeds thrive. Wear rubber gloves.

Tree Limb Trimming

Purchase an extending trimmer with a saw and pulley clipper. Beware of electric lines. Before trimming any limbs, get approval from the home owner.

Light Bulb Replacement

Sounds simple, but for some reaching up to a nine foot ceiling is a difficult chore. We offer a 60-watt light bulb with a connection card, and if they'd like we replace burned out ones.

Dog Washing

Organize a "doggie wash." Use the recommended dog shampoo that is sold in pet stores. This is done best around your neighborhood. The best workers and organizers of a dog wash are kids. Two ten-year-old boys recently touched their entire neighborhood by blanketing all the houses with a homemade flyer explaining their project. They later reported washing sixteen dogs and one reluctant cat. They also provided a flea collar to each clean pet.

Garage Cleaning

With a homeowner and half a dozen people, this unsavory task can be fun.

Fireplace Kindling

Bundle it up and give it out in the Fall. On the binding, attach your logo and phone number.

Bark and Mulch for Yards

In the spring this is a big hit. Load up a pickup truck, knock on doors, and offer it to people. You can even offer to help spread it.

De-icing

After an ice storm, a few shovels of rock salt can make a big difference on a slippery sidewalk or driveway.

House Number Painting on Curbs

With stencils, spray paint house numbers on curbs. Find decent looking stencils.

Shopping Assistance for Shut-ins

This would come by referrals. Work with shut-ins to get a list of needs, shop and deliver.

Holiday Giveaways

Target 3-4 times during the year to go house to house with a holiday giveaway. Examples: small poinsettias at Christmas, Easter baskets at Easter, picnic on Independence Day (include hot dogs, chips, beans, buns, and a watermelon), mum plants in the Fall.

More Resources:

Google: 94 Servant Evangelism Ideas by Steve Sjogren
http://helenafirst.com/pdf/seProjectsTable.pdf

How many did you place a check by? ____________

Mark 10:45 (ESV)

For even the Son of Man came not to be served but to serve, and to give His life as a ransom for many.

Today's Reading To Grow Your Faith

I Heard Good News Today 3
Read: Chapter 23—A Break in Enemy Lines

Which part of the story was the most amazing to you? That some of the national believers were injured in the church bombing and yet still wanted to go back or that the sheik agreed to not bomb the churches anymore—and why?[167]

Find the country mentioned on the map on page ix of *I Heard Good News Today 3* and pray for new believers there.

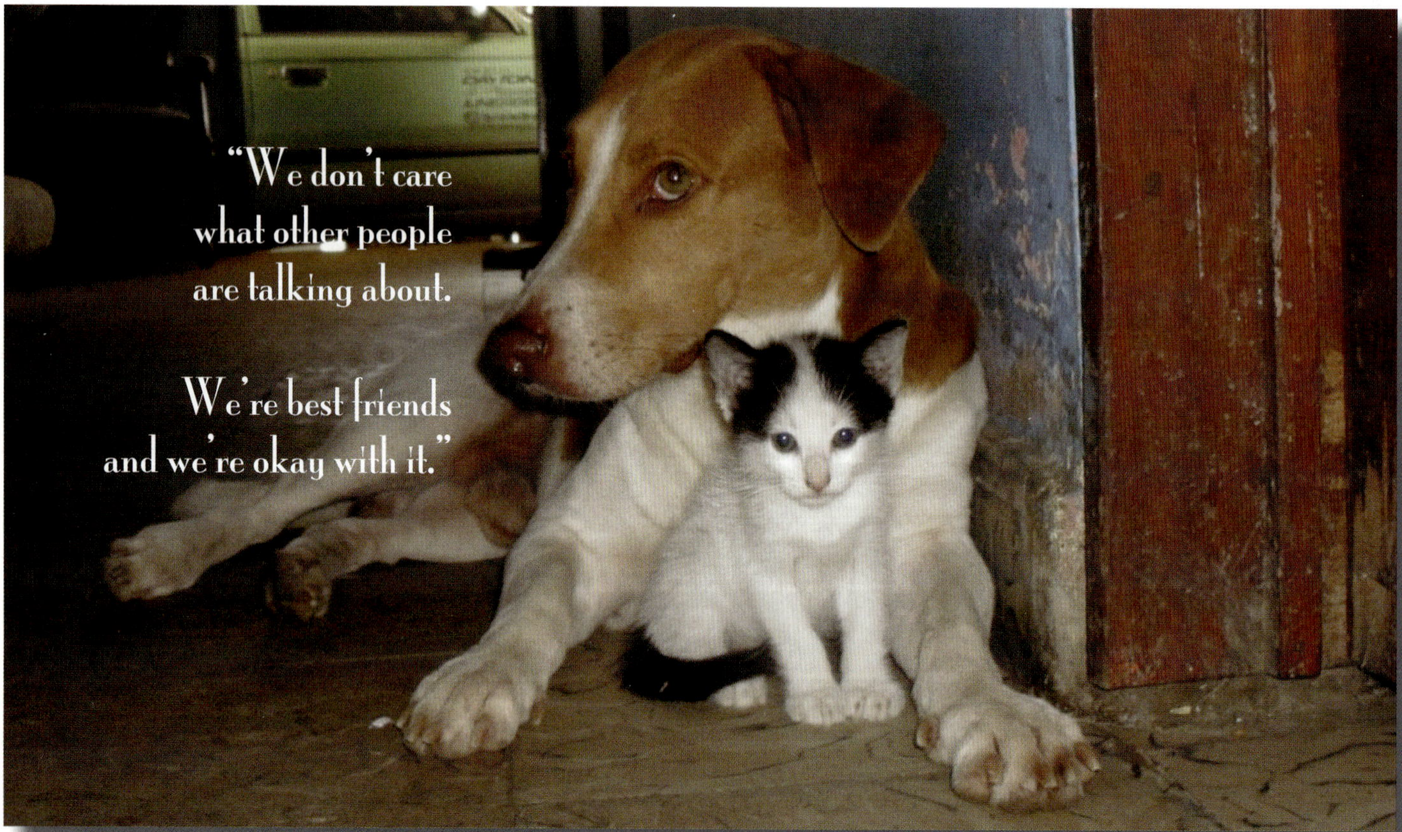

"We don't care what other people are talking about.

We're best friends and we're okay with it."

By EEIM via WikiCommons

Aah, from birth to death in the safest, softest, easiest most comfortable fashion. That's His will for my life!

Show me where to go Lord!

How Cats And Dogs Serve Their Master

Why is the Dog showing a greater willingness to serve God? [168]

____

____

Learning Life Lessons with Mrs. Debby

Start to Plan YOUR Servant Evangelism Event

You probably knew this was coming, right? You know me pretty well by now. You know that when we, Dogs, learn about some fun, crazy idea that could make us live more like Jesus, we need to teach others about it. We are "blessed to be a blessing!"

So today, I want you to pray and ask God to put a few friends or family members in your mind that you can share about **Servant Evangelism** with this week. You will be leading a Servant Evangelism Event in a few weeks, so you need to start recruiting a "team" to do it with you—and then allow them to choose what your team does!

Write their names below. Pray over your list of names. After you talk with them, mark them off if they can't serve on your team or circle if they can!

1. ______________________________
2. ______________________________
3. ______________________________
4. ______________________________
5. ______________________________

Scripture Memory

Mark 10:45 (ESV)

For even the Son of Man came not to be served but to serve, and to give His life as a ransom for many.

Check this box when you have successfully quoted the verse. 

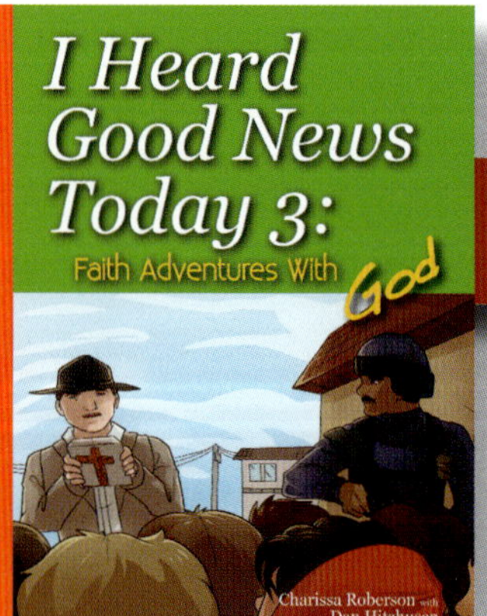

I Heard Good News Today 3

Today's Reading To Grow Your Faith

Read: Chapter 24—Let's Just Play

What did Dan love to do that helped him make friends in a foreign country? [169]

____

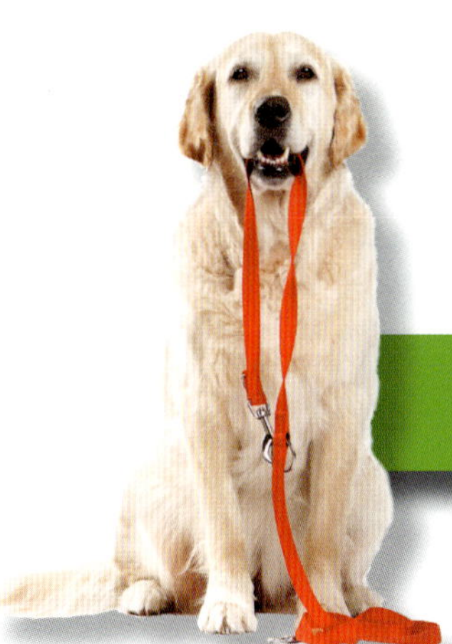

Week 19: Day 1

Lesson 55

Learning Life Lessons with Mrs. Debby

Servant Leadership in Your Family

Welcome to a new week on our Dog Walk! Recently, we've been discussing following Jesus in His example of serving others. Last week we talked about how we can serve non-followers of Jesus through doing acts of kindness that may one day lead them to love God like we do!

This week we will be looking and practicing how Jesus was a servant-leader with His closest friends and family. We will follow Jesus in ***Servant Leadership*** this week!

One fellow Dog Christian, Luke Kuepfer, has a website called "The Truth Made Simple" (www.thetruthmadesimple.org). All of his videos are one minute in length! (Not like the 45 minute pastor's, huh?!) He has almost a daily encouragement from the Bible that teaches us one insight into how to "lead, love, and serve like Jesus." Watch this very short YouTube video clip teaching on Matthew 5:14-16 to hear from him today: *www.youtube.com/watch?v=9-sK8f86nug&feature=youtu.be*

Activity For Today

Activity for Today: When our family was homeschooling, I often challenged my kids to be "secret angels" for someone else in our family. For example, choose to go and make a brother or sister's bed without them knowing or choose to do the dishes for them or another chore they are supposed to do that day. You could even write them a note of encouragement and leave it on their pillow to read at bedtime. (Mom would love this as well ☺!)

So, fellow Dogs, this is your assignment for today! You've got to choose someone in your family (or maybe a close friend if you don't have siblings) that you can bless. On the following page, fill out your assignment.

Whom will you choose to serve today? ______________________________
What will you do for them today?

Check this box when you have completed your "act of kindness." ❑

Philippians 2:5, 7a (NIV)

In your relationships with one another, have the same mindset as Christ Jesus: ...He made himself nothing by taking the very nature of a servant...

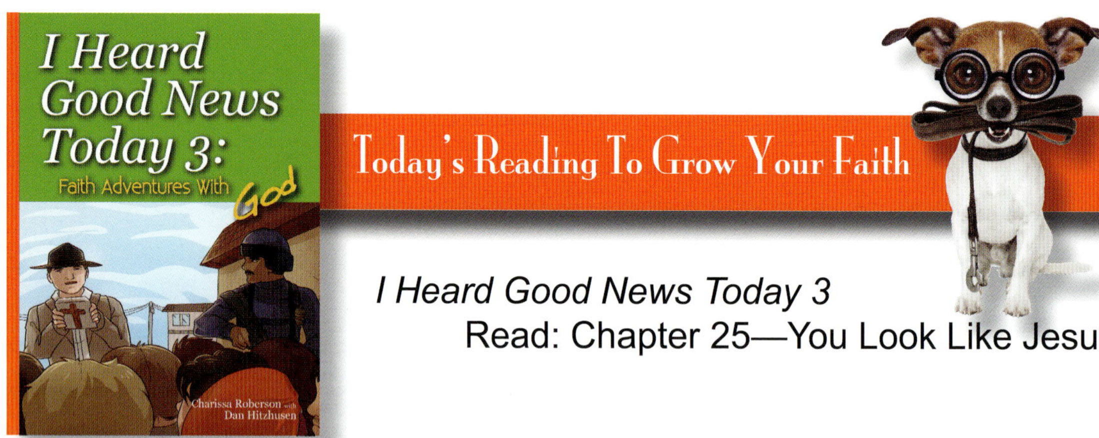

I Heard Good News Today 3
Read: Chapter 25—You Look Like Jesus

Explain the meaning of a "granddaughter church." [170]

Find the country mentioned on the map on page ix of *I Heard Good News Today 3* and pray for new believers there.

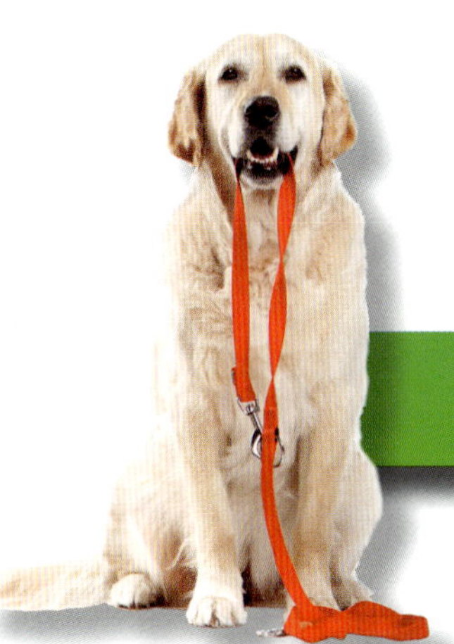

Week 19: Day 2

Lesson 56

Serve Your Parents like Jesus

So what was your sibling's (or good friend's) response when you were a "secret angel" in the last lesson?

Today, you get to be a secret angel for someone who loves you very much and serves you constantly: your homeschool teacher—Mom or Dad or whoever it is!

Watch another YouTube video lesson (Matthew 6:1) from Luke Kuepfer before you make your decision: www.youtube.com/watch?v=2Zy9vOAV6IQ&feature=youtu.be

Activity for Today: Luke Kuepfer reminds us to be humble in our serving of others. He says we are to point others to Jesus, not to ourselves. Sounds like a Dog, right?

Whom will you choose to serve today? ______________________________

What will you do for them today?

____

Check this box when you have completed your "act of kindness." ☐

Philippians 2:5, 7a (NIV)

In your relationships with one another, have the same mindset as Christ Jesus: ...He made himself nothing by taking the very nature of a servant...

I Heard Good News Today 3
Read: Chapter 26—Forgiven

What did God use to prepare the people to receive the gospel? [171]

Find the country mentioned on the map on page ix of *I Heard Good News Today 3* and pray for new believers there.

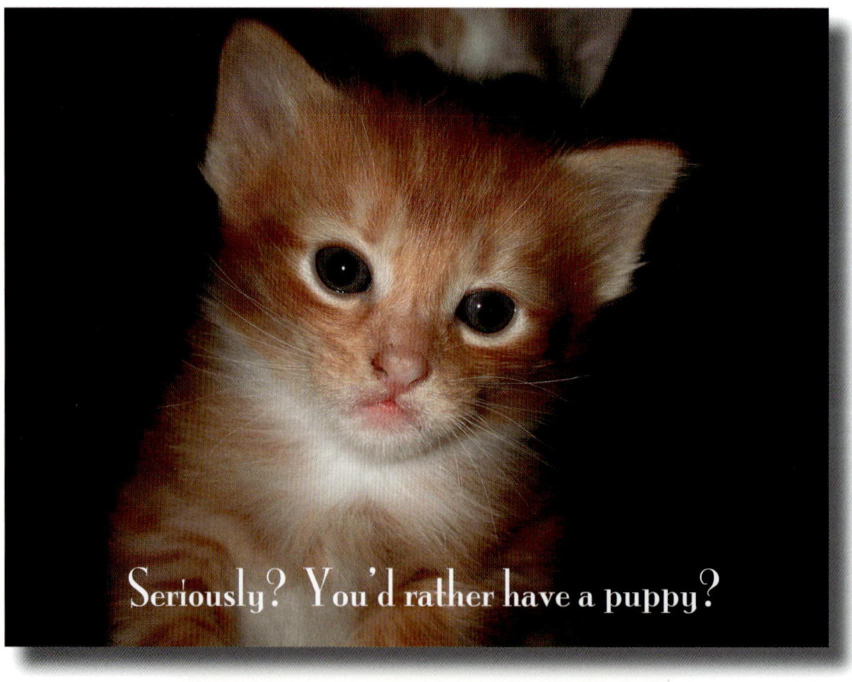

Cats Serve God How They Want.
Dogs Serve God How He Wants.

Some people think Cats don't serve God, but they do. But what is different about their service? [172]

____

____

Train Another in Servant Leadership

You knew this was coming, right? Jesus told His disciples in Matthew 28:18-20, "Go and make disciples...," so if we are walking like a Dog, we choose to follow that command of our Master as well. We are going to teach others to follow Jesus like we are!

Who in your family or circle of friends could you teach and train this week in the joy of becoming a ***Servant Leader*** who desires to "lead, love and serve like Jesus?"

When you meet with them, you can teach them your memory verse for this week and also last week as a starter: Mark 10:45. Then tell them about being a "secret angel" for a friend or family member. Challenge them to do the same in the week ahead. If you want, you can also show them one of the *YouTube* clips of Mr. Luke Kuepfer teaching on leading like Jesus.

Who will you teach and train in ***Servant Leadership*** today?

___

Write a paragraph below on what you did in your training and how they received it.

___

___

___

___

___

___

___

Scripture Memory

Philippians 2:5, 7a (NIV)

In your relationships with one another, have the same mindset as Christ Jesus: ...He made himself nothing by taking the very nature of a servant...

Check the box when you have successfully quoted the Scripture. ☐

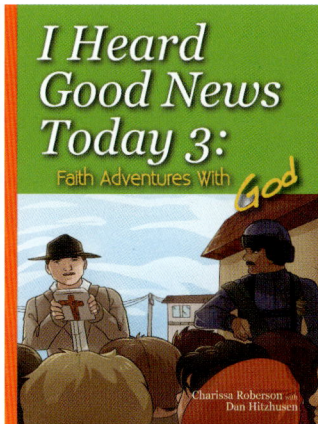

I Heard Good News Today 3: Faith Adventures With God
Charissa Roberson with Dan Hitzhusen

Today's Reading To Grow Your Faith

I Heard Good News Today 3
Read: Chapter 27—The Future in His Hands

If you were going to a village to share the gospel and heard there was a Muslim fortune-teller there, would you think she would be the first one to come to know the Lord or last one—and why?[173]

___

Find the country mentioned on the map on page ix of *I Heard Good News Today 3* and pray for new believers there.

"Look into my eyes, you are getting sleepy..."

By Vera Kratochvil via WikiCommons

Here are your memory verses so far!

Week 1: II Corinthians 5:17
Week 2: Mark 12:30-31
Week 3: Ezekiel 36:27
Week 4: John 10:10
Week 5: Psalm 118:1
Week 6: I Thessalonians 5:11
Week 7: Romans 8:28
Week 8: Colossians 2:6-7
Week 9: Psalm 16:11
WEEK 10: REVIEW WEEK

Week 11: Romans 11:17
Week 12: Revelation 1:3
Week 13: Acts 17:11b
Week 14: Psalm 119:9,11
Week 15: Psalm 1:2,3c
Week 16: Mark 1:17
Week 17: Luke 9:23
Week 18: Mark 10:45
Week 19: Philippians 2:5-7a
WEEK 20: REVIEW WEEK

Week 20: Day 1

Lesson 58

Servant Leadership in Your Church

How did last week go for you as you sought to be a servant-leader in your home and family? I have no doubt that God was pleased with your acts of kindness to your siblings and parents!!! (I know that for sure because I **was** a homeschool mother for 19 years!) And how did you feel after you did your "secret angel" good deed? Hopefully, your JOY level increased as you saw the surprised looks on their faces!

My husband has often said that God's Glory and our joy are connected: the more we, as Dog Christians, give **GLORY** to God with our lives, the more **JOY** He puts back into our hearts!

In the weeks ahead, we will be gradually practicing *Servant Evangelism* and *Servant Leadership* in areas beyond your immediate family. This week, I want to challenge you to begin extending your ***Servant Leadership*** "acts of kindness" outside of your home by investigating and planning either a one-time service project at your church or to begin regularly serving every month at your church. Let's go!

Activity For The Week: Serve Your Church

Activity For Today

Call your church secretary or youth pastor to ask if you can give two hours this week to help at church.

Ask them for a list of ways you could serve your church family. Pray and talk with your parent or teacher about it. Plan what you will do and when you will do it. Fill in your information on the next page.

Whom did you call? ___________________________________

What ideas for serving did they give you?

____

____

Which service project did you commit to with your parent/teacher's permission?

____

When will you go and serve at your church? ______________________

Scripture Memory for Week 20: No New Verses: Turn to page 214 and review the first 19 weeks!

If you haven't already done so, I highly recommend you write down these first 18 verses on 3" by 5" index cards. Even better, ask your mom or dad to buy you a small spiral-bound set of index cards that you can use for reviewing all your verses.

If you can't buy the index cards, a second best option would be to type out all 18 verses on a Word Document today. Then review the verses using the index cards on which you hand wrote them or the printed document you have typed.

Today's Reading To Grow Your Faith

I Heard Good News Today 3

Read: Chapter 28—You Have Not Because You Ask Not

What was the impossible request that Dan prayed and did it come true? [174]

____

Find the country mentioned on the map on page ix of *I Heard Good News Today 3* and pray for new believers there.

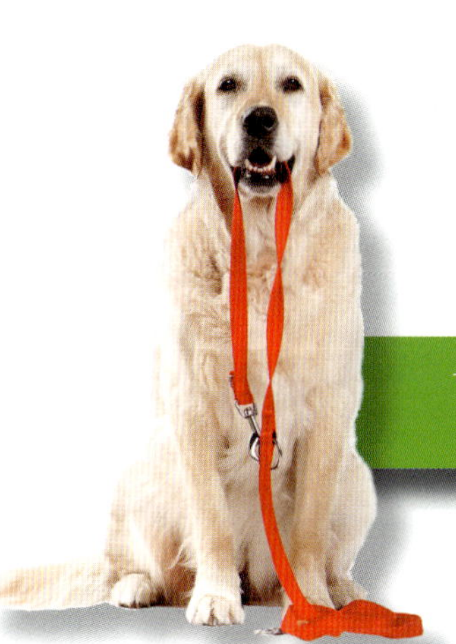

Week 20: Day 2

Lesson 59

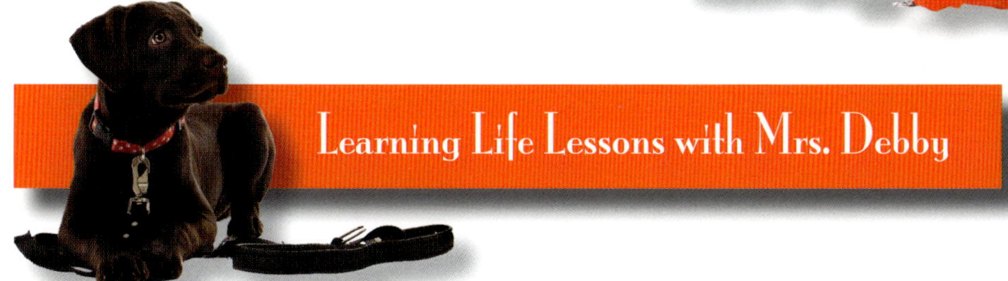

Servant Leadership in Your Church

How's it going with planning your ***Servant Leadership*** project at your church? Hopefully, your plan is in formation or perhaps you have already completed your service project. If not, keep working on it today to make it happen this week or next week.

When you have completed your Servant Leadership project at your church, then you can answer these questions:

What did you do at your church?

____

How was your JOY level when you were finished?

____

Whom did you get to bless while you were serving?

____

Today's Reading To Grow Your Faith

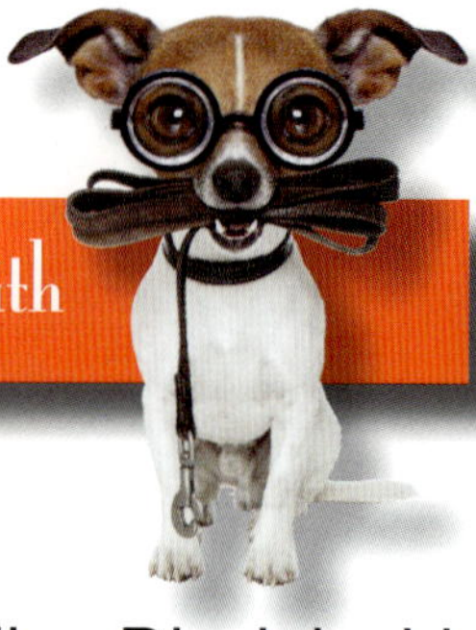

I Heard Good News Today 3
Read: Chapter 29—Duckling Discipleship

Explain how a mother duck and her ducklings relate to sharing your faith with new believers. [175]

Find the country mentioned on the map on page ix of *I Heard Good News Today 3* and pray for new believers there.

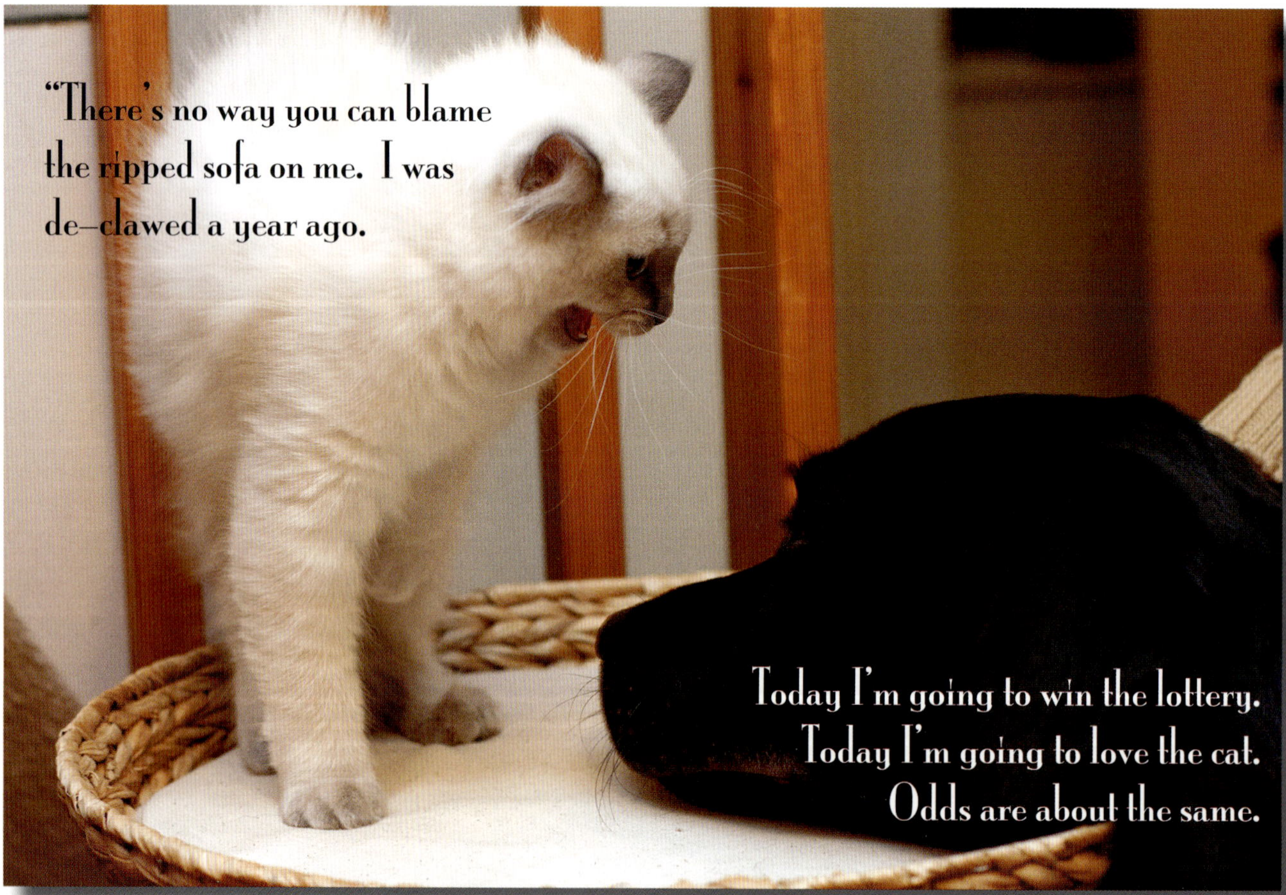

"There's no way you can blame the ripped sofa on me. I was de–clawed a year ago.

Today I'm going to win the lottery. Today I'm going to love the cat. Odds are about the same.

By Antti via WikiCommons

Cartoon Day

Week 20: Day 3

Lesson 60

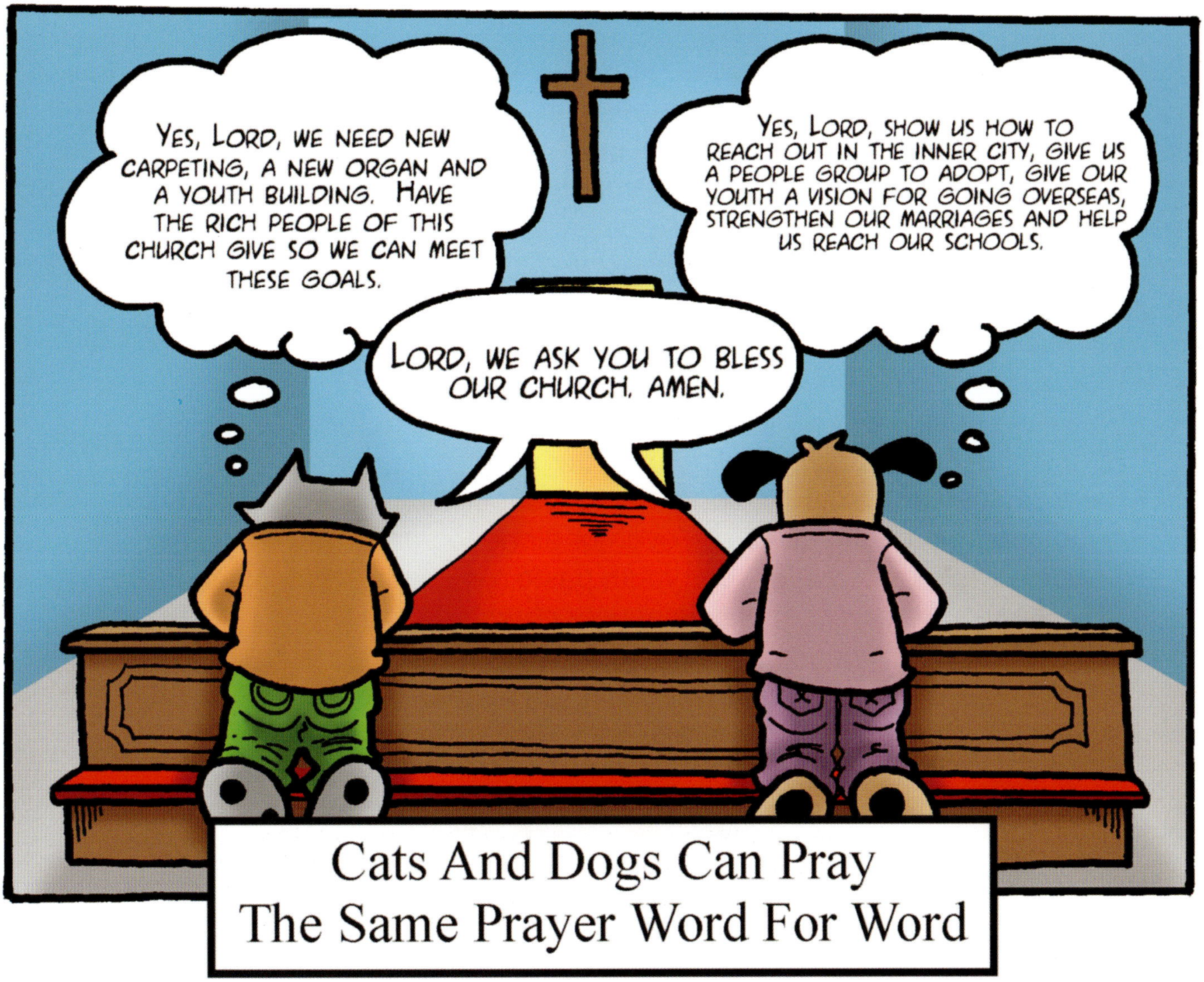

YES, LORD, WE NEED NEW CARPETING, A NEW ORGAN AND A YOUTH BUILDING. HAVE THE RICH PEOPLE OF THIS CHURCH GIVE SO WE CAN MEET THESE GOALS.

LORD, WE ASK YOU TO BLESS OUR CHURCH. AMEN.

YES, LORD, SHOW US HOW TO REACH OUT IN THE INNER CITY, GIVE US A PEOPLE GROUP TO ADOPT, GIVE OUR YOUTH A VISION FOR GOING OVERSEAS, STRENGTHEN OUR MARRIAGES AND HELP US REACH OUR SCHOOLS.

Cats And Dogs Can Pray
The Same Prayer Word For Word

Why is the Cat's prayer rather selfish? [176]

____

____

Servant Leadership in Your Church

Okay, Okay, Okay...so what's next, my fellow Dog? Well, I'd like you to begin praying and asking God to show you how you can find a place to practice Servant Leadership on a ***regular basis*** at your church. "Regular" basis means ***either weekly or monthly.***

So, talk to your parents or teacher, then talk with someone at your church to see if you can start serving as a regular volunteer in some area. Remember, as Dog Christians, we live to love God and love others much more than ourselves! And I'm sure that by now, you are seeing the blessing you receive when you live that way: your **JOY** level increases dramatically!

Here are a few ideas that our family has done over the years:

- Volunteer in the nursery
- Pick up trash in the church sanctuary or in the parking lot
- Volunteer to help in a Sunday School class or AWANA for younger kids
- Help set up chairs each week before your youth group or church service
- Bake cookies or make lunch one day for your church staff
- Invite your pastor and his family over for dinner or lunch
- Offer to babysit for **free** for your youth pastor or Sunday School teacher
- Help plant flowers or rake leaves at your church
- Wash windows at your church building
- Write a note of encouragement to your pastor, church secretary or Sunday School teacher or youth leader

If you are able to be a Servant Leader on a regular basis at your church, what have you decided to commit to for the rest of this school year?

____

Scripture Memory

Quote all 18 review verses to a family member and then place a check mark in the box after you have successfully quoted them. ☐

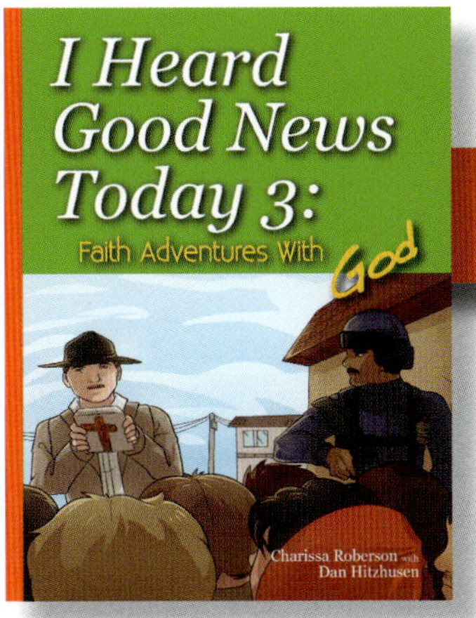

Today's Reading To Grow Your Faith

I Heard Good News Today 3
Read: Chapter 30—A Meeting With Mother Teresa

How did God overrule Dan's mistake on the prayer card for His glory and the team's joy? [177]

Find the country mentioned on the map on page ix of *I Heard Good News Today 3* and pray for new believers there.

When Abby was 17, she graduated a semester early
to go on a four-month mission trip to Mozambique
with Least Of These Ministries.

This was the day she flew home.

Have you ever thought about going
overseas for a year in between
high school and college?

Week 21: Day 1

Lesson 61

Learning Life Lessons with Mrs. Debby

Servant Evangelism Locally

Well, we are switching gears a little this week in our thinking. Are you ready? Woof! Woof! I can just hear your excitement!!!

We are going to work all this week on actually planning your **Servant Evangelism Event**. So start by turning back to pages 198-201. Remember when you checked off a few of the ideas that we learned about from Steve and Janie Sjogren? You should have written a number on page 201 indicating how many you liked.

Now, you've got to prayerfully choose one! Choose what "act of kindness" to share God's love with your city or neighborhood you feel God wants you to do. Next, look backwards again to page 204 and read over the names of friends or family members you want to challenge to serve alongside of you. Remember, our Master on our Dog Walk, Jesus, always sent His disciples out two-by-two!

Activity For Today

ACTIVITY FOR THIS WEEK:

1. Choose a **Servant Evangelism Event** from the list on pages 198-201 or create your own. What did you choose to do?

____

2. Invite people to join your team to make it happen. Whom did you invite?

____

3. Discuss with your parent/teacher your idea. With their permission, plan a day and time and place for your **Servant Evangelism Event**. When did you decide?

____

4. Make a list of any supplies you need to make or buy:

a. ____

b. ____

c. ____

5. Plan a meeting of your Servant Evangelism Team. When?

____

6. Delegate jobs for your team at the meeting.

7. Begin praying today and every day until it happens for God to use this Servant Evangelism Event to show His love to whomever He blesses through your team.

8. Guess at what a budget would be for your project.

______________________________ = $ ______________

______________________________ = $ ______________

______________________________ = $ ______________

______________________________ = $ ______________

______________________________ = $ ______________

Total = $ ______________

9. If you don't have the money yourselves, ask your parents or your teacher how you can earn money to pay for everything. (I don't recommend simply asking your parents for money.)

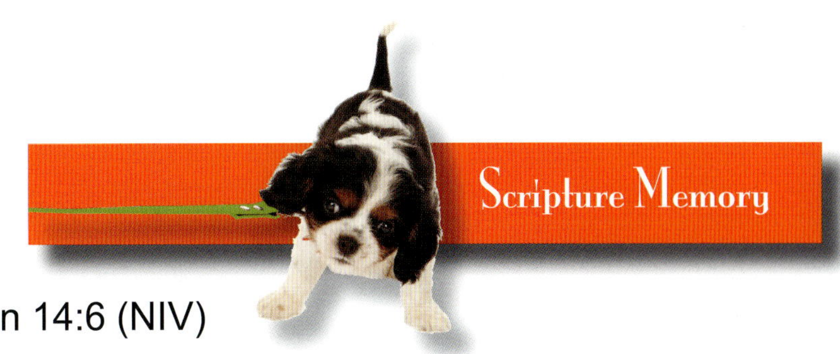

John 14:6 (NIV)

Jesus answered, "I am the way and the truth and the life.
No one comes to the Father except through me."

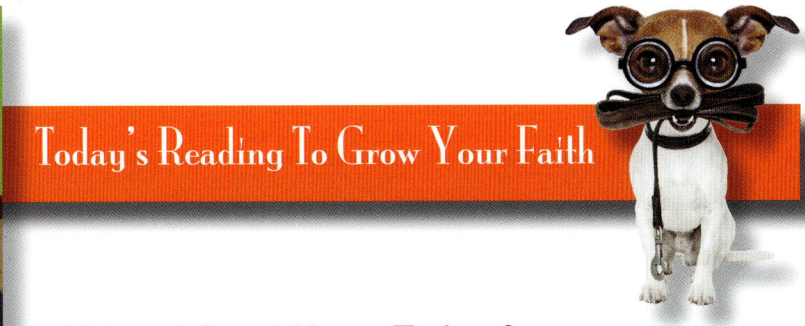

I Heard Good News Today 3
Read: Chapter 31—He Saw Me

Do you believe God still does miracles today—and why? [178]

Find the country mentioned on the map on page ix of *I Heard Good News Today 3* and pray for new believers there.

"Oh, you have a problem with my attitude?"

"Get a dog."

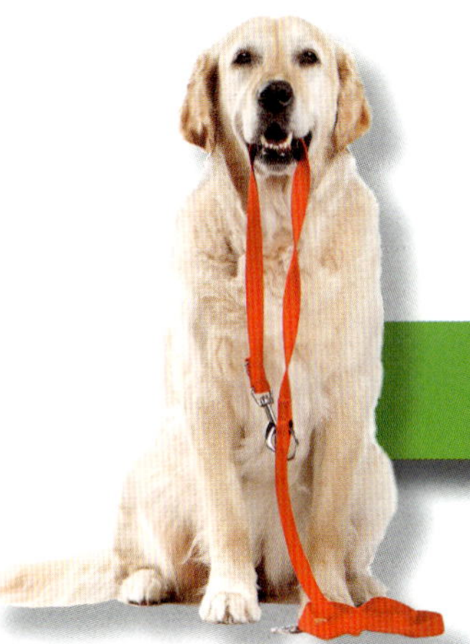

Week 21: Day 2

Lesson 62

Servant Evangelism Locally

Well, fellow Dogs, are you excited or scared about your upcoming **Servant Evangelism** project? If you are scared, that's okay. Remember, the Apostle Paul himself had to have God appear to him a few times saying, "Fear not." If you're excited, that's fantastic! Keep the enthusiasm (PMA) spreading!

******Keep planning your Servant Evangelism Event today.******
(Go back to Lesson 61, page 222, if you need to fill in your information there.)

Spend 10 minutes praying over your upcoming event:

Pray for God to be glorified.
Pray for yourself to be a humble team leader.
Pray for God to cause your team to work well together.
Pray for all the people Jesus will bless through you and your team.
Pray that this "act of kindness" will lead some people to "repentance" as the Bible says in Romans 2:4. Pray that God will bring more people into His Kingdom.

Put a check in the box when you have finished your time of prayer today. 

Scripture Memory

John 14:6 (NIV)

Jesus answered, "I am the way and the truth and the life.
No one comes to the Father except through me."

Today's Reading To Grow Your Faith

I Heard Good News Today 3
Read: Chapter 32—By the Dark of Night

What did you like the most about this story? [179]

Find the country mentioned on the map on page ix of *I Heard Good News Today 3* and pray for new believers there.

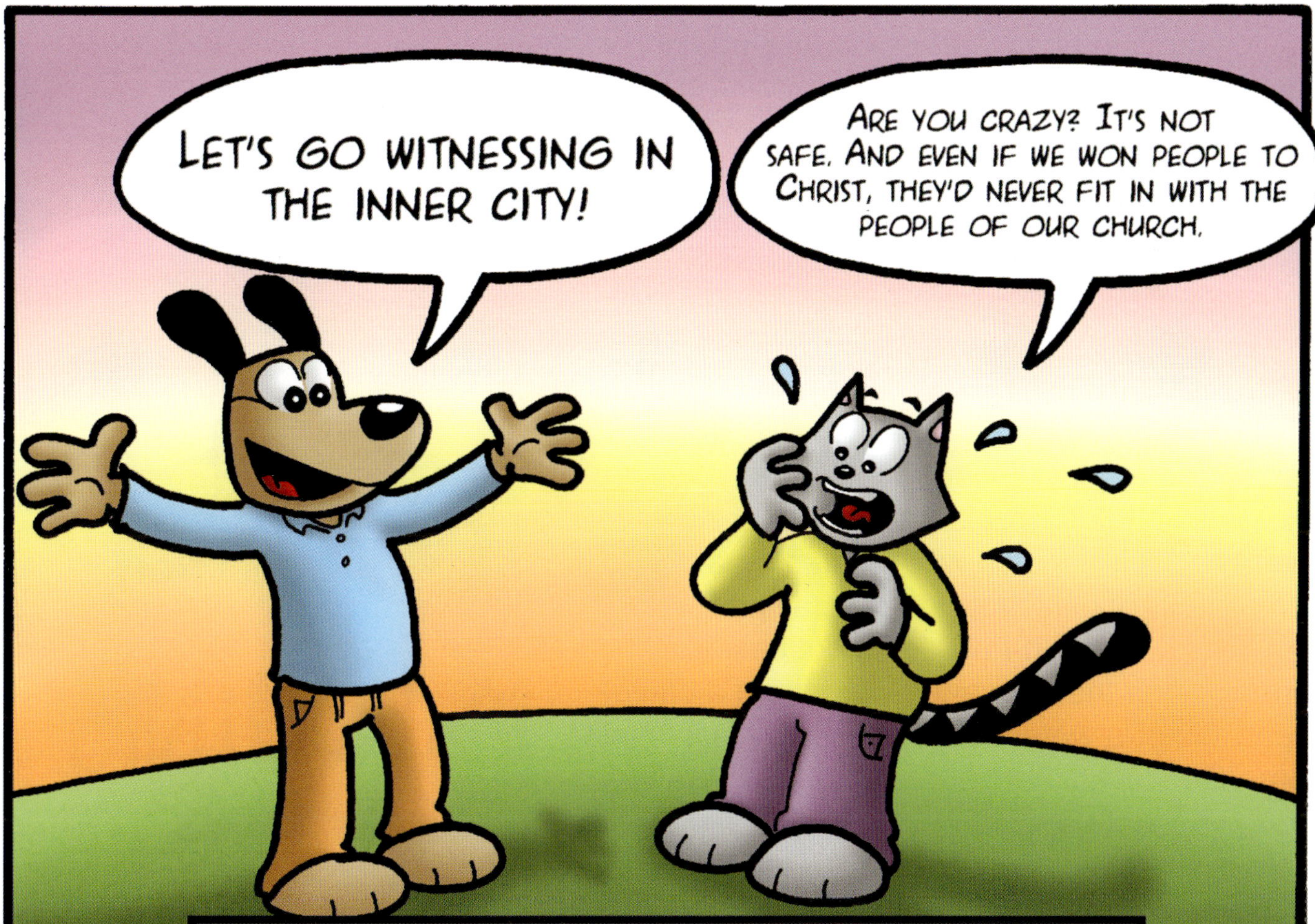

LET'S GO WITNESSING IN THE INNER CITY!

ARE YOU CRAZY? IT'S NOT SAFE. AND EVEN IF WE WON PEOPLE TO CHRIST, THEY'D NEVER FIT IN WITH THE PEOPLE OF OUR CHURCH.

Cats Love To "Protect" Their Church

Is the Cat more worried about their church or the lost, and why? [180]

____

____

Servant Evangelism Locally

I hope you have had a **great** time planning and preparing to serve your community for the glory of God this week. I can still vividly remember the first time our family held a **Servant Evangelism** project when our four children were all in elementary school or younger!

We were living in Mesa, Arizona, at the time. Our kids were 4, 6, 8, and 9 years old. My husband had learned about Servant Evangelism from his "long, lost cousin" Steve Sjogren. Because he was excited about this idea, my husband invited one other family from our church who had four boys about our kids' ages. We got permission to use our church parking lot. We created four posters that read:

FREE CAR WASH!
FREE COKES!
No MONEY!
No KIDDING!

So one Saturday morning, we went for about 2 hours and held a **free** car wash at our church parking lot! Our church was located on a busy road, so lots of cars stopped. We all had a blast! People who stopped truly could not believe we were washing their car and giving them a can of Coca Cola or a water bottle for **free**. We just told them, "God loves them and wanted to bless them through us that day."

You may be asking, "Should ours last two hours?" The answer is no. Steve Sjogren says that your project should last as long as it is fun! If the fun of serving wears off in 20 minutes, stop. If it wears off in three hours, then stop. Stop when you are no longer having fun. (Serving God doesn't have to be hard.)

In the end, we knew God was pleased. We knew He was glorified. Our hearts were full of joy!

*****Keep planning your Servant Evangelism Event today.*****
(Go back to Lesson 61, page 222, if you need to fill in your information there.)

ACTIVITY FOR TODAY:

If your **Servant Evangelism** project requires you to gather or create some posters or cards to give away to people you want to bless, then you can spend some time today working on these items. Or perhaps you need to go shopping to buy water bottles or cans of soda to give away.

Hopefully, you and your team have worked to make the money to pay for everything. (Remember, I don't recommend "mooching" off your parents for this event. God will generously reward you, eternally, for the acts of kindness you do for others in Jesus' name!)

Also, I'd love to hear or see photos of your **Servant Evangelism Event!** Please email them to debby@mmpublishers.com with a brief description of what you did.

John 14:6 (NIV)

Jesus answered, "I am the way and the truth and the life.
No one comes to the Father except through me."

Quote this verse to a family member or a friend and then check the box after you have successfully quoted it. ❏

Today's Reading To Grow Your Faith

I Heard Good News Today 3
Read: Chapter 33—Keep On in the Lord's Work

Why did the men love spending time in jail? [181]

Find the country mentioned on the map on page ix of *I Heard Good News Today 3* and pray for new believers there.

By Mary03101983 via WikiCommons

"Do you think there will be humans in heaven?"

Week 22: Day 1

Lesson 64

Servant Evangelism Globally

Buenos Dias! Guten Tag! Salamat Pagi! Bonjour! Nee How! Woof Woof! *Good morning!* You are probably thinking, "Finally, a language I can understand, right? (Though I bet you understood the "woof woof!")

Well, my fellow Dogs following the Master, today we will look at some of Jesus' ***very last words*** to his followers. Therefore, they must be **very, very** important!!!

Yes, let's read Acts 1:8 together; I really like it in the New English Translation (NET):

"But you will receive power when the Holy Spirit has come upon you,
and *you will be my witnesses in Jerusalem,*
and *in all Judea* ***and*** *Samaria,*
and *to the farthest parts of the earth."*

Wow! There are ***four*** "ands" in that ***one*** verse. Hmmm....let's think about that little three-letter word and its importance to us as Dog Christians.

Several years ago, I was sitting in our church balcony and listening to another missionary speaker talking about this verse. (Lots of missionaries like to talk about this verse.) So, I was a little bored...to be honest. But then I prayed, "Lord, what do you want me to learn today from this very familiar verse in Acts?" Well, of course, when we ask God with a pure heart ready to obey His voice, He answers. Duh...

So, that day for the first time those **four** "ands" really jumped off the page for me. What Jesus was saying to His followers (that includes you and me) is what I call a "both/and" command, ***not*** a "first, second, third, fourth" command.

Are you confused? I'm sorry if you are, but hang in here with me. Look back at the verse and read it again slowly.

Now, read it for what it does ***not*** say. (Sometimes it's very important to understand what the Scriptures do not say in order to understand what they do say!)

"But you will receive power when the Holy Spirit has come upon you,
and first *you will be my witnesses in Jerusalem,*
then *in all Judea* ***then*** *Samaria,*
then *to the farthest parts of the earth."*

Too many people in our churches read it like it is written above and say, "Well, I will start with my own family (Jerusalem), then when they all know the Lord, I will move to sharing Jesus with my neighbors (Judea). Then, after a long time of praying and sharing Jesus with my neighbors, maybe I will have time to work with people in my city who are different from me (Samaria). But I know I'm not one of those who will go "to the farthest parts of the earth." That's only for the people who are "called" to be a missionary. And that's definitely not me." This line of thinking is sequential: first, Jerusalem; second, Judea; third, Samaria; and last, the ends of the earth. But that's not what the text says.

Nor does it say:

"But you will receive power when the Holy Spirit has come upon you,
you will be my witnesses ***either*** *in Jerusalem,*
or *in all Judea* ***or*** *Samaria,*
or *to the farthest parts of the earth."*

Reading it that way would give us a choice, right? Most Christians who read it this way think, "Hmm, where would I like to serve God? I know, I'll stay here where I know the language and culture!"

But this line of thinking totally misses those **four** "*ands,*" doesn't it?

That day when I was bored in church up in the balcony, remember? Well, that day the Holy Spirit opened my eyes to see those **four** "ands" and that has made a huge difference in my life. Now, I know how to walk like a Dog according to Acts 1:8.

You see, for Dogs, we read it with the "both/and" line of thinking. So we ask the Holy Spirit to lead us to obedience by asking ourselves ***four*** questions all-at-once, not sequentially following one another. So, that day, I began to ask my Master, Jesus Christ, these four questions *simultaneously, not sequentially*:

Where is my Jerusalem... right now?
Where is my Judea...right now?
Where is my Samaria...right now?
Where is my farthest part of the earth...right now?

Got it? Do you understand where I am going with these questions?

Now did I go and live somewhere different that week? No, but I began to change the way our family would choose to spend our weekly free time after school and work were finished. Here's what Jesus showed me:

- My "**Jerusalem**" was some family members who needed us to pray for them and share Jesus by blessing them with clothes and food when needed.
- My "**Judea**" was a new neighbor family that we started a Bible Study together with weekly during one summer.
- My "**Samaria**" was volunteering with my kids in an after-school tutoring ministry with children in the inner city, a low-income area in our city. (See the picture below.)
- For the "**farthest parts of the earth**," we each chose a missionary family to pray for from our world map with photos of missionary friends around the world, and we invited international students to our Thanksgiving meal!

So, we began living out Acts 1:8 as Jesus intended, with a "both/and" mentality, not a sequential "first—second—third" or "either—or" line of thinking.

And guess what? We have not stopped living that way ever since. God certainly receives lots of glory from our free time now, and truly our joy level has increased 100% as a family!

This is Abby and the girls she tutored!

Acts 1:8 (New English Translation)

But you will receive power when the Holy Spirit has come upon you,
***and** you will be my witnesses in Jerusalem,*
***and** in all Judea **and** Samaria,*
***and** to the farthest parts of the earth."*

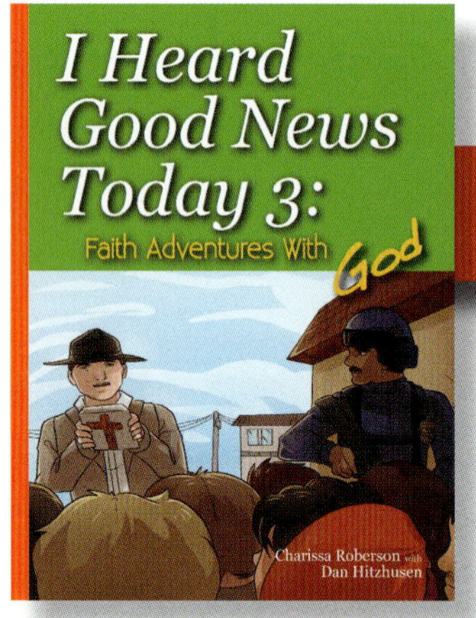

Today's Reading To Grow Your Faith

I Heard Good News Today 3
Read: Chapter 34—
Protection or Destruction?

What does Dan usually say to people who are thinking about going on one of his teams? [182]

Find the country mentioned on the map on page ix of *I Heard Good News Today 3* and pray for new believers there.

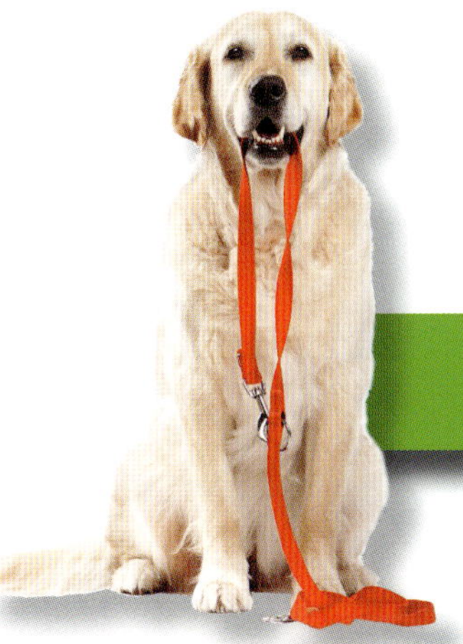

Week 22: Day 2

Lesson 65

Learning Life Lessons with Mrs. Debby

Servant Evangelism Globally

Well, yesterday's lesson was rather long...sorry, but not sorry! Why am I not sorry? Because your life will be forever changed if you begin to understand and live out loud the "both/and" principle of living according to Acts 1:8. So, how do you begin?

FIRST: Look up the word "witness" in a dictionary. Write a simple definition here as it relates to Acts 1:8.

____ 183

SECOND: Pray for God to show you personally (or as a family) how you can let the Holy Spirit make you a *witness* in all four areas of Acts 1:8.

THIRD: Spend some **"SOAK"** time with God (Go back to Lesson 29 and review if you have forgotten.), ask Him to whom He wants you to be a *witness* for His glory and their joy, and write down YOUR answers in these four areas of Acts 1:8.

1. Where is my Jerusalem...right now? (family member)

____

2. Where is my Judea...right now? (neighbor or friend)

____

3. Where is my Samaria...right now? (someone very different from you in your own city)

____

4. Where is my "farthest part of the earth"...right now? (another nation or people group in the world to pray for or a missionary family to partner with in prayer, giving, encouraging, serving or visiting)

Acts 1:8 (New English Translation)

But you will receive power when the Holy Spirit has come upon you,
***and** you will be my witnesses in Jerusalem,*
***and** in all Judea **and** Samaria,*
***and** to the farthest parts of the earth."*

I Heard Good News Today 3
Read: Chapter 35—Interrogation and the Secret Police

Whom did God have ready to help Dan before Dan even knew him? [184]

Find the country mentioned on the map and pray for new believers there.

Cartoon Day

Week 22: Day 3

Lesson 66

HERE I AM, LORD.
SEND HER.
(SHE'S NOT AS BUSY AS I AM.)

HERE I AM, LORD. I'LL
GO IF YOU WANT, JUST
MAKE IT CLEAR.

Responding To God's Heart For The Nations

Are you more the Cat or the Dog in this cartoon and why? [185]

____

____

Servant Evangelism Globally

I hope your mind has been blown away, just like mine was, when you see the true meaning of Acts 1:8 this week. The "both/and" view of that one verse can truly change the course of your life.

Cat Christians often reject this view because the "both/and" view would make them think of others above themselves. And they just don't want that. But we Dogs have learned the "Secret to Joy"—Jesus, Others, You!

Therefore, obeying Jesus' last words by spending time in prayer and loving people (both in our family, and our friends, and people who are culturally different from us) glorifies God! As a result, Dogs have extreme JOY knowing they are following Jesus' last command plus living a life "outside the Christian bubble" that truly impacts the world for God's glory! Wow! What an amazing life ***The Dog Walk*** has turned out to be!!!

Activity For Today

ACTIVITY FOR TODAY:

Find a world map or globe in your house, or on the Internet if necessary.

Research the country or people group you felt God put on your heart to pray for yesterday. Also, if you are praying for a missionary family, research the country where they live. Here is a great website to help: www.joshuaproject.net.

Spend five minutes praying for your people group or country.

If you have chosen to pray weekly for a missionary family, write them an email today to ask for any specific prayer requests. (One tip: do not use the words like missions, missionary, etc. in your email for their safety.) If you don't know of any, write me and I'll find someone who would love to have you praying for them! debby@mmpublishers.com

Check here when you have completed all the steps for today's activity. ❑

Acts 1:8 (New English Translation)

But you will receive power when the Holy Spirit has come upon you,
***and** you will be my witnesses in Jerusalem,*
***and** in all Judea **and** Samaria,*
***and** to the farthest parts of the earth."*

Quote this verse to a family member or friend and check the box once you have successfully quoted the verse. ❑

I Heard Good News Today 3
Read: Chapter 36— Painting Targets

True or False: There are times when God simply asks people to pray. [186]

Find the country mentioned on the map on page ix of *I Heard Good News Today 3* and pray for new believers there.

I loved it when my daughter, Elise,
wore the same dress at 17 years old
that I wore when I was 17!

Week 23: Day 1

Lesson 67

Learning Life Lessons with Mrs. Debby

Reflection Week on Serving Like Jesus

Finally...I hope you have completed or plan to have your very own **Servant Evangelism** project by this week (if not, there's still time!). As a fellow Dog following Jesus on our walks together, I know that being involved with **Servant Evangelism**, doing acts of kindness in Jesus' name, has been some of the best times we have had as a homeschool family. We have lots of joyful memories of blessing people in our neighborhood or our city or even in other parts of the USA or around the world!

If you still need help deciding what to do for your **Servant Evangelism Event**, here is a list to help give you ideas: http://helenafirst.com/pdf/seProjectsTable.pdf.

This week I want you to take time to reflect on what you have learned the past five weeks while we have been following Jesus by walking on the paths of **Servant Evangelism** and **Servant Leadership** in various areas of your life.

Here is Elise volunteering at a homeschool co-op.

We will start with the areas you were able to "lead, love, and serve like Jesus." Luke Kuepfer always says in his YouTube videos, encouraging us from God's Word, to be a servant-leader just like our Master on our Dog Walk. www.thetruthmadesimple.org/servant-leadership-insight-from-matthew-121/

Reflect and answer these questions thoughtfully:

1. Did your JOY increase when you practiced **Servant Leadership** in your home?

____

2. How did your parents or siblings respond when you practiced a “secret” act of kindness for them?

____

3. Did any of them follow your example?

____

4. How did you display God’s Glory to your church staff or youth pastor?

____

5. Has the friend or family member you trained chosen to live it out yet? If so, how have they become a servant to others?

____

6. What is one area of **Servant Leadership** that you plan to continue and how?

____

No New Verse This Week ☺ But Keep Reviewing!!!

I Heard Good News Today 3
Read: Chapter 37—The Two Swords

What can we learn about God's protection even in the middle of a war? [187]

Find the country mentioned on the map on page ix of *I Heard Good News Today 3* and pray for new believers there.

Reflection Week on Serving Like Jesus

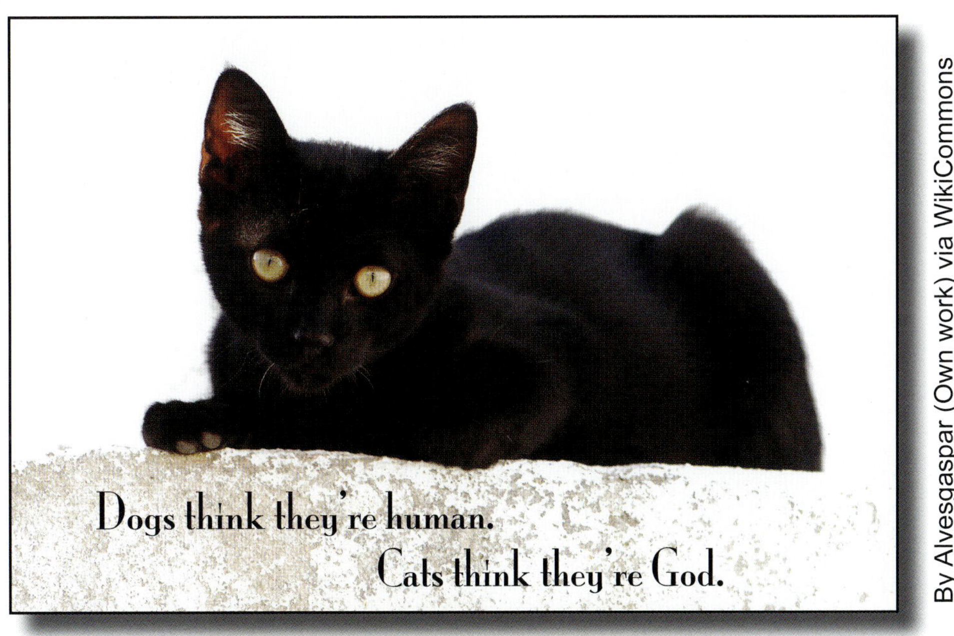

Dogs think they're human.
Cats think they're God.

By Alvesgaspar (Own work) via WikiCommons

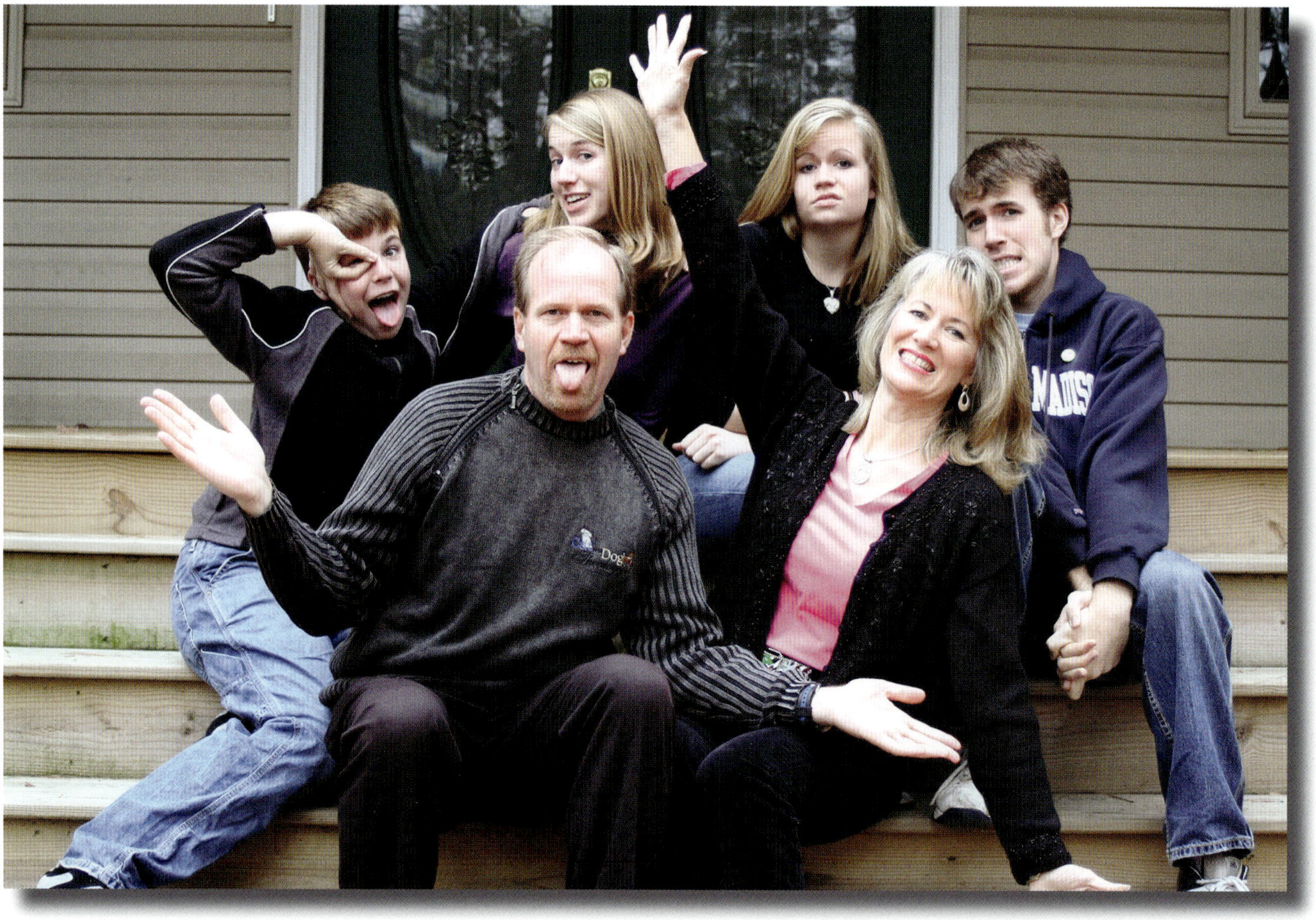

Sometimes we get crazy as a family.

Does your family ever do that?

Week 23: Day 2

Lesson 68

Yesterday, you spent time reflecting on your experiences on your Dog Walk of choosing to follow the example of Jesus, our Master, by practicing **Servant Leadership** in your home and church. Today, we will spend time answering reflection questions on your opportunities to practice "acts of kindness" for the Glory of God. We hope and pray these will lead others to repent from following their own way and want to follow Jesus with their lives like you have chosen to do.

Remember the verse that Steve and Janie Sjogren quote often when describing **Servant Evangelism** to others:

Romans 2:4 (ESV)
Or do you presume on the riches of his kindness and forbearance and patience, not knowing that God's kindness is meant to lead you to repentance?

Reflect and answer these questions thoughtfully:

1. What did you first think when you learned about **Servant Evangelism** and how has your opinion changed since you have practiced it with your team?

____

____

2. What were **three** of your favorite ideas for a **Servant Evangelism** project?

3. How did you enjoy or not enjoy leading a team for your **S.E. Event**?

4. What is your favorite "story" of a person's response to your "act of kindness" just to show them that God loves them?

5. What do you plan to change in your weekly schedule now that you have learned the meaning of Acts 1:8 with a "both/and" perspective on participating in **Servant Evangelism** locally and globally?

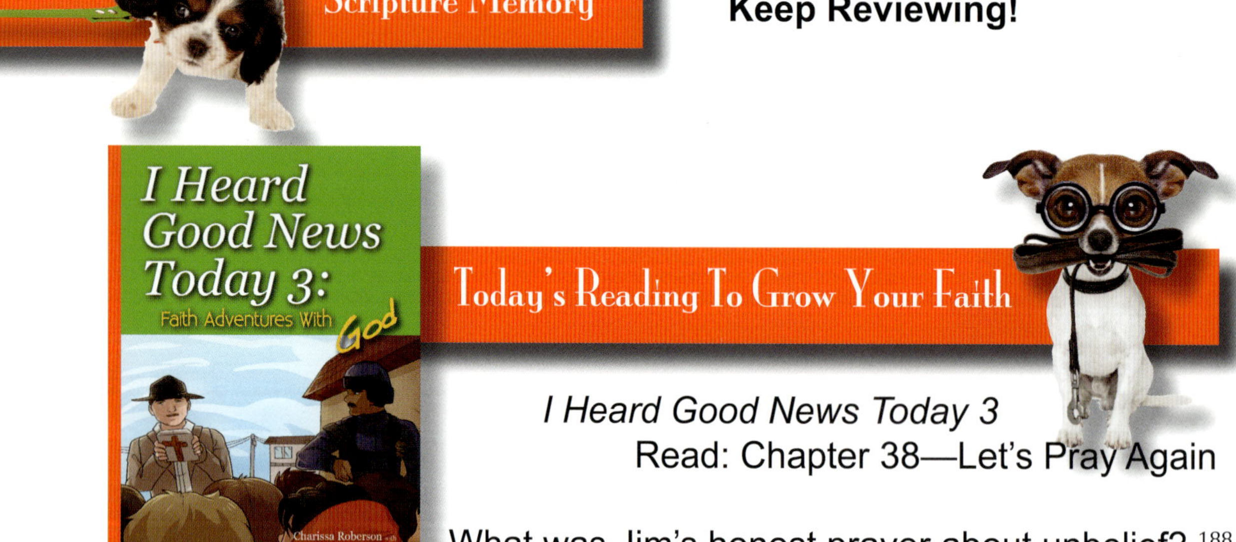

Scripture Memory
I Heard Good News Today 3:
Faith Adventures With God
Charissa Roberson with Dan Hitzhusen
Today's Reading To Grow Your Faith

Keep Reviewing!

I Heard Good News Today 3
Read: Chapter 38—Let's Pray Again

What was Jim's honest prayer about unbelief? [188]

Find the country mentioned on the map on page ix of *I Heard Good News Today 3* and pray for new believers there.

Cartoon Day

Week 23: Day 3

Lesson 69

Wow! God is really going to love me now!

Wow God! This is really going to make You famous!

Cats Serve For Acceptance.
Dogs Serve From Acceptance.

Who is the Cat focused on and who is the Dog focused on? [189]

____

____

Learning Life Lessons with Mrs. Debby

Reflection Week on Serving Like Jesus

Guess what is coming next week? **The EvangeCube!!!** Yes, after reading so many stories from *I Heard Good News Today 3: Faith Adventures with God,* you will begin learning how to use your own **EvangeCube**. Are you excited? I hope so! (You've seen it in the box for so long, you've probably already got it memorized!)

So, before we jump into that next week, I'd like you to reflect on what those stories have been doing in your own heart and mind.

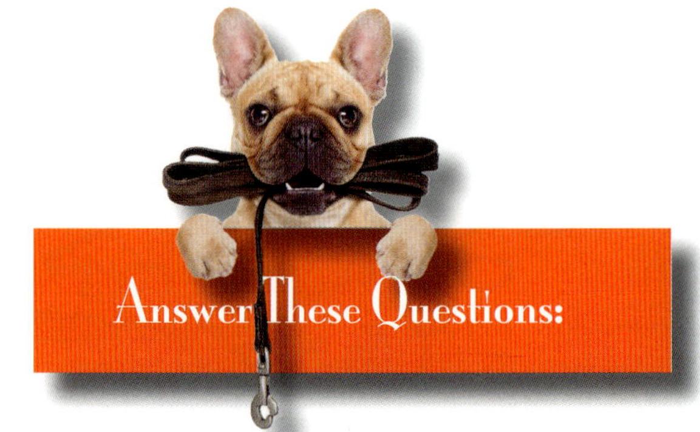

Reflect and answer these questions:

1. Have you ever shared your faith in Jesus with someone you just met before? If so, how did they respond?

____

2. Which story in *IHGNT3* has been your favorite so far and why?

____

3. Before reading these stories, did you ever think a new church could be started in a village or neighborhood in *just one week*? Circle One: Yes No

4. How has your faith in God increased through reading the stories from *I Heard Good News Today 3*?

____

____

5. If you could visit any of the countries you have read about in *IHGNT3,* which one would you pick and why?

____

Today's Reading To Grow Your Faith

I Heard Good News Today 3
Read: Chapter 39—Chicago?

Has your understanding of God's greatness changed as a result of this story, and if so, how? [190]

Find the country mentioned on the map on page ix of *I Heard Good News Today 3* and pray for new believers there.

By BrokenSphere via WikiCommons

We love to teach our kids to serve—even at our own home.
Here are Elise and Hunter cleaning windows on a spring day!

Week 24: Day 1

Lesson 70

Learning Life Lessons with Mrs. Debby

The Dog Walk: Speaking of Your Master

Welcome to our third and final section of *The Dog Walk.*

Yes, we started our Dog Walk learning how to be devoted to the Master, Jesus, in our attitudes, spiritual growth, and actions. Then we learned to follow Him in the pattern He left for us as a Servant Leader by serving those nearest to us and also those who might not follow Jesus yet. But this week we will begin the JOY of learning how to speak about our Master, our wonderful Lord and Savior, Jesus! Another way of saying it is we're going to learn how to share our faith effectively.

Before we open up our **EvangeCube** today, I want you to read over the last passage of Scripture we will be memorizing this year: Colossians 4:2-6. *Yes, I know you were excited over that piece of news! And you will have five weeks to learn it!* Here are the verses in their entirety.

Colossians 4:2-6 (ESV)

2 Continue steadfastly in prayer, being watchful in it with thanksgiving.
3 At the same time, pray also for us, that God may open to us a door for the word, to declare the mystery of Christ, on account of which I am in prison
4 that I may make it clear, which is how I ought to speak.
5 Walk in wisdom toward outsiders, making the best use of the time.
6 Let your speech always be gracious, seasoned with salt, so that your may know how you ought to answer each person.

Do you notice any parts that you have already been practicing on our Dog Walk so far this year? After you read over it, list six phrases on the next page that Paul and Timothy wanted the church in Colossae to pray for them as they ministered to others: [191]

1. ____

2. ____

3. ____

4. ____

5. ____

6. ____

ACTIVITY FOR TODAY:

1. Open up your **EvangeCube** box. Then watch this video presentation and read the paper script in your box: https://www.youtube.com/watch?v=zETUh50u8Vs

2. Here is a great script to help you practice using your new **EvangeCube**: http://www.jfhp.org/resources/downloads/discipleship_materials/nyi_evangecubescript.pdf. Also, try using verses you have already memorized!

Colossians 4:2 (ESV)

Continue steadfastly in prayer, being watchful in it with thanksgiving.

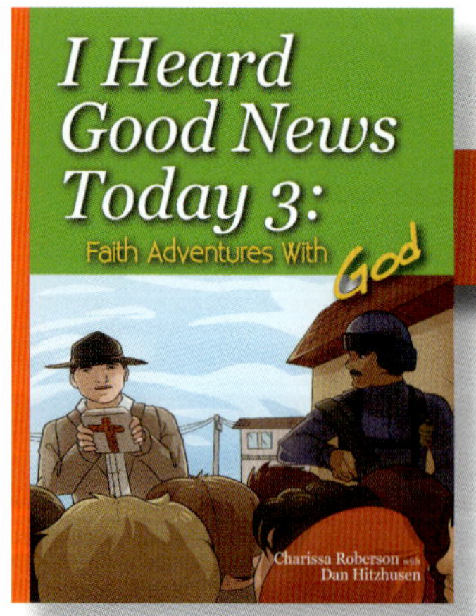

Today's Reading To Grow Your Faith

I Heard Good News Today 3

Read: Chapter 40—The Book of Acts in Action

How many churches were first planted, and how many were there three years later?[192]

____

Find the country mentioned on the map and pray for new believers there.

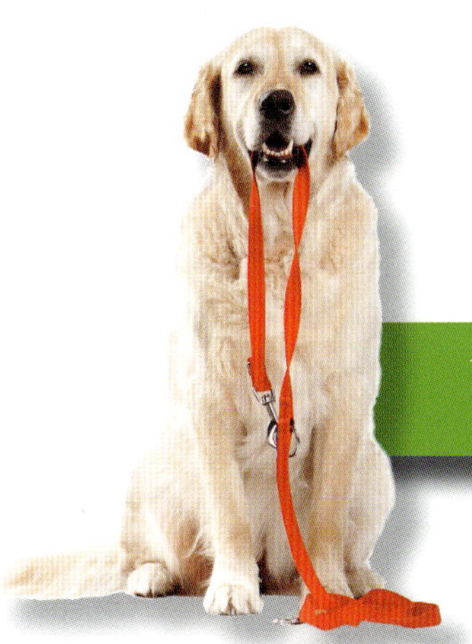

Week 24: Day 2

Lesson 71

Learning Life Lessons with Mrs. Debby

EvangeCube Practice Today!

What do you think, fellow Dogs? Isn't it so amazing to be able to tell the Good News of Jesus while using a cube full of cool pictures? And you can use it with people of any age or language because there are no words to read, right?

ACTIVITY FOR TODAY:

Activity For Today

1. Keep practicing with your **Evange-Cube**, here is another video clip you can watch for practicing: https://www.youtube.com/watch?v=IR7YDRil5Eg

2. Put some of your Scripture Memory verses into your presentation. Use at least one verse in your presentation, or you can use more verses if you want. Which verses will you include?

___

3. Spend 15 minutes today practicing with your **EvangeCube.**

4. Set up an appointment to share your **EvangeCube** with a friend or family member later this week. Who said yes? ___

Check this box when you have completed these steps above. 

Colossians 4:2 (ESV)

Continue steadfastly in prayer, being watchful in it with thanksgiving.

I Heard Good News Today 3
Read: Chapter 41—Beyond Languages

What did the Holy Spirit do through the American dancer that astounded the Indians?[193]

Find the country mentioned on the map on page ix of *I Heard Good News Today 3* and pray for new believers there.

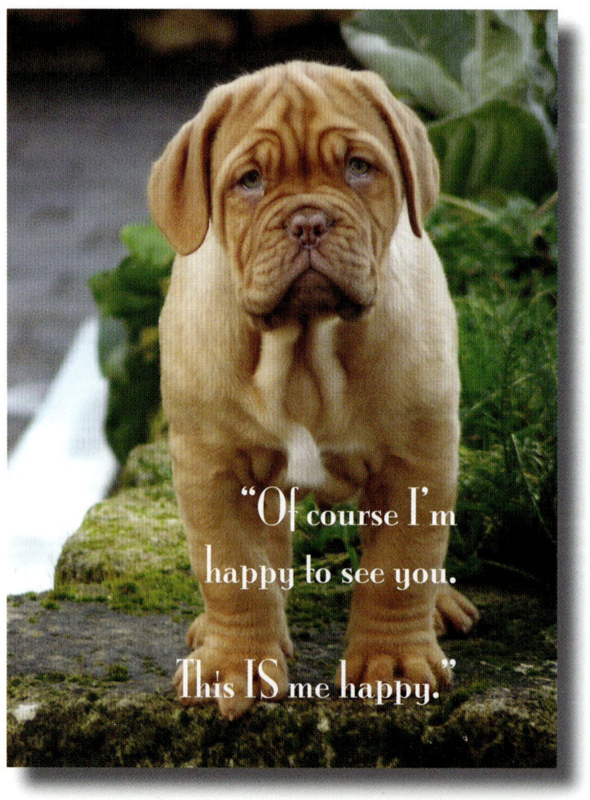

"Of course I'm
happy to see you.
This IS me happy."

By Des doyens bordelais via WikiCommons

Cartoon Day

Week 24: Day 3

Lesson 72

Trust me.

God loves you and so do I.

Cats And Dogs Take Risks Differently

Explain how Cats and Dogs respond to risk differently in the cartoon. [194]

____

____

Sharing your EvangeCube!!

Today is **THE DAY!** Hopefully you have scheduled your appointment to practice using the **EvangeCube** with a friend or family member for today or later this week.

One very important truth to remember is this simple definition of "successful witnessing" that my husband and I both learned when we were in college from a ministry now called Cru: *Success in witnessing is simply taking the initiative to share Christ in the power of the Holy Spirit and leaving the results to God.* (Credit: http://www.cru.org/content/dam/cru/legacy/2012/01/successfulwitnessing.pdf)

Just like we talked about earlier this year in Lesson 9, the pressure is off when our only responsibility is to speak of Jesus; however, the person's response is dependent upon the Holy Spirit drawing them to a relationship with God Himself. As it says in Ephesians 2:8–10:

> *8 For by grace you have been saved through faith. And this is not your own doing; it is the gift of God, 9 not a result of works, so that no one may boast. 10 For we are his workmanship, created in Christ Jesus for good works, which God prepared beforehand, that we should walk in them.*

Begin this lesson by spending some **SOAK** time with God (Lesson 29) and talking to Him about preparing your heart to be His messenger today or later this week.

Pray also for the heart of the person with whom you will be sharing the Good News of Jesus. Pray that the Holy Spirit will draw them to Jesus if they don't have a relationship with God yet (John 14:6).

Put a check in the box after you have done both. ☐

ACTIVITY FOR TODAY:

1. Whom did you practice your **EvangeCube** presentation with today?

2. How did they respond to the Good News of Jesus?

3. Will you make any changes in your presentation next time?

4. Do you think God received glory by your obedience to Acts 1:8 today?

5. Did your JOY increase after using the **EvangeCube**?

Scripture Memory

Colossians 4:2 (ESV)

Continue steadfastly in prayer, being watchful in it with thanksgiving.

Quote this verse to a family member and then place a check in the box after you have successfully quoted the verse. ☐

I Heard Good News Today 3

Read: Chapter 42—Tell Them Why We're Here

Why was Michelle so scared and why didn't she need to be afraid? [195]

Find the country mentioned on the map on page ix of *I Heard Good News Today 3* and pray for new believers there.

"Knock, Knock..."

"Oh, please, not another one."

By Prskavka via WikiCommons

Week 25: Day 1

Lesson 73

What's Your Story? Testimony Time!

Fellow Dogs! Welcome to a new week in *The Dog Walk*! I am so excited about teaching you how to quickly share "your own story" of following Jesus with whomever God leads you to share it. Often, in the church, we call telling "your own story" of coming to faith in Jesus a fancy word: ***testimony***.

Write a brief definition related to sharing your faith for the word ***testimony***:

____ 196

When I was younger, I was taught a simple way to share "my own story" or ***testimony.*** They said to think of an object to use for an illustration, combine that with a Bible verse, then share "your own story" in three parts. I was also encouraged to try and keep it to about 3-5 minutes. The three parts might include:

- **My life before following Jesus**
- **Who or what led me to repent, believe and follow Jesus**
- **How my life has changed since I started following Jesus**

<u>Here is my own example:</u>

The first 13 years of my life, I was like a donut with a hole in the middle.

Even though my parents took me to church and prayed for me, I was trying to fill that hole in my life with lots of friends and with achievements like good grades and other honors. But I soon realized that none of these really filled the hole inside my heart. My life looked good on the outside like a glazed donut, but I felt "empty" on the inside.

Something was definitely missing.

Then one summer, around the 4th of July, I attended my Jr. High Church Camp for a week. The first night there one of the counselors shared how he was trying to find peace and happiness in many different places and people, but he still felt "empty." Then he tried a personal relationship with Jesus and found what he was looking for!

Because I also was missing peace and true joy in my life, I really started listening at that point. Later that night in my bunk bed, I asked Jesus to come into my life and forgive all my sins, and then to fill the empty hole in my heart with His peace, love and joy. And He did!

As the summer went along, one of the female counselors began meeting with me to help me grow in my relationship with Jesus. I am forever grateful for her! She taught me how to make Jesus my BFF, best friend forever. I began to see the Bible come true in my own life like it says in II Corinthians 5:17, "Therefore, if anyone is in Christ, he is a new creation. The old has passed away; behold, the new has come."

So now, my life is no longer like a glazed donut with a hole in the middle, but a chocolate-covered, cream-filled donut. Since then I have experienced the true peace and joy that only Jesus can give us that will last for all of eternity!

ACTIVITY FOR TODAY:

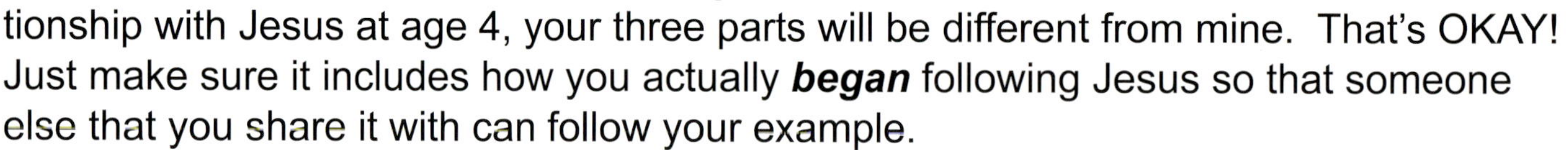

Take some time to think about "your own story" or ***testimony*** of starting your walk with Jesus. If you are like my own children who all began a relationship with Jesus at age 4, your three parts will be different from mine. That's OKAY! Just make sure it includes how you actually ***began*** following Jesus so that someone else that you share it with can follow your example.

Divide your ***testimony*** into three parts with a few sentences using one of the two outlines that follow. (You will write the actual paragraphs in your next lesson.)

Option 1:

- **My life before following Jesus.**
- **Who or what led me to repent, believe and follow Jesus.**
- **How my life has changed since I started following Jesus.**

Option 2:

- **How I learned about Jesus when I was young.**
- **When and how I decided to follow Jesus.**
- **How my life has changed since I started following Jesus.**

Check here when you have finished writing your three-part outline. ❏

Scripture Memory

Colossians 4:3 (ESV)

At the same time, pray also for us, that God may open to us a door for the word, to declare the mystery of Christ, on account of which I am in prison.

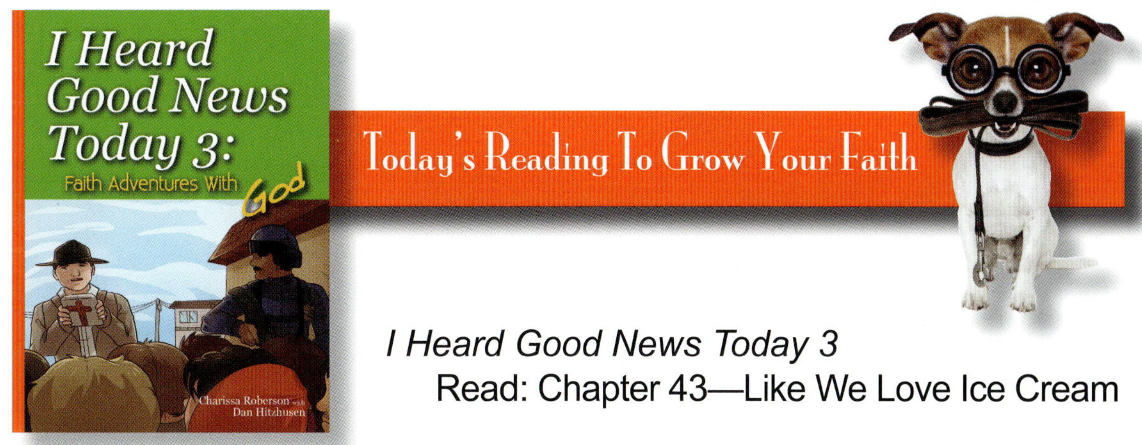

I Heard Good News Today 3
Read: Chapter 43—Like We Love Ice Cream

What language did God use in Rebecca's dream to speak to Michelle? [197]

Find the country mentioned on the map on page ix of *I Heard Good News Today 3* and pray for new believers there.

This is Hunter when he was in Peru.
He learned to share his faith there using the EvangeCube.

Week 25: Day 2

Lesson 74

Learning Life Lessons with Mrs. Debby

What's Your Story? Write "Your Own"

Today, you will spend some time determining which illustration and Bible verse you will use for your ***testimony***. Then you will type or write your own 3-5 minute story of following Jesus.

ACTIVITY FOR TODAY:

Activity For Today

Take some time to pray and think about an object or example that you could weave into your ***testimony*** like I used a "donut" in my own ***testimony***. (Of course, this is not necessary, but it does help people relate to your story.)

Next, see if one of your Scripture Memory verses, or any other Bible verse that you feel God wants you to use, can be woven into your ***testimony***. Also, ask your parents if you need help finding a Bible verse that you could weave into your story to point people to God's Word.

On a separate sheet of paper, spend time today typing or writing the three paragraphs that will help you easily share your personal ***testimony*** of following Jesus.

Check here when you have finished writing your testimony. ❑

Forward a copy of your ***testimony*** to me at debby@mmpublishers.com. I'd love to read it and give you feedback! (Please know that as the years go by, your testimony may change. So don't be afraid to update it every now and then!)

Colossians 4:3 (ESV)

At the same time, pray also for us, that God may open to us a door for the word, to declare the mystery of Christ, on account of which I am in prison—

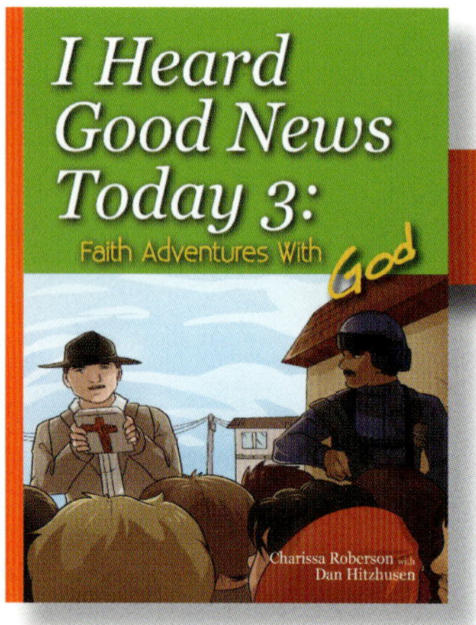

Today's Reading To Grow Your Faith

I Heard Good News Today 3
Read: Chapter 44—Freedom Behind Bars

Dan preached about Paul and Silas. Where were they and what made Paul and Silas different from the other prisoners?[198]

Find the country mentioned on the map on page ix of *I Heard Good News Today 3* and pray for new believers there.

Lord, I'm all Yours. Just don't ask me to suffer please, or go overseas either.

Anywhere. Anytime. Anyplace. No limits God. Use me to make You famous.

Surrendering Before God

Do you feel you are completely surrendered to God like the Dog? If not, what is holding you back? [199]

Learning Life Lessons with Mrs. Debby

What's Your Story? Share with Someone

Good morning, my fellow Dogs! I hope this week has not been too intense for you. I'm sure writing your ***testimony*** in a more simple and creative way wasn't that easy for some of you, but hopefully you enjoyed the challenge once you got into it!

You will see next week how it all weaves together...sharing the **EvangeCube** and sharing your ***testimony*** to point people God brings into our lives to Him. As Dogs, we want to bring more worshipers to God. We want to be Dogs who will point to His glory with our lives. When we do that, we can fully experience the joy of the Lord both now on earth and for all of eternity!

So, today you get to be a Dog Trainer. I want you to find someone in your family or a friend to whom you can read or tell your newly written ***testimony.*** Then, take about 10-15 minutes to teach them how to write their own personal testimony if they haven't already done that in the past. (Refer back to Lessons 73 and 74)

Whom did you share your testimony with today? ___________________________

Did you get to train them in how to write their own? Circle One: Yes No

Check this box when you have completed the actions above. ❑

Scripture Memory

Colossians 4:3 (ESV)

At the same time, pray also for us, that God may open to us a door for the word, to declare the mystery of Christ, on account of which I am in prison.

Quote Colossians 4:2-3 to a family member and then check the box after you have successfully quoted it. ❑

Today's Reading To Grow Your Faith

I Heard Good News Today 3
Read: Chapter 45—Do You Believe The Same As Billy Graham?

Do you think God could use you in answer to someone else's prayer? Why or why not? [200]

Find the country mentioned on the map on page ix of *I Heard Good News Today 3* and pray for new believers there.

This is my 435th day of captivity. The saddest thing is they seem far more interested in what's on T.V. than in me.

By Juanedc from Zaragoza via WikiCommons

To Be Used For Lesson 77: How It Went Sharing Your Faith!

Week 26: Day 1

Lesson 76

Learning Life Lessons with Mrs. Debby

Speaking of Jesus: Testimony + EvangeCube

Today, we will begin to put it all together so you will be prepared to point people to Jesus when you meet anyone who hasn't started on his or her *Dog Walk* with the Master!

How does it all work? Let me give you a great example of when I was in Ethiopia a few years ago. You see, it was on my first e3 Partners trip with Dan Hitzhusen (www.e3partners.org) when I had to learn to use the **EvangeCube**! There were 14 people on that mission team to a place called Arba Minch, Ethiopia. (Ethiopia is a country in East Africa. Look it up on a globe or map if you have time.) Before we left the USA, we had to practice sharing our testimony and the **EvangeCube** with at least three other people. *You see the more you share it, the easier it gets!*

When we finally got to Arba Minch, we were assigned different villages or parts of the city to go to each day with a translator and a disciplemaker (someone from a local church who will follow up with the new believers). My area of the city was just outside a university. We hung out in some coffee shops and talked with the college students.

At the beginning of each day, we would pray for God to bring just the people He wanted for us to share the Good News of Jesus with that day. So, then I would walk up to small groups of students and often begin by saying, "Hi, my name is Debra, and I have come all the way from America to tell you my story. Could I have a few minutes of your time today?"

Usually, they would give me a few minutes, mostly because I looked and dressed differently from them. But I would dive into my 3-5 minute ***testimony*** first (the shorter the better to not lose their attention), and then I would ask if I could show them my **EvangeCube**.

They were very curious about the **EvangeCube** and usually would stay around and listen to the end.

Later in the week, I was even given the privilege of training about 11 students in how to share the **EvangeCube** with others and start small Bible study groups at their university. All Glory to God for the work He began in those students in that one week!

ACTIVITY FOR TODAY:

Practice in front of a mirror today. Yes, I know it sounds crazy... but do it! Start with your 3-5 minute ***testimony,*** then move right into sharing your **EvangeCube.**

.

Go through all of it at least twice. *The more you do it, the easier it gets!*

Check when you have gone through your ***testimony*** and **EvangeCube** twice. ☐

Scripture Memory

Colossians 4:4 (ESV)

that I may make it clear, which is how I ought to speak.

Today's Reading To Grow Your Faith

I Heard Good News Today 3
Read: Chapter 46—God of the Storm

What two things did God use to bring the flight attendant to Himself? [201]

Find the country mentioned on the map on page ix of *I Heard Good News Today 3* and pray for new believers there.

Week 26: Day 2

Lesson 77

Learning Life Lessons with Mrs. Debby

Speaking of Jesus: Witnessing with the EvangeCube

The more you share it, the easier it gets! You've heard that phrase before this week, haven't you? Well that applies to sharing your faith, too! (Is your mirror wearing out?!!)

But there is something that is even more important than having your testimony memorized or knowing what to say with the **EvangeCube**. It is realizing your dependence upon God. We must never forget that the Holy Spirit will take over when we begin to share the Good News of Jesus! Look at this verse below:

But when they arrest you, ***do not worry*** *about what to say or how to say it.* ***At that time you will be given what to say,*** *for it will not be you speaking, but the* ***Spirit of your Father speaking through you.*** (Matthew 10:19-20, NIV)

God wants to bring more worshipers to Himself even more than we do, much more for sure! Two verses in the New Testament are proof of that Truth:

For God so loved the world that he gave his one and only Son, that whoever believes in him shall not perish but have eternal life. (John 3:16, NIV)

The Lord is not slow in keeping his promise, as some understand slowness. Instead he is patient with you, not wanting anyone to perish, but everyone to come to repentance. (2 Peter 3:9, NIV)

Honestly, sometimes you can't believe the words that come out of your mouth when telling others about Jesus! It is so exciting to be God's voice or messenger while on this earth. Just like Acts 1:8 taught us, we are to be His *witnesses* wherever we go and leave the results up to God.

ACTIVITY FOR TODAY:

1. Keep practicing your ***testimony*** plus sharing the **EvangeCube**, but practice on a sibling or friend or parent today.

2. Next, spend some ***SOAK*** time with God today (Lesson 29), asking Him who, outside of your family and close friends, He might want you to actually be a *witness* to this week (Acts 1:8). Make a list of at least five names below:

a. ______________________________

b. ______________________________

c. ______________________________

d. ______________________________

e. ______________________________

3. Now that have your list, begin to pray your Scripture Memory verses (Colossians 4:2-6) over those names. Pray also that God will orchestrate a time where it is super comfortable and easy for you to share the **EvangeCube** with at least one of them in the week ahead, and your ***testimony*** if you feel that would be best to start or end your time with them.

Check this box when you had the chance to share with someone not in your family this week. Go back to page 268 and write briefly who it was and what happened. ❑

Scripture Memory

Colossians 4:4 (ESV)

that I may make it clear, which is how I ought to speak.

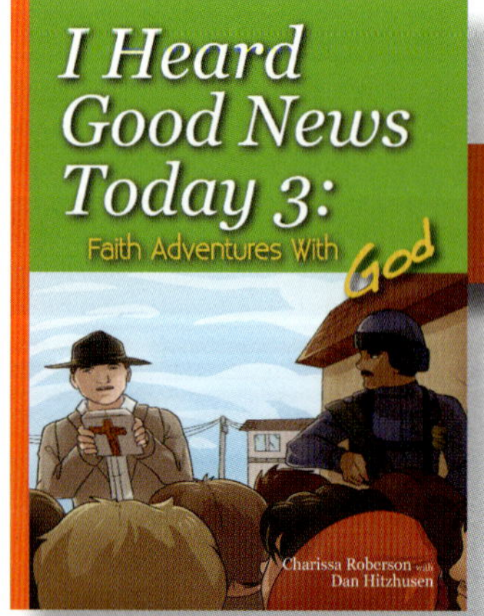

Today's Reading To Grow Your Faith

Read: Chapter 47—Commencement Address

What did Dan do that was so bold—and would you have done it?[202]

Cartoon Day

Week 26: Day 3

Lesson 78

WE WANT YOU TO KNOW THAT WE ARE LITERALLY TRUSTING GOD FOR MIRACLES IN THIS CHURCH, WE WANT TO SEE THIS CHURCH TAKE OFF FOR GOD!

WE WANT YOU TO KNOW THAT WE ARE TRUSTING GOD FOR LITERAL MIRACLES IN THE CHURCHES IN THIS CITY. WE WANT TO SEE OUR CITY TAKE OFF FOR GOD AND IMPACT THE WORLD.

Pastoral Goals

Why could the Cat pastor's prayer be selfish? [203]

____

____

Speaking of Jesus: Dog Training Day

You knew this was coming, right? It is the 3rd day of the week, isn't it? Time to go into Dog Training mode, okay? Ask God to show you who He wants you to train in sharing the **EvangeCube**. Make a list of three names, then plan a time to teach and train at least ***one*** of them this week, or each of them, or all of them together.

Whom do you plan to train in using the **EvangeCube**?

1. ______________________________
2. ______________________________
3. ______________________________

When will you meet with them and where? (Or do it as a large group.)

1. Day and Time: ____________________ Where: ____________________
2. Day and Time: ____________________ Where: ____________________
3. Day and Time: ____________________ Where: ____________________

Check here when you have completed today's assignment. ☐

Scripture Memory

Colossians 4:4 (ESV)

that I may make it clear, which is how I ought to speak.

Quote verses 2-4. ☐

I Heard Good News Today 3: Faith Adventures With God

Charissa Roberson with Dan Hitzhusen

Today's Reading To Grow Your Faith

Read: Chapter 48—A Strategic Photograph

What did God use to bring this entire village the gospel? [204]

____

Week 27: Day 1

Lesson 79

Learning Life Lessons with Mrs. Debby

Orality: Storytelling like Jesus

How has your time sharing the **EvangeCube** been going? I hope you are having as much fun sharing it as the 10-year-old boy I met in Ethiopia a few years ago. Remember my story about being on a team in Arba Minch, Ethiopia (Africa)? Well, most of my time was with college students at the coffee shops on the side of the road by their university, but I really wanted to see inside an Ethiopian home.

Therefore, one day my translator and disciplemaker said we could walk down a side road, praying as we went that God would prompt a family to invite us into their home. After several attempts at knocking on the gates, because they have a courtyard in front of their homes, we finally met a nice family who invited us inside.

With a big smile, I introduced myself—through my translator speaking what I had just said in their language—and asked if I could share a most important story with them. They said, "Yes!" I was so excited! There was a mother and father and baby and their 10-year-old son. After sharing the **EvangeCube**, I discovered they also loved Jesus and were excited we were sharing the Good News of Jesus in their area. The 10-year-old boy was really intrigued by the **EvangeCube**, so I asked him if he wanted to learn how to share it with others. With a light in his eyes, he nodded "yes."

I was thrilled to quickly teach him when to open each panel and what to basically say. It was easy for him since he was raised in the church and knew the story of Jesus. Then came the defining moment: he turned around and shared the **EvangeCube** with us! Of course, it was still done through a translator, but my new younger friend did a fantastic job. Overjoyed and delighted at his enthusiasm, I offered to give it to him as a gift if he would agree to share it with his relatives and friends and neighbors. With a huge smile, he shook his head and shook my hand as I handed him his very own **EvangeCube**. What a beautiful memory for me!

But, are there other ways to share the gospel, especially with people who don't read well and who love to listen to stories? Yes! Another method of sharing the Good News of Jesus is called *Orality* or called *Bible Storying.* What is *Orality*?

The President of Living Water International, Jerry Wiles, says, "Orality is really a superior way of Bible teaching: telling stories so it's more interactive, it's engaging, it's participatory, and it sticks." He explains that the behavior change is more evident when people are engaging in the Word actively and together rather than when they read it on their own.[205]

Did you know that 2/3 of the world prefer hearing stories over reading them? It doesn't always mean they *can't* read, but they'd prefer *hearing* something rather than reading it. The same is true even here in America. Most people love to watch movies more than read books. It's because those movies are simply stories they can see and hear.

If we understand the power of this, it helps us discover a great way to share the gospel through stories. Specific stories with engaging questions really grab your listener's attention and allow you to talk to their heart!

The goal of *Orality* or *Bible Storying* is ***not*** to get the whole gospel out in a few minutes. Rather, it is to get them interested in talking about spiritual things. When someone shares a story wherever they are, they don't always get to the "Jesus died for your sins" part. They may simply get someone talking about something spiritual for the first time in years.

And you know what's the coolest thing about it? It's so easy to do! You can start off by saying, "Hey, that reminds me of a story," or "Hey, would you mind if I tell you a story?" Everyone's open to that! Jim Thurber (who trains people in *Bible Storying*) told my husband that out of the 800 times he has asked someone if he could tell a story (Yep—he was keeping count!) only five said "no." And those people had to say "no" because they were late to catch a plane or do something important. It wasn't because they didn't want to hear a story!

Can you imagine engaging people on spiritual matters and never having them say, "No, I don't want to hear?" This is what I want to introduce you to over the next few lessons. Eventually it may lead to having you share your testimony or sharing the EvangeCube with them. But it can all start with a story!

ACTIVITY FOR TODAY:

1. I want you to watch two videos for your assignment today. The first is less than two minutes in length. See what you think. The title of the video clip is: "Paul Eshleman - Orality"

https://www.youtube.com/watch?v=J_ZzM1pEkE0

2. The second is a great 10 minute video clip describing the *Orality*: "Storytelling the Gospel" in India. Listen all the way through this one. The title of the video clip is called, "Scriptures In Use—Orality Training Overview."

https://www.youtube.com/watch?v=RoIXjubHyPU

3. Also I want you to research "Orality in Sharing the Gospel" on the Internet. Spend 10 minutes today studying at least **one** of the following websites:

https://orality.imb.org/resources/?id=232

www.water.cc/orality

www.mnnonline.org/news/orality-getting-back-to-the-basics-of-gospel-sharing/

Check this box when you have completed your three assignments for today. ☐

Colossians 4:5 (ESV)

Walk in wisdom toward outsiders, making the best use of the time.

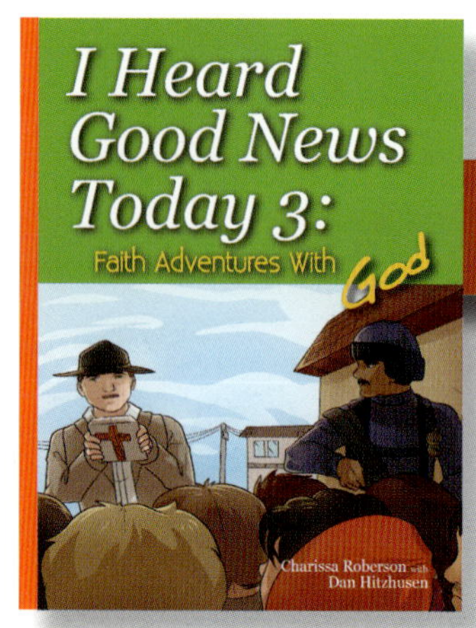

Today's Reading To Grow Your Faith

I Heard Good News Today 3

Read: Chapter 49—And God Stopped the Hurricane

God used Dan's love for basketball to lead many people to Christ. What do you love to do and how could God use it? [206]

Find the country mentioned on the map on page ix of *I Heard Good News Today 3* and pray for new believers there.

By 0x010C via WikiCommons

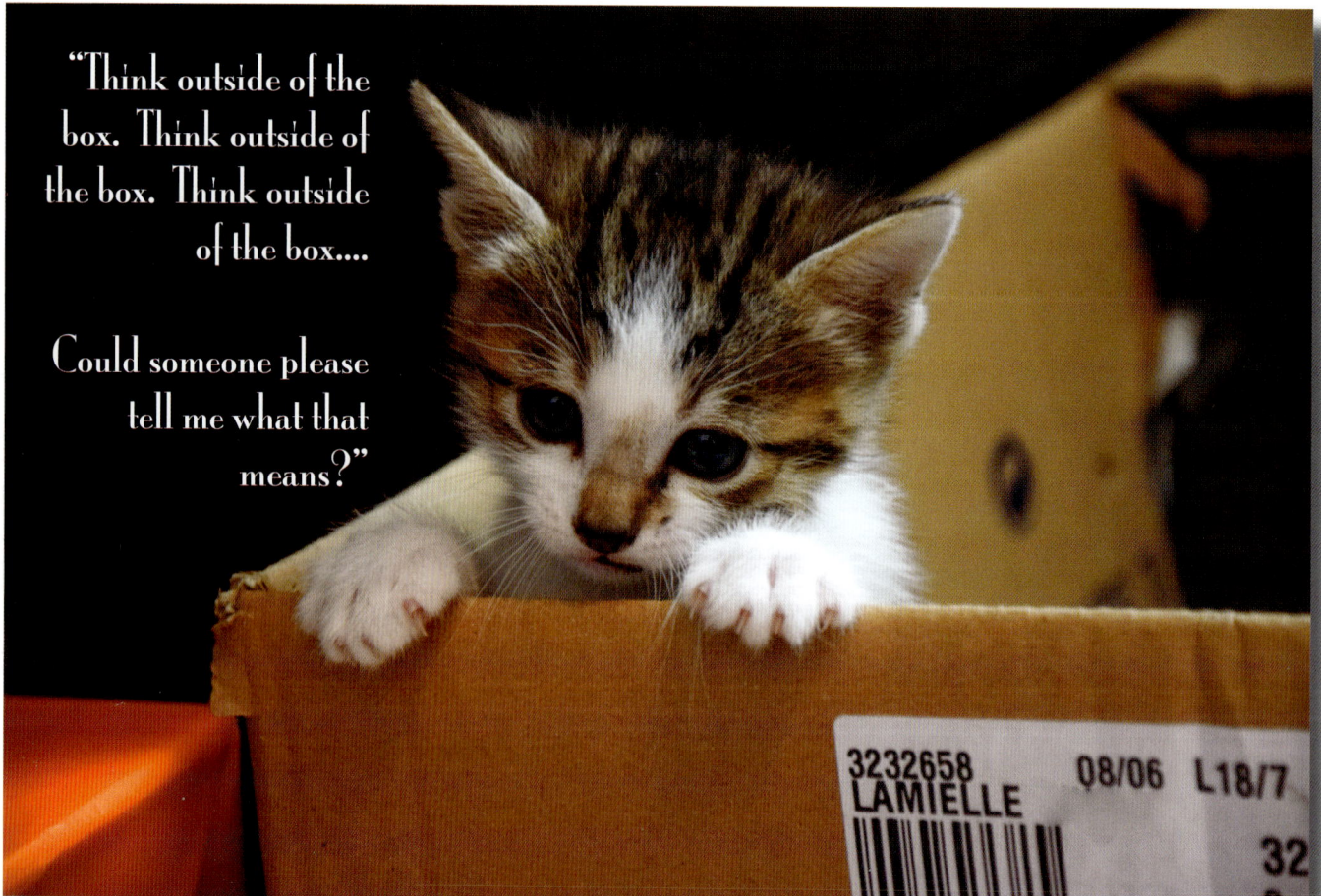

"Think outside of the box. Think outside of the box. Think outside of the box....

Could someone please tell me what that means?"

3232658 08/06 L18/7
LAMIELLE
32

Week 27: Day 2

Lesson 80

Orality: Storytelling like Jesus

I hope you enjoyed your research during your last lesson on *The Dog Walk.* Personally, I find it fascinating that 60-70% of the Bible is in narrative format or "stories." When you link of the fact that 70% of the world today (5.7 billion people) are truly "oral learners," it makes total sense that we should learn how to share the Good News of our Master, Jesus, through ***Bible Storying***.

Do you realize that this is what Jesus did? We call them "parables" in the New Testament—but they're basically stories! Look what Mark says about Jesus:

> 33 *With many such* ***parables*** *he spoke the word to them,*
> *as they were able to hear it.*
> ***34 He did not speak to them <u>without</u> a parable,***
> *but privately to his own disciples he explained everything.* (Mark 4:33,34)

If that's what Jesus did, and we're trying to be like Jesus, shouldn't we be telling stories, too? Of course we should!

So, fellow Dogs, where do we start? You've probably already guessed it! By learning a Bible story. So this week, we're going to focus on one Bible story and then learn the questions to ask after you've told the story. I've underlined key words in the story to help you memorize it!

There are three steps to learning these stories. They are listed below.

1. Knowing when to use the story.
2. Learn to tell the story itself.
3. Learn the questions that go with the story.

ACTIVITY FOR TODAY:

Learn the three parts to your first story. [207] It's an easy one and I'm sure you've heard it before. You will find it in the beginning of the Bible. It's the story of Adam and Eve being tempted by Satan. You know that one, don't you?

Part 1—When would you use this story?

- To teach children the importance of obeying God.
- To train children to choose the truth over a lie.
- To teach children that Satan will try to tempt them to disobey God.

Part 2—The Story (Genesis 3:1-7):

1 The serpent was clever, more clever than any wild animal God had made. He spoke to the Woman: "Do I understand that God told you not to eat from any tree in the garden?"

2-3 The Woman said to the serpent, "Not at all. We can eat from the trees in the garden. It's only about the tree in the middle of the garden that God said, 'Don't eat from it; don't even touch it or you'll die.'"

4-5 The serpent told the Woman, "You won't die. God knows that the moment you eat from that tree, you'll see what's really going on. You'll be just like God, knowing everything, ranging all the way from good to evil."

6 When the Woman saw that the tree looked like good eating and realized what she would get out of it—she'd know everything!—she took and ate the fruit and then gave some to her husband, and he ate.

7 Immediately the two of them did "see what's really going on"—saw themselves naked! They sewed fig leaves together as makeshift clothes for themselves.

Part 3 — Follow Up Questions:

1. The Serpent was pretty smart in deceiving Eve, wasn't he? (Yes)
2. Instead of deceiving her, what could he have done? (Told the truth)
3. What do we learn about Satan? (He lies and deceives people.)
4. What do we learn about God? (He knows everything.)
5. Do you think Satan still deceives people today? If so, how? (Answers vary)
6. How can this story help you in the future? Affirm any answer. (Possible answers: Choose to obey God when tempted or choose the truth over a lie.) [226]

Wow, this is a long day, huh? And guess what? I want you to practice in the mirror. (Yep! Back to the mirror again.) Tell the story with hand motions and expressive faces maybe even moving your body like a snake.☺ **Remember it is important to get your listeners *engaged in the story*!**

Scripture Memory

Colossians 4:5 (ESV)

Walk in wisdom toward outsiders, making the best use of the time.

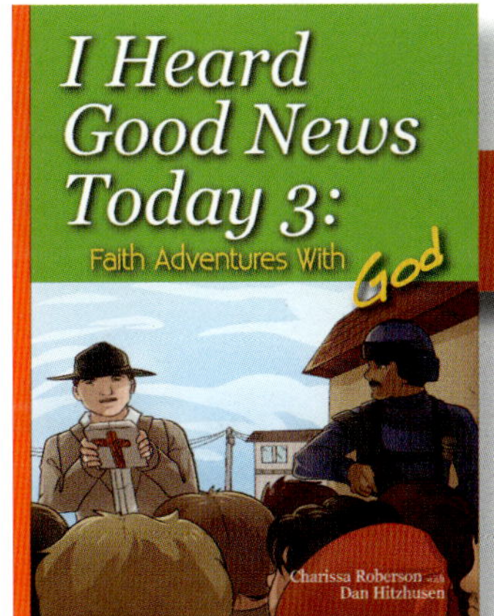

Today's Reading To Grow Your Faith

I Heard Good News Today 3
Read: Chapter 50—Say Yes

What valuable lesson did Lorie learn? [208]

Find the country mentioned on the map on page ix of *I Heard Good News Today 3* and pray for new believers there.

Here we are with our Middle Eastern friend who got his doctorate
at Virginia Commonwealth University.
He texted us the day before and asked us to come to his graduation.
Wanting to encourage him, we changed our schedule and went the next morning.
We love to tell him stories of Jesus.

Cartoon Day

Week 27: Day 3

Lesson 81

What other fun things can we do to entertain these kids so our meeting will get bigger?

Let's not worry about numbers. Let's figure out who's hungry for God and disciple them and train them to evangelize and disciple others.

How Cats And Dogs Strategize To Reach The Youth

What's is the Cat's primary focus? [209]

____

____

Learning Life Lessons with Mrs. Debby

Orality: Bible Storying

Hi, fellow Dogs, how's the memorization going for Bible Storying? It's tough isn't it? But I know you can do it because kids your age have memorized—not only entire chapters—but entire books on the Bible. You can do this!

But if you are struggling, let me give you some good news. **You don't have to memorize the story word-for-word.** People don't care if you memorize every word. They only want to hear the basics to the story. That is why I underlined those key words. If you get the basics down, that's what you need! Tell the stories in your own words as best you can. Whew, the pressure's off, right?

Whether you have memorized it or not, you are "graduating from the mirror." Do you have your cap and gown ready? ☺ *Today* I want you to practice your exciting *Orality* or *Bible Storying* on someone else. Ask your parent and make a few phone calls to arrange a time with your siblings or cousins or grandparents or friends to demonstrate *Orality* or *Bible Storying*.

Remember, the story doesn't have to be perfect. Just give them the basics. Tell the story with enthusiasm and engaged them with asking the questions. If you like, you could also have them act it out. And the more you practice, the better you'll get! Feel free to end your time asking if they have any questions or needs you can pray for them.

Now, write the names of two to three possible people you can practice on today or later this week:

1. ____________________

2. ____________________

3. ____________________

Check this box when you have practiced *Orality* or *Bible Storying* this week. ☐

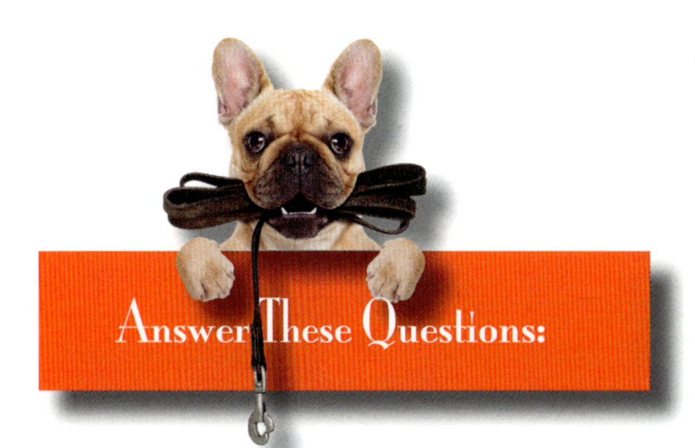

Answer these questions afterwards:

1. To whom did you share your story with actions, questions, and excitement?

____

2. What was their response?

____

3. Did you enjoy practicing *Orality/Bible Storying* this week?

____

4. Rank which "Speaking of Jesus" method you have enjoyed doing the most:

Sharing the **EvangeCube**
Telling your ***testimony*** or
Orality/Bible Storying?

First choice:

Second choice:

Third choice:

Colossians 4:5 (ESV)

Walk in wisdom toward outsiders, making the best use of the time.

Quote Colossians 4:2-5 to a family member and put a check mark in the box after you have done it successfully. ❑

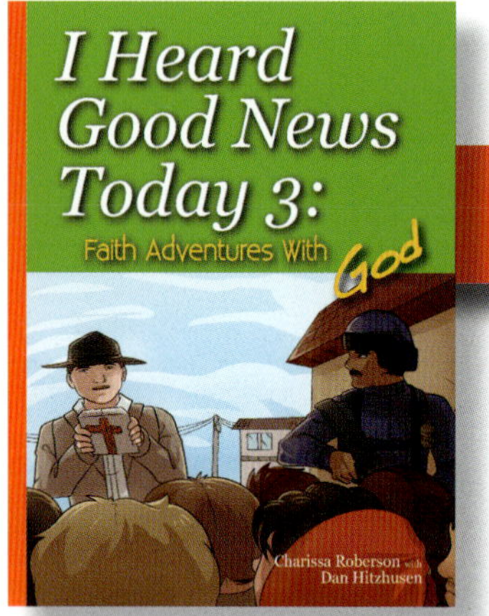

Today's Reading To Grow Your Faith

I Heard Good News Today 3
Read: Chapter 51—A Way In

What was Dan missing that was a big problem in the story? [210]

Find the country mentioned on the map on page ix of *I Heard Good News Today 3* and pray for new believers there.

Week 28: Day 1

Lesson 82

Learning Life Lessons with Mrs. Debby

Sharing the Gospel Through Games!

Hey fellow Dogs, do you like to play games? I'll bet you do if the sun rises in the east each morning! And it does, so I'll bet you love games!!!

Wouldn't it be great to play games and through the games teach about Jesus! Do you want to know what's exciting? You can do exactly that!!! There's a man named D.J. Bosler who has created an entire ministry by teaching children through games. It is called GameLife™ and has three components:

Game:

In this section, you play a game with the kids. It is fun, and there's lots of action so nobody "falls asleep" like they might if you were just speaking.

Discovery:

Once the game is over, you do a Bible study that parallels the game they just played. Pretty cool, huh?

Life:

Once they've heard the Bible story, you can then teach them how that game and Bible story apply to their lives. They then learn a deep lesson about God and are now better equipped to reflect God's glory in their everyday lives!

Go to his website now (www.gamelife77.com) and watch a four-minute video about it! It is really cool!!! Check this box when you have watched it. ☐

When my husband met D.J. Bosler, Mr. Bosler told him a story. It went something like this:

> "So our team had played the game Red-Rover and the kids loved it. We then sat them down and talked about how Nehemiah was rebuilding the weakest part of the walls. Then we applied it to their lives saying, "Why did you choose which set of arms to run through?" Most replied, "Because they looked the weakest."
>
> We'd then say, "Just like Nehemiah built up the weakest part of the walls, what are the weakest parts in your life that you think you need to strengthen?" They then started talking about "obeying their parents" or "having a better attitude" or "meeting more with Jesus."
>
> At the end of the day, one of the kid's dad walked in. I saw the father and said to his son, "Derek, tell him about what you learned in Nehemiah today!" Derek had a blank stare on his face. He didn't know what to say.
>
> I looked at him and smiled. "Derek, tell him what you learned about Red-Rover." Derek lit up! He didn't stop talking for about five minutes. He remembered the Bible lesson from the game far more than from the Bible passage. Kids really learn from games!"

So today, you are going to learn a brief lesson about Nehemiah because you're going to get some kids and teach them about God through Nehemiah. But, my fellow Dogs, there are two ways you can teach a lesson. First, you can play the game and then sit them down and tell them about the story of Nehemiah. Secondly, you can simply tell them the story of Nehemiah and maybe even have them act it out with you. Either is okay.

Which will you choose to do? ______________________________

In either case, you need to learn the "Big Picture" of Nehemiah and be able to tell it to the kids you are teaching. You'll find it on the next page. Again, key points are underlined. You might want to read through it five or six times. Don't worry about learning it word-for-word, just learn the gist of it so you can tell it your own way.

Back in the Old Testament, the people of Israel lived in a place called the Promised Land for a long time. But after years went by, they forgot God. Because of that, God was angry with the people of Israel and had other nations defeat them. Their city was destroyed and the Israelites were taken to many other nations around the world.

After 70 years in captivity, Nehemiah's heart was broken. Being a Jew, he wanted to rebuild the city of Jerusalem and restore it to its former glory. So God gave him favor in the eyes of the king he was under and he set out to repair the walls.

When he first got to Jerusalem it was a mess. The walls had been broken through and the gates had been torn down. There was no protection at all for the city.

So Nehemiah gathered a bunch of other Jews and they went to work. They first repaired the weakest parts of the walls. Then they filled up the holes. Finally they rebuilt the gates.

Because the people worked at it with all their heart, it got finished in 52 days. Everyone was amazed, even people from other nations!

Can you close your eyes and retell the basic story of Nehemiah above? Give it a try. Check this box after trying. ☐

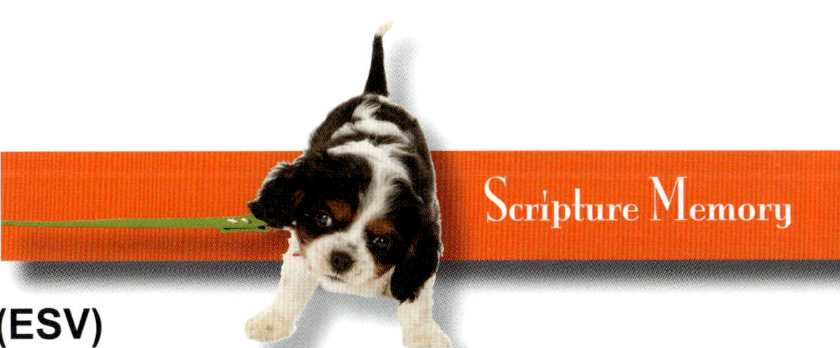

Colossians 4:6 (ESV)

Let your speech always be gracious, seasoned with salt,
so that your may know how you ought to answer each person.

I Heard Good News Today 3
Read: Chapter 52—Two Prayers, One Answer

What were the two prayers that were answered? [211]

Find the country mentioned on the map on page ix of *I Heard Good News Today 3* and pray for new believers there.

Seriously? You like cats better than me? This is such a sad day.

By Ildar Sagdejev (Specious) via WikiCommons

Week 28: Day 2

Lesson 83

Learning Life Lessons with Mrs. Debby

Sharing the Gospel Through Games

Okay, fellow Dogs—I hope you're as excited as I am about sharing the gospel through games! Now that you understand the Bible story, you need to know a little bit about the game (if you don't know it already.)

The game is called Red-Rover. If you don't know it (odds are you do!), ask your mom or dad, or go to: https://www.youtube.com/watch?v=DGnSveGKtSU.

Now that you know the game and know the Bible story, you're missing one thing! The questions that come at the end to help them understand the importance of what the game was all about. So what are those questions?

For Red-Rover, you can ask these questions:

1. Did you choose the weakest set of arms to run through or the strongest?
   (Hopefully they'll say "weakest.")
2. Nehemiah strengthened the weakest areas of the wall. What do you think is the weakest part of your friendship with God?
   (Encourage them in any answer they give.)
3. How can you strengthen those areas?
   (Encourage them in any answer they give.)

ACTIVITY FOR TODAY:

Let's do this, fellow Dogs! You're now ready! You've been taught all three parts to help you teach those younger than you. You've learned:

The Game: Red-Rover

The Discovery: The Story of Nehemiah

Life Lessons: The Questions

Now, go out and find three-to-six younger kids (or family members) and walk them though GameLife! Place a check in the box after you have completed it. ❑

If you had fun teaching this way, we have more games to use. Go to http://www.unveilinglory.com/content/view/77 and look under the Middle School section.

Scripture Memory

Colossians 4:6 (ESV)

Let your speech always be gracious, seasoned with salt, so that your may know how you ought to answer each person.

Today's Reading To Grow Your Faith

I Heard Good News Today 3
Read: Chapter 53—At The Right Time

Why did God want Britney to be obedient immediately? [212]

Find the country on the map and pray for new believers there.

Cartoon Day

Week 28: Day 3

Lesson 84

It's not safe there and I could never love those kinds of kids. Forget it.

Wow! That sounds challenging, but let me pray about it and see what the Lord wants.

Responding To A Two-Week "Hug Team" To Help Orphaned Children In Mozambique*

*TO FIND OUT MORE ABOUT "LEAST OF THESE" MINISTRY, E-MAIL BECKY BATES @RBATES1049@AOL.COM

Do you think you'd ever want to work at an orphanage overseas, why or why not?[213]

____

____

Dog Training Day!

By now you know the drill, right? Today is your day to train someone in "GameLife.™"

Find someone who is around your age and train them in these three areas: The Game, The Discovery, and The Questions. Then have them find three-to-six younger kids and play the game with those kids and have them learn their life lesson!

Check this box after you have trained someone else in GameLife.™ ❑

Colossians 4:6 (ESV)

Let your speech always be gracious, seasoned with salt,
so that your may know how you ought to answer each person.

Quote Colossians 4:2-6 to a family member and then place a check in the box after you have successfully quoted the entire passage. ❑

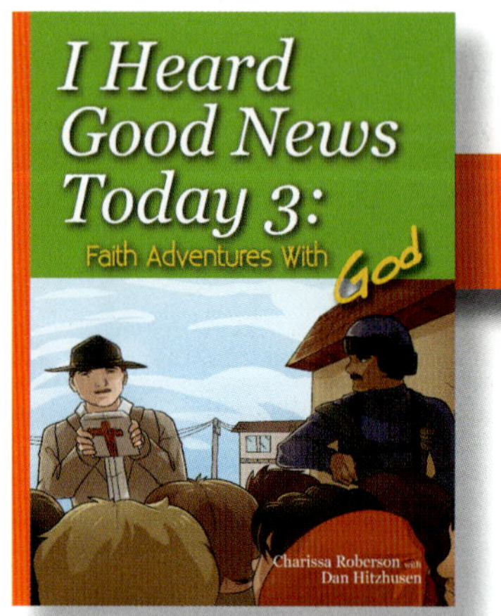

Today's Reading To Grow Your Faith

I Heard Good News Today 3
Read: Chapter 54—Midnight Miracle

What was the midnight miracle? [214]

Find the country mentioned and pray for new believers there.

Week 29: Day 1

Lesson 85

Learning Life Lessons with Mrs. Debby

Speaking of Jesus Cross Culturally

Well, last week was fun, I hope! Getting kids to play games and then teaching them about the gospel can be a blast—all Glory to Him forever and ever!

So this week, I have a new challenge for you. I'm getting pretty BOLD these last weeks of *The Dog Walk*, aren't I? Jesus certainly challenged His disciples to take risks for the glory of His Father God, so should we be any less challenged? We are His followers here in this century, especially those of us on *The Dog Walk*!

Have you had fun learning to "Speak of Jesus" by using the **EvangeCube**? How about giving your personal ***testimony*** with a creative twist, shortened to 3-5 minutes? And finally, discovering a new way to tell the world about our wonderful God and His Son, especially those who don't read, using *Bible Storying/Orality*?

Well, this week I want to challenge you to "Speak of Jesus" ***cross-culturally***! What does that mean? Well, be willing and take a risk to befriend someone, perhaps an international student, from another country where they have a different language than you do. They may also eat different foods than you normally do, and maybe they even dress a little differently than you do.

How do you do this? The first step is to pray! Ask God to show you someone who lives right around you who is from another nation that you could befriend. Maybe it is a Hispanic child. Maybe they are from Asia. And maybe they even live in your neighborhood or go to your school. In most cases, they are very close.

If that doesn't work, contact your church office to see if they know anyone you could contact to introduce you to an international student living in your hometown right now. If you have a university near where you live, that is a great place to start.

Perhaps your mother or father or teacher could call the university office that welcomes the international students.

If none of that works, look for a local Chinese take-out fast food restaurant in your area or a nail salon where many people from Vietnam or other Asian countries usually work.

What do you do next? When you start to talk with them, be a “learner” not a “teacher” at first. Ask them lots of questions about their home country. They usually love to tell you about their family and their life back “home.” Facebook or pictures are great for this.

If they need help speaking better English, perhaps you could offer to teach them some English words and greetings. When we had a French high school student live with us for three months, my husband started putting sticky-notes all over our kitchen to teach Felix the words for those items in English. It worked great, and he quickly learned some new words.

What is the BEST idea you could do for them? INVITE THEM TO YOUR HOUSE FOR DINNER. Seriously? Yes, I am very serious. Why? Because statistics say that around 80% of international students never get invited into an American home. Some churches or ministries call this becoming a “Friendship Partner.” Here are some frequently asked questions with good answers from a ministry called International Students Inc. (ISI): http://www.isionline.org/Home/ChurchPartners/FAQs.aspx

Review Colossians 4:2-6 (ESV)

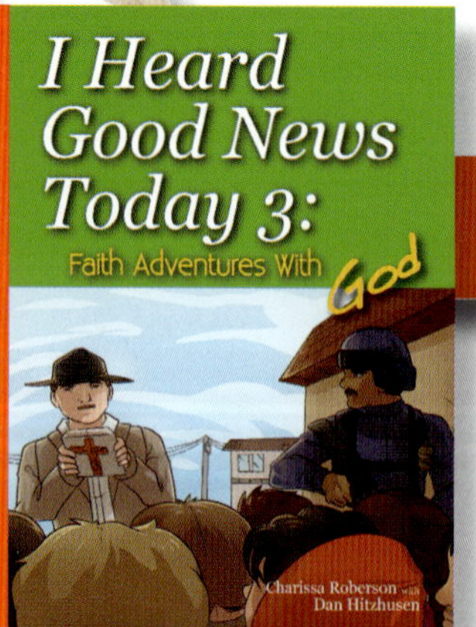

I Heard Good News Today 3

Today's Reading To Grow Your Faith

Read: Chapter 55—A Chess Game

What did Dan tell his team to do in order to share the gospel clearly? [215]

Week 29: Day 2

Lesson 86

Speaking of Jesus Cross Culturally

Hello, my Dog friends! Have you thought about what we talked about in your last lesson? Have you mentioned it to your parents? Have you prayed about it—I know what God will say, remember Acts 1:8, and the "both/and" instructions from Jesus?

Hopefully my own story about this desire and God's answer will encourage you!

When my four children were very young, my husband and I wanted to have a friendship with some international students to be able to love them, share our culture with them, learn about theirs as a family, and speak of Jesus with them.

With not much time to drive over to the university 20 minutes away, I began to pray for God to bring students to us. Would you believe He did just that??? The house next door to us in our suburban neighborhood just happened to be a rental home. Lo and behold, after two years of living on that cul-de-sac, a new "family" moved in one day. Not really a "family," but three international students from Taiwan and one from Korea.

I was so excited! We went over to meet them with a plate of chocolate chip cookies. We learned their names, even though they were not easy for us to pronounce. We invited them to our house for Thanksgiving Dinner and my kids acted out the First Thanksgiving story. We talked all about our love for God. We became their friends. Later on, we did speak of Jesus with them, and they even asked us to pray for them. *God heard my heart's desire and prayer for international friends for our family! And He answered in a way that was much better than I could ever imagine!*

ACTIVITY FOR TODAY:

Pray and ask God to clearly show you whom you can reach out to **cross-culturally**. Discuss the idea of inviting an international student into your home for a meal with your parents. If they say "yes," then call your church office to ask for help with whom to contact in your local area.

If the church office or your parents cannot help you, go to a local restaurant that serves food from other countries. Pray when you go there that you could meet a new friend from another part of the world. *God will often surprise you with quick answers when you are asking for something that is important to His heart and plan for all nations!*

Remember, it can be as simple as, "Hi, my name is ____________ and I've got a project for school I'm working on. I'm suppose to ask someone from another culture over for dinner, so my mom and I would like to know if you could come to our house for dinner?"

Plan a meal you would like to serve to an international student that could introduce them to some of your favorite American foods. Keep praying for God to lead your family to just the right ***cross-cultural*** friendship right in your own city or even your own neighborhood.

Check this box when you have completed today's activities. ☐

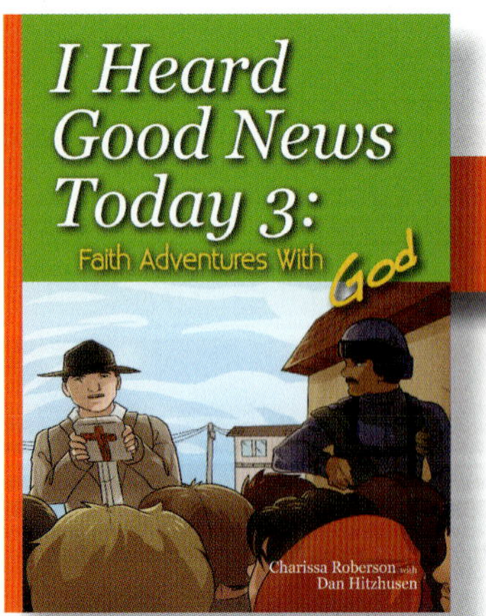

Today's Reading To Grow Your Faith

I Heard Good News Today 3

Read: Chapter 56—The Most Important Thing Ever

What was the greatest thing in the world to Ricky? [216]

Yes Lord, let my heart rejoice!

Yes Lord, let the Muslims, the Buddhists, the Hindus, the Chinese and Tribals rejoice in You!

When Cats And Dogs Sing
"Let The Whole World Rejoice"

If God answered all of your prayers today, would different parts of the world be changed? [217]

Speaking of Jesus Cross Culturally

"What could she challenge us with today?" That is what you are thinking, right?

Well, today you need to really think "outside of the box"—"outside of the homeschool bubble"—even "outside of our nation's borders." ***WHAT ?!?!?***

Yep, I want you to go on the e3Partners website today, and dream about joining an e3 Partners mission team one day in the future. Go to: www.e3partners.org.

You know all these amazing faith adventure stories you have been reading the past 20 weeks from our newest book, *I Heard Good News Today 3: Faith Adventures with God?* Just about all of those stories were about the life of Dan Hitzhusen, my husband's good friend who is on staff with e3Partners.

E3Partners specializes in taking people overseas to share the gospel with the **EvangeCube**! The stories you've been reading were all under the leadership of E3.

Let me tell you about the girl to the right. She is homeschooled as well. At 15 years of age, she came with us to Peru on an e3 Team. She came with her brother, and they had to raise over $6,000 for both of them! Want to know how they did it? Go to https://www.youtube.com/watch?v=4qs35Mp-jZU

Here is Samantha (15 Years old) in Peru loving on a little girl!

Samantha (Sam) had never shared her faith before. (Too bad this curriculum hadn't been written for her when she was in middle school!) But on this trip, she ended up "on fire" for the Lord, leading many people to Jesus using the **EvangeCube**.

You can be like Sam. You can do this too! Going overseas is something God may want for you. Pray and ask Him to show you.

ACTIVITY FOR TODAY:

Spend 15 minutes surfing the **e3Partners** website: www.e3partners.org Dream **BIG DOG** dreams with God and make a list of three to five countries you would like to possibly go to one day and speak of Jesus with your **EvangeCube**.

My Dream Countries For the Future

1. ____________________________________
2. ____________________________________
3. ____________________________________
4. ____________________________________
5. ____________________________________

Finish this week thanking God for all you have learned this year about being devoted to your Master, serving and leading like Jesus, and speaking of Jesus.

Give your **BIG DOG DREAMS** of speaking of Jesus one day in another country back to God, saying, "If the Lord wills, I will go there one day." (James 4:15)

Scripture Memory

Colossians 4:2-6 (ESV)

2 Continue steadfastly in prayer, being watchful in it with thanksgiving.
3 At the same time, pray also for us, that God may open to us a door for the word, to declare the mystery of Christ, on account of which I am in prison —-
4 that I may make it clear, which is how I ought to speak.
5 Walk in wisdom toward outsiders, making the best use of the time.
6 Let your speech always be gracious, seasoned with salt, so that your may know how you ought to answer each person.

Place a check here after you have successfully quoted it. ☐

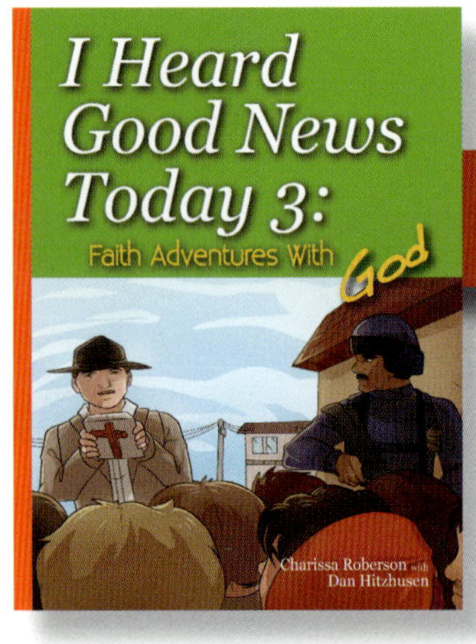

Today's Reading To Grow Your Faith

I Heard Good News Today 3
Read: Chapter 57—Down The Jungle Path

How did God answer the woman's prayer? [218]

Find the country mentioned on the map on page ix of *I Heard Good News Today 3* and pray for new believers there.

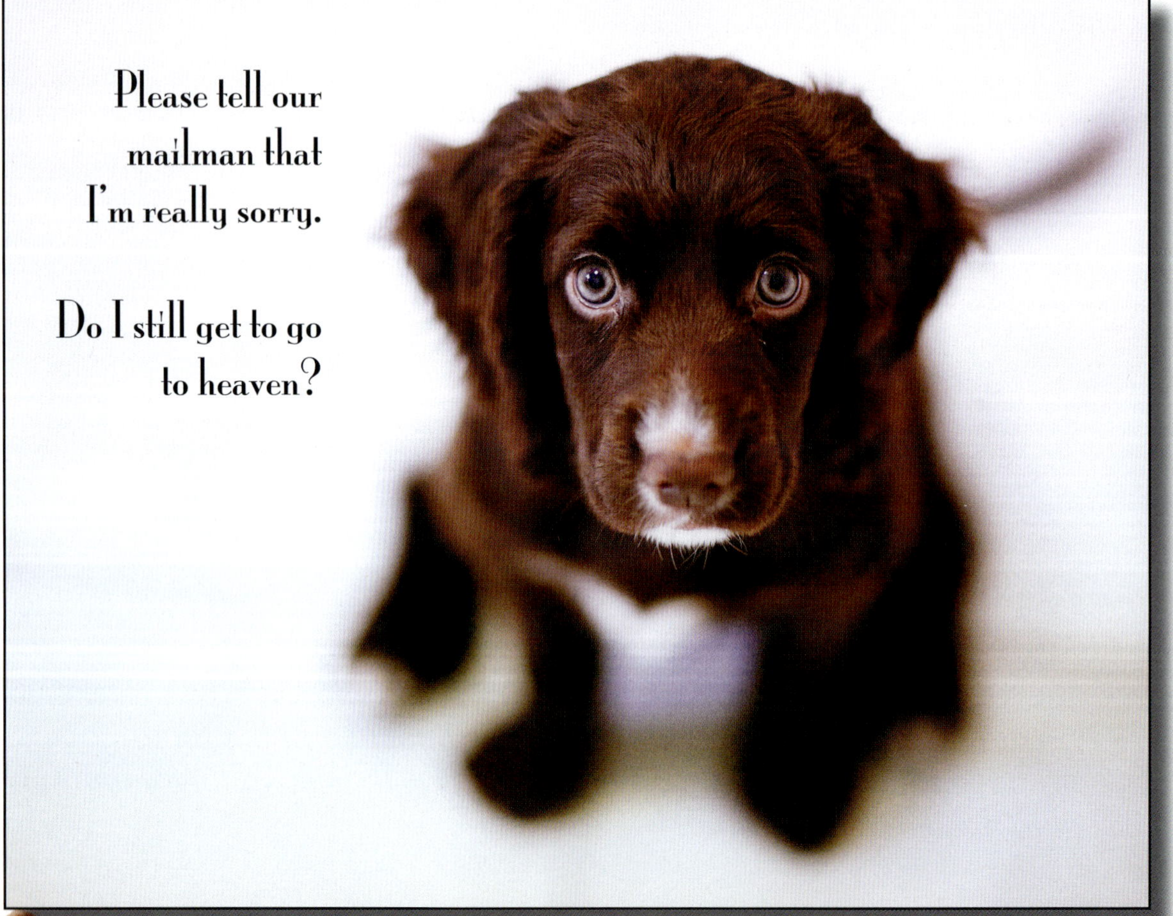

Please tell our mailman that I'm really sorry.
Do I still get to go to heaven?

By PhotKing □ from Cambridge , UK via WikiCommons

Week 30: Day 1

Lesson 88

Refection & Review of *The Dog Walk*

Well, my Dog friends, my fellow followers of our Master and BFF, Jesus Christ, here we are—we made it! Thanks for the honor you have given me by reading about my life-walk with Jesus over the past 40 years! Yep, I am *that old*. But I don't feel that old because following Jesus on *The Dog Walk* through life definitely keeps me feeling much younger than my years. It is because of the JOY I have knowing that my every day life does bring God great glory. I hope and pray you will continue *The Dog Walk* for the rest of your life. You won't be sorry, I promise!

To start this week on a lighter note, take a few minutes to listen to this song, "Do Everything," while you watch a fun music video by Steven Curtis Chapman on the internet: http://www.shazam.com/track/53379940/do-everything#referrer=shz.am

Don't you think his song, "Do Everything," truly summarizes *The Dog Walk* in everyday life? The chorus is so catchy; it certainly sticks in my brain all day long after I listen to it. Does it do the same for you? (By the way, if your mom has never listened to it, have her watch it with you. As a mom, I know she'll be greatly encouraged!)

For this final week, I have decided to help you summarize what you have learned and gained these past 29 weeks by asking you a few questions each day this week.

You could call this your ***final exam***, but don't be scared...there are no right and wrong answers. Your answers are truly your own. However, it is very important to reflect and remember all that God has taught you this year so you can "keep on keeping on" the rest of your days! If you are willing and interested in helping us with future revisions of *The Dog Walk*, when you finish the next three lessons, please copy and paste the 30 final reflection questions and your answers into a Word Document (10 each day for the next three lessons), then email the document to me at debby@mmpublishers.com. Your answers will help us make this curriculum even better for future Dogs!

Today we will reflect on the first section of *The Dog Walk*: Heart Attitudes and Becoming Devoted to the Master. Then tomorrow the next section: Following Our Master by learning to "lead, love, and serve like Jesus." Finally, our last day together (boo hoo!) we will reflect on the section called: Speaking of Jesus.

Alright, my fellow Dogs, let's do this!

Devoted To The Master

1. From "The Most Important Command of our Master" Part 1 (Lesson 4), which part of "Loving the Lord Your God with ALL your..." is most difficult for you? Circle here:

HEART **SOUL** **MIND** **STRENGTH**

Why?

____

____

2. Review the lessons on "Cause Me vs. Help Me Prayers" (Lessons 7-9). Do you think your prayers have changed because of learning these lessons? If so, how?

____

____

3. Can you still quote the "Secret to JOY!" What do the three letters stand for?

J -

O-

Y- .

4. How has your life been different after learning this "Secret to JOY"?

____

____

5. Think about what you learned from *Emma's Story*. Can you share the most important truth about God you learned from reading that book?

____

____

6. Do you remember our canine friends, Matt and Bubba, from *The Positive Dog*? List one-to-three life lessons you learned from that book that have changed your life:

1. ____

2. ____

3. ____

7. Which plan (Lessons 22-30) did you most enjoy that caused you to spend time growing in your friendship with God? Circle your favorite:

READ, NEED, DEED **CINCO DEVO** **SOAK**

8. Have you continued to spend time with God using either or all of these plans? If so, which ones?

____

9. Do you feel you have grown in your friendship and dependence on Jesus by using these plans? Circle: Yes or No

10. Can you still name the four fingers and thumb represented by *The Word Hand* which teach us how to use The Bible? Write what you can below.

A:

B:

C:

D:

THUMB:

11. From Lessons 31-45, which part of *The Word Hand* was the most challenging for you?

____

12. Which part was the most meaningful for you?

____

13. Do you still remember and practice "*HWLW*" *(His Word Last Word)* at night before sleeping? Circle: Yes or No

14. If your answer was Yes, with whom do you practice "*HWLW*"?

____

15. Regarding the "Dog Training Days" at the end of each week, did you like or not like teaching others? Circle One: Liked or Didn't Like

17. Do you see the value in training others to follow Jesus on *The Dog Walk*?
Circle One: Yes or No

18. If yes, describe how God has impacted someone else through you:

____

____

19. What was your favorite Scripture Memory verse from the first 15 weeks?

____ (Just give the reference!)

No New Verses: Review!

If you haven't already done so, I highly recommend writing down these verses on 3" by 5" index cards or ask your mom or dad to buy you a small spiral-bound set of index cards that you can use for reviewing all your verses.

If you can't buy the index cards, a second best option would be to type out all your memory verses on a Word Document today. Then review the verses using the index cards on which you hand wrote them or the printed document you have typed.

Here is your list so far:

Week 1: II Corinthians 5:17	Week 11: Romans 11:17	Week 21: John 14:6
Week 2: Mark 12:30-31	Week 12: Rev. 1:3	Week 22: Acts 1:8
Week 3: Ezekiel 36:27	Week 13: Acts 17:11b	Week 23: off
Week 4: John 10:10	Week 14: Psalm 119:9-11	Week 24: Col. 4:2
Week 5: Psalm 118:1	Week 15: Psalm 1:2,3c	Week 25: Col. 4:3
Week 6: I Thessalonians 5:11	Week 16: Mark 1:17	Week 26: Col. 4:4
Week 7: Romans 8:28	Week 17: Luke 9:23	Week 27: Col. 4:5
Week 8: Colossians 2:6-7	Week 18: Mark 10:45	Week 28: Col. 4:6
Week 9: Psalm 16:11	Week 19: Phil. 2:5,7a	Week 29: Col. 4:2-6
Week 10: REVIEW	Week 20: REVIEW	Week 30: REVIEW

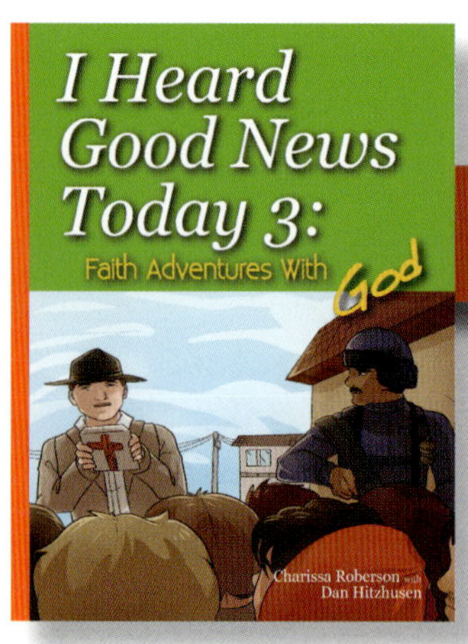

I Heard Good News Today 3

Read: Chapter 58—A Letter to the Island of Youth

Explain how Dan was an answer to the woman's prayer without even realizing it.[219]

Don't forget to pray for these people!

Find the country mentioned on the map and pray for new believers there.

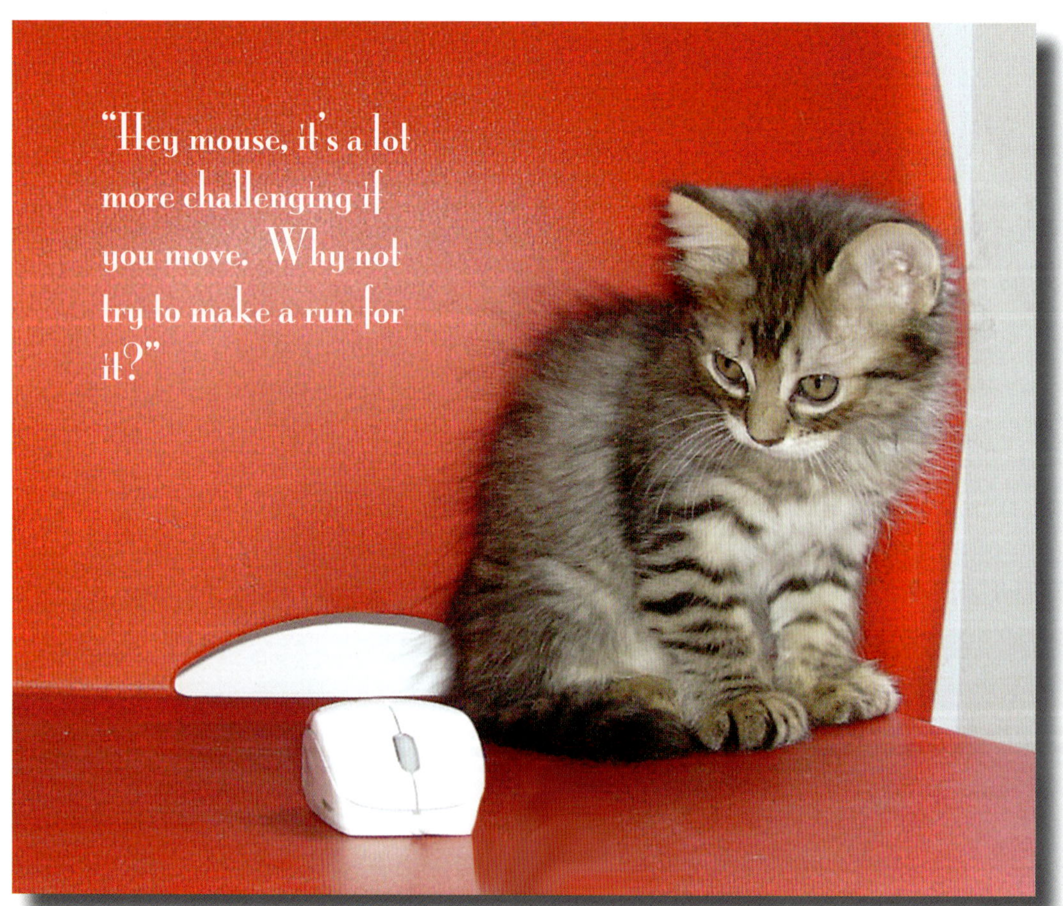

"Hey mouse, it's a lot more challenging if you move. Why not try to make a run for it?"

By Canopus49 (Own work) via WikiCommons

Week 30: Day 2

Lesson 89

Reflection & Review of *The Dog Walk*

So hopefully yesterday's lesson wasn't too painful, my Dog friends ☺!

Yes, I totally feel like we are friends now, having walked *The Dog Walk* together all year long...30 weeks is a long time, isn't it? And guess what? We can continue to be best buddies and grow together in following Jesus for the next four years of your life. How? Check out our four years of high school Bible curriculum on www.CatandDogTheology.org. We start with a much deeper look at *Cat and Dog Theology*, then we study *RG3: Revealing God's Greatest Glory*. Next we move into *E267: Preparing for Eternity*, and finally a whole year's study on *Heaven* (but I promise it won't be boring!).

You will love the books you read, cartoons to think about, and especially "The Chris and Sarah Stories" that relate the lessons you are learning to your life as teenagers. Check it out online or come and meet us at our *Cat and Dog Theology/UnveilinGLORY* booth at your local homeschool convention!

Following Our Master

1. Which Scripture Memory verse in this section (Weeks 16-22) is the most challenging for you to live out in following Jesus? ________________________________

2. Write why it was the most challenging.

___

___

3. Place a check by which person's story in this section impacted you the most.

- ❑ St. Francis
- ❑ Helen Roseveare
- ❑ Jim & Elisabeth Elliot
- ❑ Elise Sjogren

4. How did their story impact your life?

___

___

5. When you did your Servant Evangelism Event, write a highlight about what took place.

___

___

6. What was the hardest part of your event?

___

___

7. How do you think God was glorified through your Servant Evangelism Project?

___

___

8. Are there other Servant Evangelism Projects you would like to do in the future? Make a list of 3—4 possible future S.E. projects you hope to do (Lesson 53):

1. ______________________________

2. ______________________________

3. ______________________________

4. ______________________________

9. Write the best lesson you learned watching Luke Kuepfer's video clips on Servant Leadership.

____

____

10. Was it easier to practice Servant Leadership at home or at church and why? Circle one: Home or Church

____

____

11. How do you think God was glorified in your Servant Leadership in your home or at church?

____

____

12. How has learning the "both/and" lesson of Acts 1:8 changed the way you plan to spend your free time in the future?

____

13. Now that you are almost finished with *The Dog Walk*, fill in possible people or places you plan to live out Acts 1:8 as a *witness* in the days ahead:

Your Extended Family (Jerusalem)? ______________

Your Neighborhood (Judea)? ______________

Your City (Samaria)? ______________

Cross-Culturally (To the Ends of the Earth)? ______________

14. Has God placed a country or a missionary family on your heart that you plan to continue to support in prayer, giving, encouraging, serving or maybe going?

Circle: Yes or No

15. If yes, which country or which family/person?

Today's Reading To Grow Your Faith

I Heard Good News Today 3
Read: Chapter 59—Five-Minute-Old Believers

How long do you have to be a believer before you can effectively share your faith?[220]

Find the country mentioned on the map and pray for new believers there.

Somehow
I just don't
think this is
my mommy.

By AyBars (Own work) via Wiki Commons

AND FINALLY LORD, WE WANT TO REMIND YOU OF OUR NEED FOR THE NEW GYMNASIUM....

AND FINALLY LORD, WE WANT TO PRAY FOR OTHER CHURCHES IN OUR CITY AND ALSO IN IRAQ....

Ending The Church Prayer Meeting

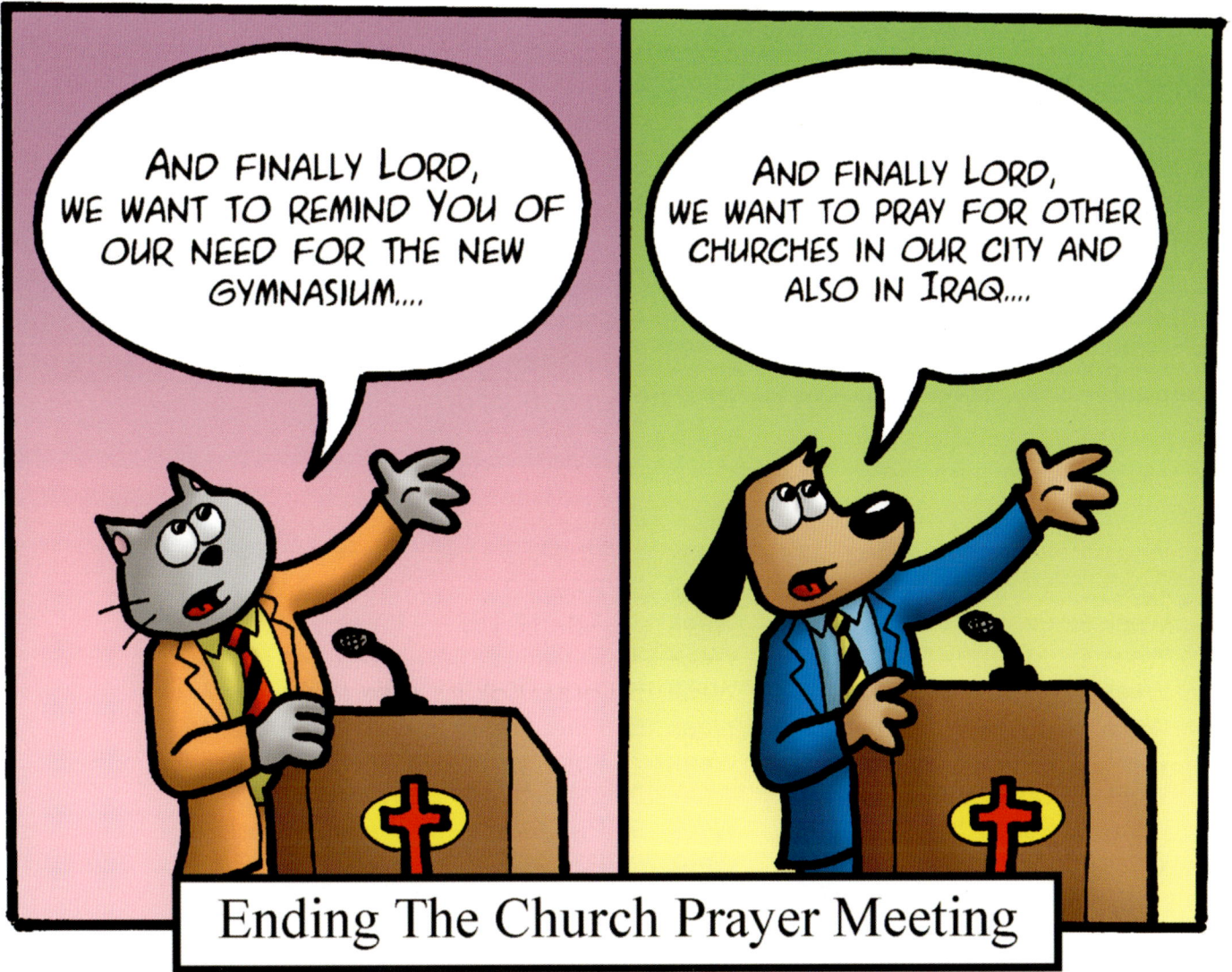

Why is the Cat's prayer self-centered compared to the Dog's prayer? [221]

____

____

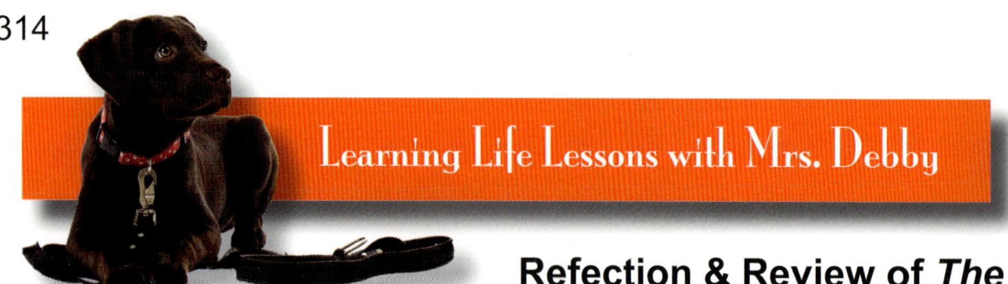

Refection & Review of *The Dog Walk*

Wow! Bow Wow! ☺ Are we really completing our last lesson in *The Dog Walk* today? I want to end by saying, "Congrats to ALL of you DOGS who have completed this curriculum!"

The Dog Walk is definitely not an easy curriculum to work through, but my prayer for you is that your relationship with your Master and BFF, Jesus Christ, has grown deeper and stronger as a result of our walk together this year. I also pray that you will continue to follow Jesus and speak of Jesus the rest of your life. Truly, to God be the glory, great things He has done!

Since today is your ***last, final, totally done*** lesson in *The Dog Walk,* please accept this challenge before you finish your lesson today: Take a few minutes to review all your Scripture Memory verses for this year, then ***quote them all*** to your parent or homeschool teacher. ***You can do it! I believe in you!!***

Here is your list:

Week 1: II Corinthians 5:17	Week 11: Romans 11:17	Week 21: John 14:6
Week 2: Mark 12:30-31	Week 12: Rev. 1:3	Week 22: Acts 1:8
Week 3: Ezekiel 36:27	Week 13: Acts 17:11b	Week 23: off
Week 4: John 10:10	Week 14: Psalm 119:9-11	Week 24: Col. 4:2
Week 5: Psalm 118:1	Week 15: Psalm 1:2,3c	Week 25: Col. 4:3
Week 6: I Thessalonians 5:11	Week 16: Mark 1:17	Week 26: Col. 4:4
Week 7: Romans 8:28	Week 17: Luke 9:23	Week 27: Col. 4:5
Week 8: Colossians 2:6-7	Week 18: Mark 10:45	Week 28: Col. 4:6
Week 9: Psalm 16:11	Week 19: Phil. 2:5,7a	Week 29: Col. 4:2-6
Week 10: REVIEW	Week 20: REVIEW	Week 30: REVIEW

Put a check in this box when you have quoted ALL your verses on your Dog Walk. ❑

Speaking Of Our Master

1. Did the YouTube video clips help you to learn how to use your **EvangeCube**?
   Circle: Yes or No

2. About how many times have you been able to share your **EvangeCube** with another person so far? ___________

3. Do you plan to use it in the future? Circle: Yes or No

4. Was figuring out a 3-5 minute version of your ***testimony*** difficult or easy for you?
   Circle: Easy or Difficult

5. Did you enjoy helping someone else write their own ***testimony***?
   Circle: Yes or No

6. Are you finding it easier to speak of Jesus or be a witness of your faith in Him to others now that you have been trained with the **EvangeCube** and you have "your own story" with Jesus ready to share? Circle: Yes or No

7. Have you seen the Holy Spirit bring anyone to repent and follow Jesus yet when you used the **EvangeCube** or shared your ***testimony***? Circle: Yes or No

8. If yes, can you briefly describe what happened here?

____

____

9. What did you learn about *Orality/Bible Storying* that was new for you?

____

____

10. Write down what was a highlight for you in BibleStorying or GameLife:

____

____

11. Do you think you'll ever use BibleStorying/GameLife in the future?
Circle: Yes or No

12. Do you plan to befriend or invite to dinner an international student? Circle: Yes or No (Of course, your parents need to agree to this idea.) If yes, what favorite American meal do you plan to serve them for dinner?

____

____

13. Finally, would you recommend *The Dog Walk* to other middle school students?
Circle: Yes or No

14. Why or Why not?

____

____

15. Describe how reading the 60 stories from *I Heard Good News Today 3* this year has impacted your life?

____

____

If you are willing and interested in helping us with future revisions of *The Dog Walk*, please type your answers from the last three days of review questions and email the document to me at debby@mmpublishers.com.

Your answers will help us make this curriculum even better for future Dogs!

Today's Reading To Grow Your Faith

I Heard Good News Today 3
Read: Chapter 60—A Symbol of Salvation

Look up Matthew 10:16. How did it apply to Dan that night? [222]

Find the country mentioned on the map and pray for new believers there.

The Answer Key

The Answer Key

[1] To encourage Tara
[2] Becky and Graham Bates
[3] God
[4] Children in Turkey, especially at the orphanage for Tara
[5] Thank You, Jesus, for all that you have done for me.
[6] Answers may vary: Cat was "me-focused" and Dog wanted to make God famous.
[7] Answers will vary, but should equal 100%
[8] an entire year
[9] "we admire your persistence" (after meeting with the orphanage board)
[10] Alan Grant, a missionary from Turkey OR Pastor George who told them about Alan
[11] The Bates could not speak the Turkish language to explain why they had 6 large duffel bags OR the demons, Confusion & Doubt, also help to create the problem
[12] "I'm here to protect you, little one. No need to fear."
[13] The Cat relies on a prayer. The Dog relies on a changed life and the fruit of the Spirit.
[14] To lay down his life for his friends
[15] friends
[16] all that He has heard from His Father
[17] the Lord
[18] the angels OR Spirit had surrounded them
[19] It's okay. Peace for you, little one. I'm not going to hurt you.
[20] Holy, holy, holy is the Lord God Almighty!
[21] Love, God, heart, soul, mind, strength, love, neighbor, yourself, 12, 31
[22] Least of These Ministries
[23] the dark one OR Satan
[24] her grandparents, Ulma and Halime
[25] an earthquake
[26] Amy
[27] a rescue dog
[28] Hug Teams
[29] get help for her in the States (USA) or even possibly adopt her
[30] Because they are yelling at the person.
[31] no
[32] wheelchair
[33] about 20
[34] Emma
[35] heart, soul, mind, strength, neighbor
[36] Courage
[37] Beth and Becca
[38] her friend, Ruth
[39] foreign adoption had never occurred, especially not a handicapped child
[40] God
[41] No.
[42] There is no right answer to this, but words like, "repentive, kind, loving, gentle, obedient" would be appropriate words.

The Answer Key

---

[43] His Holy Spirit
[44] God is.
[45] Fatima
[46] Yasmur
[47] Chaos
[48] sell her or kill her
[49] There is no reference to the glory of God.
[50] Jealousy and Impatience
[51] Ahmed
[52] Her father, Mark
[53] Graham
[54] Satan
[55] Jesus
[56] full and meaningful
[57] His grandmother, Becky Bates, came to his classroom and showed photos and told the story of Least of These Ministries.
[58] Her brother, Adam
[59] Justice and six other angels
[60] thief, steal, kill, destroy, they, life, abundantly
[61] Beth, it's time to pray.
[62] Emma Ruth Sneed
[63] God can make a way.
[64] Answers will vary. It should reflect a time of great self-centeredness.
[65] A positive dog and a negative dog
[66] Positivity makes us happier, healthier, helps us live longer, improves our relationships, makes us better leaders, and leads to greater success.
[67] A smile
[68] Laugh and smile more often
[69] Positive or negative: Whichever one you feed grows.
Positive dogs live longer, happier and healthier lives.
Feed the positive dog with real smiles and big laughs!
[70] Gratitude and appreciation OR thankfulness
[71] what is good in your life, what you are thankful for, and what you appreciate
[72] a thank-you walk
[73] gratitude
[74] You can't be stressed and thankful at the same time.
Gratitude is like muscle. The more you do with it, the stronger it gets.
Abundance flows into your life when gratitude flows out of your heart.
[75] The dog for the positive attitude.
[76] Gratitude, complaining
[77] tell yourself "get to" instead of "have to" everyday OR change "have to" to "get to"
[78] blessed, stressed
[79] friends
[80] think of 3 things you are thankful for anytime you feel stressed

The Answer Key

---

81 you are not going to complain unless you identify 1 or 2 solutions to your complaint.
82 To choose faith instead of fear
83 a future that hasn't happened yet. Fear believes in a negative future. Faith believes in a positive future.
84 opportunities
85 stronger
86 doing something he enjoyed & focusing on the present moment
87 what was good in his life
88 prayer or meditation (on the Scriptures as followers of Jesus)
89 everyone around you
90 you not only make yourself better, you make everyone around you better.
91 To grow closer to Jesus through trust.
92 By being kind OR simple acts of kindness
93 Your kindness feeds others and changes the world.
Kindness is a gift that is always returned to you.
94 We are afraid of getting hurt.
95 Love dissolves hate, soothes anger, comforts pain, heals relationships, casts out fear, and transforms us and those who receive our love.
96 encouragement
97 optimists, encouragers, and inspirers
98 I believe in you.
99 Negativity actually helps you see & appreciate the positive.
Negativity forces you to feel those painful emotions so you can appreciate the positive ones.
Negativity builds character & strength when we persevere and overcome it.
Builds our positive mental and emotional muscle when we face negative others.
100 Matt mentored other dogs. Matt taught the importance of feeding the positive dog and shared strategies to help them do it. Matt loved everyone and put his love into action. He listened and coached other dogs having problems. He gave constant encouragement. He believed in the other dogs more than they believed in themselves. Matt also made the time to share his appreciation with those who helped around the shelter and recognized the dogs that had become more positive.
101 Gratitude and prayer
102 Any of these are correct: Matt knew that positivity was a choice. Matt had become an expert at feeding the positive dog and starving the negative dog. Matt had more fun, joy, love, health, and friends. Matt still felt negative at times, but these negative emotions no longer defined him. Matt enjoyed a thank-you walk everyday. Matt was grateful and prayed for others. Matt didn't let other negative dogs affect him in a negative way, but saw them as teachers who taught him to be more positive.
103 Answers will vary. If you would like to share with me how this book has changed your attitude or your life, please email your answer to debby@mmpublishers.com.
104 All they want to do is be blessed by God. They don't want to bless anyone else.
105 Plan his night out beforehand so he was ready and rested or go to sleep earlier.

---

[106] The Dogs, because they want to meet with God more often.
[107] Answers will vary.
[108] Yes, because He loves all people no matter what they are like.
[109] Answers will vary.
[110] Answers will vary, but hopefully they want to obey God.
[111] She knew so many people and became their "person of peace."
[112] Kurt
[113] word, Christ
[114] faith, please, God, rewards
[115] We are to love each other.
[116] 39
[117] 27
[118] The Dogs because they are spending time in God's Word.
[119] It could have been a trap and he could have been killed.
[120] to check and make sure that what the preacher, Paul, said was true.
[121] A powerful joy beginning to swell deep within him.
[122] We can rightly handle the word of truth, we are unashamed of God, we are doing our best for God and His Glory
[123] After they took off for India and in Singapore.
[124] Answers will vary, but yes, it is okay to question a pastor's words if you research it from the Bible. Pastors aren't perfect, but you should approach them humbly and respectfully.
[125] There were men who wanted to know about Jesus.
[126] His family would forsake him, he would have no place to go and the villagers would beat him.
[127] False
[128] to remind us not to sin against God
[129] to treasure God's Word and to live (for His Glory!)
[130] for teaching, rebuking, correcting and training in righteousness, and so we as God's servants may be thoroughly equipped for every good work
[131] to be fruitful for God, to not wither in our faith, and to prosper in all that we do
[132] to be prepared to give an answer to everyone who asks
[133] You have to really want it and stay focused for a long period of time.
[134] The dictator had taught the people of his country that God did not exist.
[135] Answers may vary: To engage in thought or reflect; to contemplate; to ponder
[136] a fruitful life OR leaf does not wither (strength) OR will prosper (successful life)
[137] causes us to carefully obey the Lord OR we will have success and be prosperous
[138] our words and thoughts will be pleasing to the Lord
[139] we will love God's Word more
[140] causes us to depend on God more OR more power in our prayers
[141] Because it was under martial law and there were riots.
[142] http://www.navigators.org/About-Us/Stories/Navigator%20Stories/March%202006/How%20to%20Meditate%20Day%20and%20Night
[143] He danced out of joy! Answers will vary from this point on.

The Answer Key

---

[144] The first thing he does is have a Quiet Time with God.
[145] A relationship.
[146] Follow Me
[147] Follow Me
[148] Follow Me
[149] Follow Me
[150] Following Jesus every day
[151] Answers will vary, but they must have really hungered for God's Word.
[152] all the world
[153] Holy Spirit
[154] The Word of God
[155] our good deeds
[156] our love for one another
[157] Dan and Debbie could be forced to leave the country. The local believers would lose their job, be jailed or killed.
[158] Because they are expecting God to serve them. They don't serve God.
[159] It was that those with physical healings were more thankful for the spiritual healing.
[160] The hotel staff wanted to come to know the Lord too.
[161] Nothing. The church wouldn't have been planted.
[162] Because they don't yield to God. They expect God to fit into their life.
[163] Answers will vary.
[164] To glorify His Father
[165] To serve and to give His life as a ransom for many.
[166] He went back to a town to share the gospel where he had been beaten.
[167] Answers will vary.
[168] Because they are willing to go anywhere for the Lord.
[169] Play volleyball
[170] This is when a church starts a daughter church and that daughter church starts their own daughter church—which is a granddaughter church to the first church!
[171] War, forgiving one another and the President's decision to hold courts every Tuesday.
[172] They serve God their way, not God's way.
[173] Answers will vary.
[174] For the plane to miss the city of Awassa and go straight to Arba Minch.
[175] Just as all the ducklings follow the duck in front of them as they all follow the mother duck, when we lead someone to Christ, we should get them to immediately follow our example and share their faith with others.
[176] They are only praying for things involving their church, to make it a bigger, better place for themselves.
[177] Dan's forgetfulness/mistake caused many people in America to be praying that they would meet Mother Teresa.
[178] Answers will vary, but hopefully yes!
[179] Answers will vary.

The Answer Key

---

[180] They seem to be more worried about the church than the lost because they wouldn't "fit in."
[181] They could spend deeper time reading God's word and praying. God was teaching them many things.
[182] You don't need a call. God has already commanded you to go through the Great Commission. Really, you should say to God, "Lord, I am going—unless you tell me not to."
[183] Answers may vary: "open profession of one's religious faith in words or actions"
[184] Abdul
[185] Answers will vary.
[186] True
[187] God is powerful enough to keep us safe even in the middle of a war.
[188] Lord, I know you can heal this man if you choose. Please, don't let my unbelief get in the way of your power.
[189] The Cat is focused on themselves. The Dog is focused on God.
[190] Answers will vary, but hopefully it will blow it away! God is huge!
[191] Answers may vary: That God may open a door for the Word, That they will declare the mystery of Christ, That they may make the Good News of Jesus clear, Walk in wisdom toward outsiders, Make the best use of time, Speech always be gracious & salty, Know how to answer each person
[192] 42 / 3,000
[193] Her dance moves matched perfectly the words to the song.
[194] Cats don't want to take risks. Dogs know there may be a risk involved, but are willing to take it.
[195] She was afraid because her husband wasn't with her. She didn't need to be afraid, because Jesus was with her.
[196] Answers may vary: "a public recounting of a religious conversion or experience"
[197] English
[198] Paul and Silas were in jail, yet they could praise God because of God living in them.
[199] Answers will vary.
[200] Answers will vary, but hopefully yes, because of the power of the Holy Spirit inside of you!
[201] A storm and fear of death.
[202] He went to talk to the principal of the school. Answers will vary.
[203] They are only concerned about their church. They seem to be communicating that they don't want people to go to others churches, just theirs.
[204] Answers may vary: A little girl in a canoe, Dan's desire to be a photographer, a boy's broken leg, etc.
[205] Credit: www.mnnonline.org/news/orality-getting-back-to-the-basics-of-gospel-sharing/
[206] Answers will vary.
[207] Credit: www.mnnonline.org/news/orality-getting-back-to-the-basics-of-gospel-sharing/
[208] Once the children know about Jesus' love and salvation, they can turn and tell their families about Christ.
[209] They are primarily focused on getting a bigger and bigger youth group.

The Answer Key

---

[210] Dan didn't have the hotel vouchers that he needed to get through customs.
[211] Dan was wanting a guitar and the family was praying to sell their guitar.
[212] Because the man was about to take his own life.
[213] Answers will vary.
[214] The police office changed from being mad and angry to kind.
[215] Find everyday objects from their culture, pray for God's wisdom, and use the objects to share the gospel.
[216] Knowing Jesus and telling others about Him.
[217] Answers will vary. The key is to help you see that God wants you praying about different parts of the world.
[218] By bringing Jim and his team to their village to share the gospel.
[219] He had letters to those women before he even started the trip.
[220] Five minutes!
[221] The Cat Pastor is only focused on the needs of their church. They are not worried about what is happening around the world.
[222] He had to be wise as a serpent.

[223] The hills full of horses and chariots of fire all around Elisha.
[224] The Lord struck the army with blindness.
[225] Yes (See Hebrews 13:5)
[226] Credit: These questions were modified from Jim Thurber's teaching.

If you loved *The Dog Walk,* here's your next curriculum when you are ready for high school credit!

For Students In
Grades 8-12:

Cat and Dog Theology

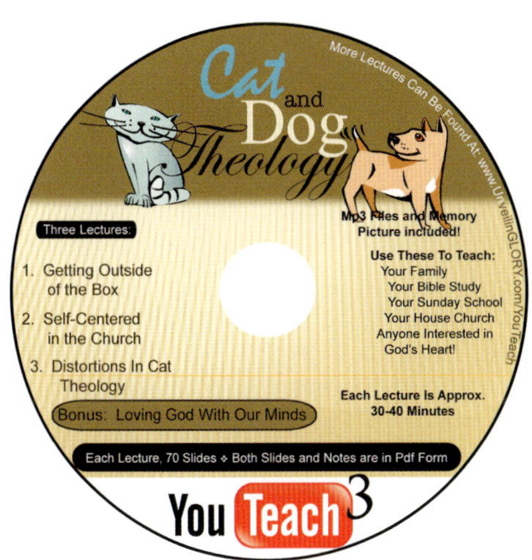

To find out more, go to www.UnveilinGLORY.com/homeschool.